COUNTRY WALKS
in the Chicago Region

by Alan Fisher

RAMBLER BOOKS

Baltimore

COUNTRY WALKS in the CHICAGO REGION

By Alan Fisher
Maps and photographs by the author

Rambler Books
1430 Park Avenue
Baltimore, MD 21217

If you notice errors in the text or maps, please point them out in a letter to the publisher.

Printed in the United States of America.

SECOND EDITION
The prior edition of this book was called *Country Walks Near Chicago*. Changing the title to emphasize the *regional* scope of this new edition is intended to reflect the growth of the Chicago area and the inclusion of more than a dozen new walks, some of them fairly far afield. Of course, the text has been updated, and all the maps have been re-drawn in a larger format.

ISBN 0-9614963-9-8

On the cover: Indiana Dunes State Park (Chapter 19).

CONTENTS

MAP 1 — Orientation

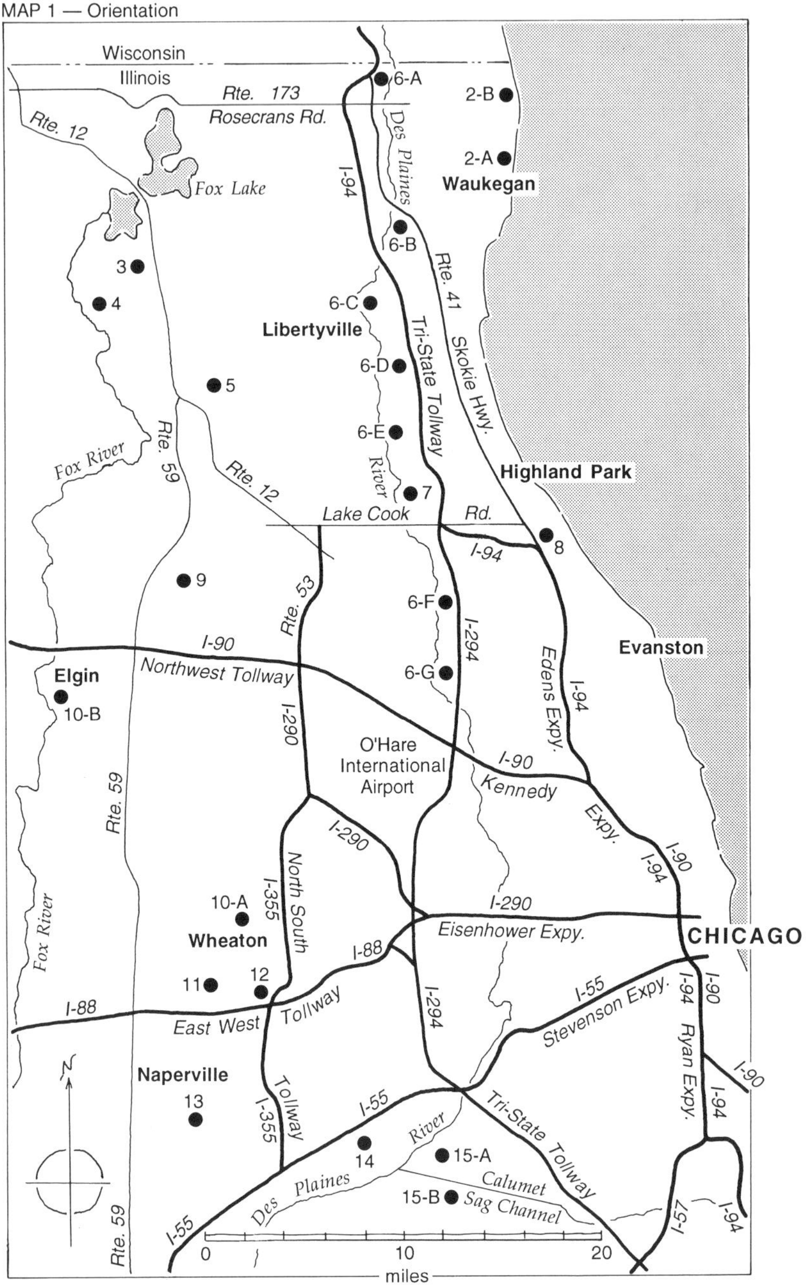

Wisconsin
Illinois

Rte. 173
Rosecrans Rd.

Rte. 12

Fox Lake

Des Plaines

6-A

2-B

2-A
Waukegan

I-94

6-B

Rte. 41

3

4

6-C
Libertyville

Tri-State Tollway

Skokie Hwy.

6-D

5

Fox River

Rte. 59

Rte. 12

6-E

River

7

Highland Park

Lake Cook   Rd.

I-94

8

9

Rte. 53

6-F

I-294

Evanston

I-90
Northwest Tollway

Elgin
10-B

Rte. 59

6-G

Edens Expy.

I-94

I-290

O'Hare
International
Airport

I-90
Kennedy

Expy.

I-90

I-94

I-290

10-A
Wheaton

North South

I-355

I-88

Eisenhower Expy.

CHICAGO

Fox River

11   12

Tollway

East West   Tollway

I-88

I-294

I-55
Stevenson Expy.

I-94

I-90

Ryan Expy.

I-90

Naperville

13

N

Tollway

I-355

I-55

Des Plaines   River

14   15-A

Tri-State Tollway

Calumet

15-B   Sag Channel

I-94

I-57

I-94

Rte. 59

I-55

0   10   20
miles

6

MAP 2 — Orientation

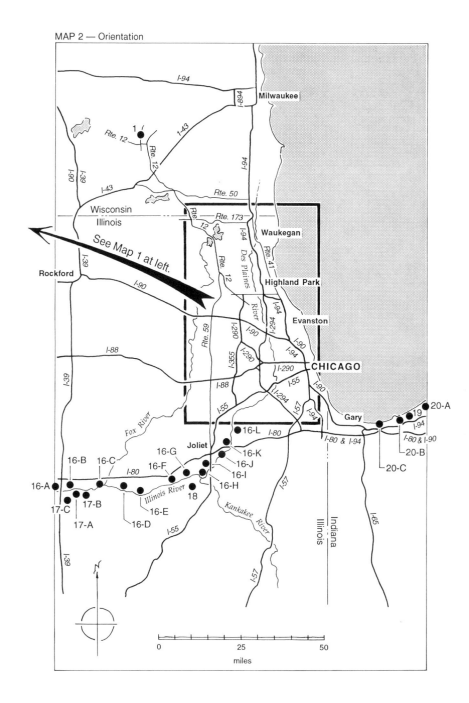

PREFACE

THIS BOOK IS FOR PEOPLE who want an outing in a country setting without wasting half the day getting there and back. If you live in the Greater Chicago region, the excursions described here are close at hand. The walks show the best of our area's parks and trails, some of which are suitable also for ski touring and bicycling. The excursions cover the gamut of the region's landscapes. Successive visits during different seasons—to see the changing foliage, views, wildflowers, and birds—provide an added dimension of enjoyment.

Automobile directions: Because readers will be driving from different places to reach the sites described here, the automobile directions sometimes outline different avenues of approach. Necessarily, there is much repetition, so focus on the set of directions that applies to you and skip the others. Of course, you may find it quicker to rely on the road maps—both regional and local—that are included in each chapter.

Walking directions: Again, I hope that the maps are good enough so that they suffice. Nonetheless, there are verbal directions to provide clarification in case of difficulty.

The following people helped me with this book in various ways, including providing information, reviewing material, and making suggestions: Nan Buckhardt, Gail Cross, Charlene Giardina, Jill Jackson, Stacey Miller, Ronni Whitmer, and Ron Vasile.

Alan Fisher

COMFORT AND SAFETY

PLEASE READ THIS. It is customary, in guidebooks such as this, to include a catalog of cautions about possible nuisances and hazards. Such matters do not make for amusing reading, but really, I think that you will be glad to focus here on a few potential problems, so that you can avoid them, rather than recall them belatedly through unpleasant (or even dangerous) experience. Please also read the introductory matter for each walk before you go.

First, about footwear: The main thing is to wear shoes that can withstand getting wet and that have thick soles to protect your feet. The waterproof liners found in the better grade of walking shoes and hiking boots really work.

Other gear for a comfortable outing includes a small knapsack or pouch containing a snack and drink, insect repellent, and an extra layer of clothing, such as a windbreaker or rain parka. Kids in particular will be glad when the food appears.

Every year the newspapers carry stories about people who pick up a squirrel, a raccoon, or some other animal and get bitten. They then have to undergo a series of painful anti-rabies shots. Don't be one of these people; don't handle *any* wild animals.

During winter, all too often drownings occur when people fall through the ice after venturing out onto frozen ponds and rivers or the shelf of ice that sometimes extends into Lake Michigan. I am sure that you have heard this before; everybody has. And yet each winter a few more people die in this manner. Don't be one of them; stay off the ice. And tell your kids.

Other sound advice that is ignored with puzzling regularity concerns lightning. If you are in an exposed or elevated area and a storm approaches, return to your car immediately. That is the safest place to be. And if lighting occurs before you get back to your car, hunker down in a low spot. Don't worry about getting wet or feeling stupid as you crouch there with the rain pouring down. Clearly it is better to get wet and yet be safe than to try to stay dry by huddling under an isolated tree or park pavilion or some other target for lightning.

Where the trails follow roads for short distances, walk well off the road on the shoulder to minimize the risk of being hit by a car, and use caution, especially at dusk or after dark, where the trails cross roads. Studies show that in poor light conditions, motorists typically cannot even see pedestrians in time to stop, so your safety depends entirely on you.

Finally, one of the pitfalls of writing guidebooks is that conditions change. Just because this book recommends something does not mean that you should forge ahead in the face of obvious difficulties, hazards, or prohibitions.

ABOUT TICKS: Many parks post warnings about ticks and tick-borne diseases, chiefly Lyme disease and Rocky Mountain Spotted Fever. Ticks live in wooded areas, tall grass, and brush. The likelihood of picking up ticks is minimal if you stick to well maintained trails. Other standard precautions are to wear long pants and a long sleeved shirt, and to spray your clothes and shoes with insect repellent containing DEET (N-diethylmetatoluamide), which also, of course, will help repel mosquitoes. If your clothes are light colored, it will be easier to spot any ticks that may get on you. Inspect yourself occasionally during your outing and when you return to your car. And when you get home, wash your clothes and examine your body closely. Deer ticks, which are the chief carriers of Lyme disease, are tiny: about the size of a caraway seed in spring and summer, slightly larger in fall and winter. Dog ticks, which may carry Rocky Mountain Spotted Fever, are much larger.

If you are bitten by a tick, remove it immediately. Grasp the tick with sharp-pointed tweezers, as near to your skin as possible, and gently but firmly pull straight out until the tick comes off, then blot the bite with alcohol. Some authorities say to save the tick in alcohol for identification and to make a note of when you were bitten. If the tick's mouthparts break off and remain in your skin, call your doctor to have the pieces removed. Research suggests that ticks must feed for a day in order to transmit disease, so there is a fairly big margin of safety if you remove the tick promptly.

The main early symptom of Lyme disease is a circular, slowly expanding red rash, often with a clear center, that may appear a few days or as long as two months after being bitten by an infected tick. As its name indicates, Rocky Mountain Spotted Fever too produces a rash, usually first on the extremities, then spreading to the torso. For both diseases, flu-like symptoms are common, including fever, a headache, swollen glands, a stiff neck, muscle aches, nausea, and general malaise. If you develop any of these symptoms after being bitten by a tick, see your doctor promptly so that blood tests and treatment with antibiotics can be administered.

1

KETTLE MORAINE STATE FOREST

Maps 4 and 5 on pages 21 and 22 show the extensive trail system at the Kettle Moraine State Forest in southeastern Wisconsin. Trails are marked with colored blazes that outline ten circuits ranging in length from 1.2 to 10 miles (1.9 to 16 kilometers). The paths climb, dip, and wind through a landscape of irregular hills and abrupt depressions that make the moraine an extraordinary—and sometimes strenuous—place for walking, snowshoeing, and cross-country skiing. In the jargon of geologists, this is *knob and kettle* topography at its fullest development.

The Kettle Moraine State Forest is open daily from 6:00 a.m. to 11:00 p.m. Dogs must be leashed. A user fee is charged. The area is managed by the Wisconsin Department of Natural Resources. For information, telephone (262) 594-6200 or go to www.dnr.state.wi.us/org/land/parks.

For automobile directions, please turn to page 18. Walking directions start on page 20.

THE BIZARRE LANDSCAPE of ridges, humps and hollows that is the Kettle Moraine has long been the focus of research into glacial processes. The moraine and other examples of glacial landforms in Wisconsin—and the fieldwork and speculation that they have attracted among geologists—are the main reason that the most recent incursion of continental ice is termed the Wisconsin glacial phase, even though it also affected most of Canada and the entire northern tier of the United States east of the Rocky Mountains.

The Kettle Moraine stretches 150 miles from the Green Bay peninsula south-southwest to the vicinity of Palmyra. It varies in width from one to thirty miles, and the deposits of clay, sand, and boulders of which it is composed are as much as three hundred feet thick. As described by Thomas C. Chamberlin, a geologist who specialized in the study of glacial deposits, the Kettle Moraine is made up of a "series of rudely parallel ridges, that unite, interlock, separate, appear and disappear in an eccentric and intricate manner. . . . The component ridges are themselves exceedingly irregular in height and breadth, being often much broken and interrupted. The united effect of all the foregoing features is to give to the formation a strikingly irregular and complicated aspect."

By far the most remarkable thing about the moraine is the numerous pits or *kettles* for which it is named. Some of these depressions have the shape of an inverted cone; others are oval or irregularly shaped. They can be merely shallow saucers or more than a hundred feet deep. Some are marshy at the bottom and others are occupied by ponds and lakes. The slope of the sides varies greatly, but in the deeper kettles, it often reaches an angle of 30 or 35 degrees—or that is, about as steep as the earth material will lie. The pits range in diameter from a few hundred feet to thousands of yards, although those popularly recognized as kettles seldom exceed five hundred feet across. Referring to the kettles, one early geological investigator (Charles Whittlesey) wrote in 1860: "In traveling through such a region the explorer frequently finds them so near together, that he no sooner rises out of one than he is obliged immediately to descend into another, the diameter of which may not be more than twice or thrice its depth." The region is also characterized by countless rounded hills and knobs that might aptly be styled inverted kettles.

Among geologists, the Kettle Moraine is known as the Kettle Interlobate Moraine, signifying that it was formed between two immense tongues of ice, one occupying the basin of Lake Michigan and the other the valley of Green Bay and Lake Winnebago. The Lake Michigan and Green Bay lobes both advanced primarily southward, but they also spread to each side—or that is, grew wider—so that the ice at the western edge of the Lake Michigan Lobe actually moved toward the southwest, and the ice at the eastern margin of the Green Bay Lobe advanced toward the southeast. As with all glaciers, each lobe was relatively thin at the edge and far thicker at the center. Eventually the two glacial lobes met and merged, at least to some extent. Although the land at the seam where the two lobes touched was completely covered by the glaciers, the surface of the ice still sloped down from each lobe to form a trough or valley between the two.

This trough of ice became the locus for creation of the Kettle Moraine. When the climate warmed and the ice started wasting away, streams of meltwater gushed out into the valley between the glacial lobes. Loaded with earth, sand, and gravel that had been picked up as the ice advanced, the streams shifted among braided channels where the current sorted the material and deposited it in beds. Bolstered on each side by the stagnant glacial lobes, the material partially filled the valley, burying the lower reaches of the ice slopes. As the glacial margin deteriorated and fragmented, the deposits also covered isolated blocks of ice, some of which were huge. Still, of course, the glacial lobes and buried blocks of ice continued to melt, and as a result the earth material in the trough gradually settled onto the underlying ground to form the range of knobby hills seen today, pockmarked with kettles showing where previously there were blocks of buried ice. When the lobes shrank still further, streams deposited more sediments along the foot of each lobe. These deposits now form an apron bordering the Kettle Moraine. Moreover, as melting progressed, the process recurred continuously farther and farther north along the opening seam between the wasting glacial lobes.

At the southern end of the interlobate moraine, the morainic system splits in two. The branches are *end moraines* produced when the rate of forward movement of the ice was matched by melting at the glacial front. While movement and melting were thus in equilibrium, earth material within the ice was transported forward and dumped in a line along the glacial front to form a range of hills, somewhat like piles of sand and gravel at the end of a vast conveyor belt. One branch of the moraine heads west through Janesville and then north through Madison and central Wisconsin, where it marks the outer limit of the Green Bay Lobe. The other branch heads south past Lake Geneva and into Illinois, where it merges with the morainic systems that ring present-day Lake Michigan. On a grand scale and in simplified outline, the configuration of moraines resembles a nicely rounded cursive double-U (although the right-hand U is longer and wider than the left). The Lake Michigan Lobe occupied the U to the right, the Green Bay Lobe the smaller U to the left, and the Kettle Interlobate Moraine constitutes the vertical stroke between the two.

≈   ≈   ≈   ≈

AUTOMOBILE DIRECTIONS: The **Kettle Moraine State Forest** is located in Wisconsin about 20 miles north of Lake Geneva. (See **Map 3** at right.) Three approaches—from the **Northwest Tollway**, from **Lake Cook Road**, and from the **Tri-State Tollway**—are described below. All eventually join **Route 12** as it heads northwest into Wisconsin.

To the Kettle Moraine from the Northwest Tollway (Interstate 90): The Northwest Tollway is the extension of **Kennedy Expressway** out of Chicago.

Leave the Northwest Tollway at the exit for Route 53 north toward Rolling Meadows and the northwest suburbs. (This exit is part of the big interchange where **Interstate 290** joins from the south.) Follow Route 53 north more than 7 miles to the exit for Lake Cook Road westbound. Go just 0.8 mile west on Lake Cook Road, then turn right onto Route 12.

Follow Route 12 west more than 60 miles, which will take you into Wisconsin and past exits for Lake Geneva and Elkhorn. There are a few abrupt turns along the way, so heed the signs closely. Eventually, Route 12 west is joined by Route 67 north. At an intersection where Route 12 turns left and Route 67 goes straight, turn left to continue west on Route 12. Go 2 miles, then turn right in the village of La Grange onto County Route H (Kettle Moraine Scenic Drive). Follow County Route H north 1.5 miles to the parking lots for the Nordic Hiking and Skiing Trails on the right and the John Muir Hiking and Off-Road Biking Trails on the left.

To the Kettle Moraine from Lake Cook Road: Lake Cook Road runs east-west along the boundary between Lake County and Cook County. Linking Highland Park, Deerfield, Buffalo Grove, and Barrington, Lake Cook Road can be reached by exits off **Edens Expressway**, the **Tri-State Tollway**, and **Route 53**.

Once you are on Lake Cook Road, go to the intersection with Route 12 halfway between Buffalo Grove and Barrington. From there follow Route 12 west more than 60 miles, which will take you into Wisconsin and past exits for Lake Geneva and Elkhorn. There are a few abrupt turns along the way, so heed the signs closely. Eventually, Route 12 west is joined by Route 67 north. At an intersection where Route 12 turns left and Route 67 goes

MAP 3 — Access to the Kettle Moraine State Forest, Southern Unit

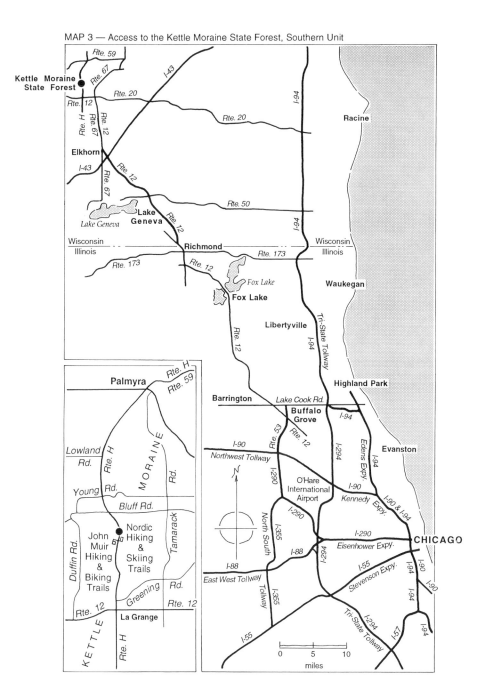

straight, turn left to continue west on Route 12. Go 2 miles, then turn right in the village of La Grange onto County Route H (Kettle Moraine Scenic Drive). Follow County Route H north 1.5 miles to the parking lots for the Nordic Hiking and Skiing Trails on the right and the John Muir Hiking and Off-Road Biking Trails on the left.

To the Kettle Moraine from the Tri-State Tollway *northbound* **near Wisconsin:** The Tri-State Tollway is designated **Interstate 294** as it circles west of Chicago **but is Interstate 94** where it links with Edens Expressway and continues toward Wisconsin.

Leave the Tri-State Tollway at the exit for Route 173, then follow Route 173 west 18.3 miles to an intersection with Route 12 in the town of Richmond. Turn right onto Route 12 and follow it northwest 30 miles into Wisconsin and past exits for Lake Geneva and Elkhorn. Eventually, Route 12 west is joined by Route 67 north. At an intersection where Route 12 turns left and Route 67 goes straight, turn left to continue west on Route 12. Go 2 miles, then turn right in the village of La Grange onto County Route H (Kettle Moraine Scenic Drive). Follow County Route H north 1.5 miles to the parking lots for the Nordic Hiking and Skiing Trails on the right and the John Muir Hiking and Off-Road Biking Trails on the left.

≈   ≈   ≈   ≈

WALKING: The Nordic and Muir trail systems of the **Kettle Moraine State Forest** each have several circuits marked with blazes of different colors. Nearly all of the trails for each system start together—that is, they are congruent—then the shortest loop peels off to return to the parking lot; later the next shortest loop peels off, and so on. The lengths of trail loops are noted on the maps. Of course, you do not have to follow any blazed circuit but can instead use the maps and the blazes to navigate a route of your own choosing. For current trail conditions, call the DNR hotline at (262) 594-6202.

Map 4 at right shows the **Nordic trails**, which are open for hiking when there is no snow. When there *is* snow, the trails are groomed specifically for cross-country skiing, so walking and snowshoeing are prohibited. Off-road bicycling is *never* allowed on the Nordic trails.

MAP 4 — Kettle Moraine: Nordic Hiking & Skiing Trails

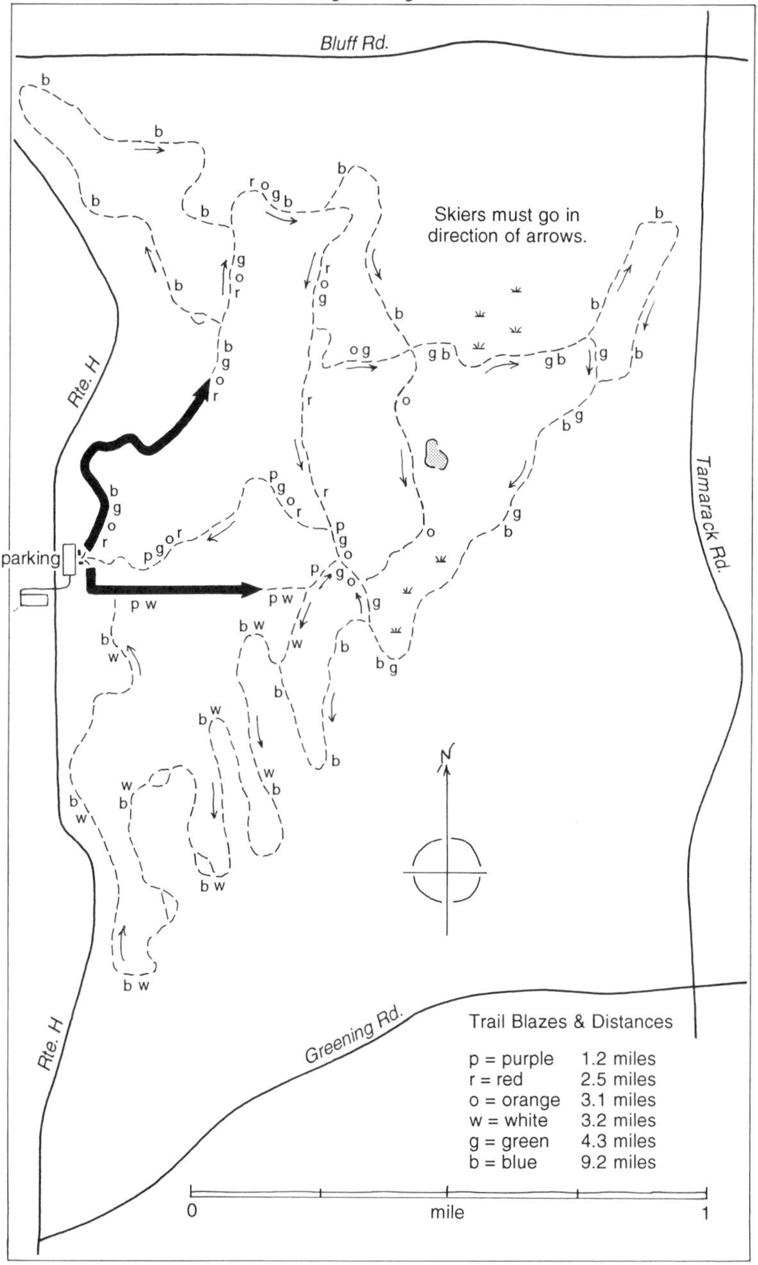

MAP 5 — Kettle Moraine: John Muir Hiking & Biking Trails

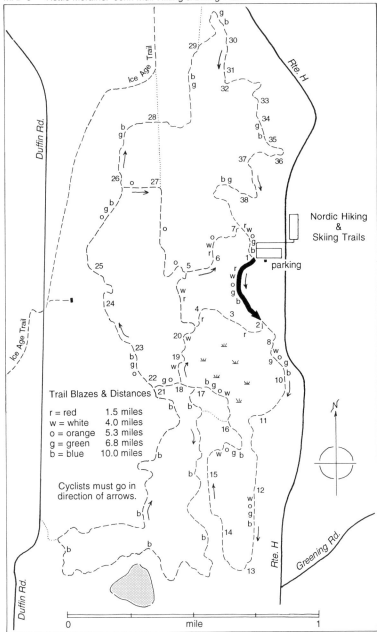

Nordic Hiking
&
Skiing Trails

parking

Trail Blazes & Distances

r = red   1.5 miles
w = white   4.0 miles
o = orange   5.3 miles
g = green   6.8 miles
b = blue   10.0 miles

Cyclists must go in
direction of arrows.

N

0   mile   1

To get started on the **Nordic Trails** shown on page 21, locate the map board between the shelter and the lavatories. Bear left and follow the posts marked with red, orange, green, and blue blazes into the woods and around whatever route you choose. Or if you want to take the white-blazed circuit, turn right from the map board and follow a path behind the lavatories, then left into the woods. Finally, there is a very short purple-blazed loop that is intended for beginning skiers.

≈   ≈   ≈   ≈

Map 5 at left shows the **Muir trails**, which are suitable for hiking—and also for off-road bicycling if the trails are not too wet. Bikers should always call the DNR hotline at (262) 594-6202 beforehand—and hikers too if they want to avoid bikers by going at times when biking is barred. Cross-country skiing and snowshoeing are also permitted, but the trails are not groomed for that purpose.

Start at the corner of the parking lot by a signpost and follow the red, white, orange, green, and blue blazes into the woods and around whatever route you choose.

2

ILLINOIS BEACH STATE PARK

Located north of Chicago near Waukegan, Illinois Beach State Park has a Southern Unit and a Northern Unit separated by the Commonwealth Edison power plant that fronts on Lake Michigan. Of the two units, the southern one is the more interesting, so go there first.

Map 7 on page 31 shows a route of 5 miles (8 kilometers) at the **Southern Unit.** The path follows the bank of the Dead River overlooking the marsh, then continues north, south, and north again through an area of low, parallel ridges (old beach dunes) covered with oak forest and prairie grasses. You can end your outing by walking along the beach itself.

Map 8 on page 32 outlines a route of 3 miles (4.8 kilometers) at the **Northern Unit.** The loop explores woods and marsh inland from the lake.

Illinois Beach State Park is open daily from sunrise to 8:00 p.m. Pets must be leashed. The area is managed by the Illinois Department of Natural Resources; telephone (847) 662-4811 or go to www.dnr.state.il.us and look for the link to state parks.

For automobile directions, please turn to page 28. Walking directions for the Southern Unit start on page 30 and for the Northern Unit on page 33.

AERIAL PHOTOGRAPHS of Illinois Beach State Park show a series of parallel ridges and troughs like oversized corrugations of a plowed field. The ridges and furrows follow the trend of the lakeshore, but they curve slightly inland toward the southern end of the park, as indicated by the stippled ridge outlines on **Map 7** on page 31. (To avoid congesting the map, the ridges are not shown north of the Dead River, but they are there in reality.) Because the difference in elevation between the dry ridges and moist troughs is slight, the shift from one to the other is sometimes defined only by subtle changes in vegetation that are apparent in the excellent photomosaic exhibited at the park's nature center. The hairpin turns of the Dead River also reflect the ridge-and-trough topography.

What accounts for this peculiar terrain, with a surface like a washboard? The ridge nearest the lake is a feature familiar to everyone: It is simply a foredune made of sand blown inland from the beach and anchored by marram grass, cottonwood, and other dune plants, as shown at right. The other ridges are the same feature repeated many times—a series of ancient foredunes now arrayed in ranks one behind the other and altogether bulging eastward into the lake. Each ridge marks the location of the shore at a different time during the last two thousand years or so. During this period, sand that was eroded from the lakeshore north of the park has been washed southward by the longshore current and deposited here. From the beach, the big bulge continues as an underwater apron of sand stretching offshore several thousand feet.

Aside from the ranks of ancient foredunes, other evidence supports the view that the lakeshore in the vicinity of Illinois Beach State Park has been building eastward as sand has accumulated. About a mile inland from the present shoreline is a clay bluff rising twenty or thirty feet above the level of the lake. Almost certainly the lake once lapped against this bluff, just as it does now along the shore in much of Lake Bluff, Lake Forest, Highland Park, and Glencoe. Also, borings at the state park show a vertical profile that is consistent with eastward movement of the shore. Below the present-day dunes there is a layer of coarse sand and gravel such as is commonly seen at the water's edge, where finer sand is washed away by the churning action of waves. And below the layer of coarse sand (and thus laid down previous to it) is a layer of very fine sand such as accumulates in a deeper offshore environment far from breaking waves.

The most direct evidence that the *beach ridge complex* (as geologists call the entire formation) has been growing eastward is provided by marine surveys conducted within the last one hundred years. The shoreline and underwater topography in the vicinity of Illinois Beach State Park were charted in 1872-1873 by the U.S. Lake Survey. The area was charted again in 1950-1955 by the Illinois Division of Waterways. A comparison of the two

surveys shows that during the eighty-year interval, the land at the southern end of Illinois Beach State Park advanced into the lake about one thousand feet and that a blanket of sand about ten feet thick was added to the lake bottom near the shore. However, in the vicinity of the present-day nature center and for a distance of about two miles to the north and two miles to the south, the shoreline remained more or less static. And farther to the north, in the vicinity of the boundary with Wisconsin, the shore receded westward about seven hundred feet and the lake bottom became deeper. This is the area from which sand has been removed by erosion and swept southward by the longshore current to build the beach ridge complex seen today at the state park.

The process of erosion in the north and deposition in the south suggests that the entire beach ridge complex—a body of sand about 9 miles long and .75 to 1.1 miles wide—is slowly migrating southward along the shore of Lake Michigan. Areas currently undergoing accretion will later reach equilibrium followed by gradual and steady loss. Thousands of years in the future, the giant bulge of sand may arrive at Chicago and eventually at the Indiana Dunes.

≈　　≈　　≈　　≈

AUTOMOBILE DIRECTIONS: Located north of Chicago near Waukegan, **Illinois Beach State Park** has a two sections—the **Southern Unit** and the **Northern Unit**—which are separated by the Commonwealth Edison power plant. (See **Map 6** at right.) Directions to both units from the **Tri-State Tollway** and from **Skokie Highway** are given below. Because the Southern Unit is more interesting, I suggest that you go there first.

To Illinois Beach State Park from the Tri-State Tollway: The Tri-State Tollway is designated **Interstate 294** as it circles west of Chicago **but is Interstate 94** where it links with Edens Expressway and continues toward Wisconsin.

Leave the Tri-State Tollway at the exit for Grand Avenue (Route 132) eastbound. In doing so, you will ignore the sign saying that traffic for Illinois Beach State Park should exit from the tollway at Rosecrans Road, which entails longer mileage and an extra toll.

From the top of the exit ramp, follow Grand Avenue east 3.2 miles, then turn left onto Green Bay Road (Route 131). Go

MAP 6 — Access to Illinois Beach State Park

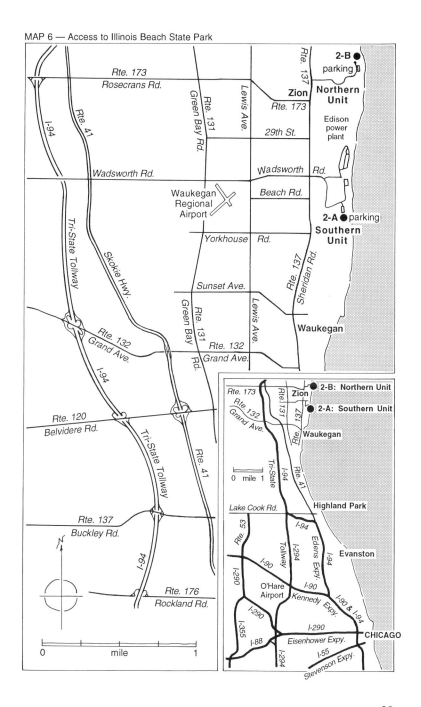

north 4.1 miles, then turn right onto Wadsworth Road. Follow Wadsworth Road east 2.6 miles to the intersection with Sheridan Road (Route 137).

For the Southern Unit (•2-A), continue straight into Illinois Beach State Park. After 1.5 miles, turn right toward the nature center and nature preserve. Walking directions for the Southern Unit start at the bottom of this page.

For the Northern Unit (•2-B) follow Sheridan Road north 2.3 miles to 17th Street in the town of Zion, and there turn right. Go 1.6 miles to the end of the road at the Dune Day Use Area. Walking directions to the Northern Unit start on page 33.

To Illinois Beach State Park from Skokie Highway (Route 41): Skokie Highway is the northward extension of **Edens Expressway** past Highland Park, Lake Forest, Lake Bluff, and Waukegan.

Leave Skokie Highway at the exit—it is on the left—for Grand Avenue (Route 132). From the bottom of the exit ramp, follow Grand Avenue east 0.7 mile, then turn left onto Green Bay Road (Route 131). Go north 4.1 miles, then turn right onto Wadsworth Road. Follow Wadsworth Road east 2.6 miles to the intersection with Sheridan Road (Route 137).

For the Southern Unit (•2-A), continue straight into Illinois Beach State Park. After 1.5 miles, turn right toward the nature center and nature preserve. Walking directions for the Southern Unit start at the bottom of this page.

For the Northern Unit (•2-B), follow Sheridan Road north 2.3 miles to 17th Street in the town of Zion, and there turn right. Go 1.6 miles to the end of the road at the Dune Day Use Area. Walking directions to the Northern Unit start on page 33.

≈   ≈   ≈   ≈

WALKING AT THE SOUTHERN UNIT OF ILLINOIS BEACH STATE PARK: The somewhat convoluted route outlined on **Map 7** at right is contrived to stretch out this walk to a total of 5 miles. The beach ridge complex is a beautiful and unusual area, and I think you will enjoy exploring it thoroughly by looping south and north—and then again—and then down the shore and back. But before you start, stop in at the **nature center**, which is located on the right as you enter the parking lot. Among the displays is an excellent panel of aerial photographs showing the parallel beach ridges.

MAP 7 — Southern Unit of Illinois Beach State Park

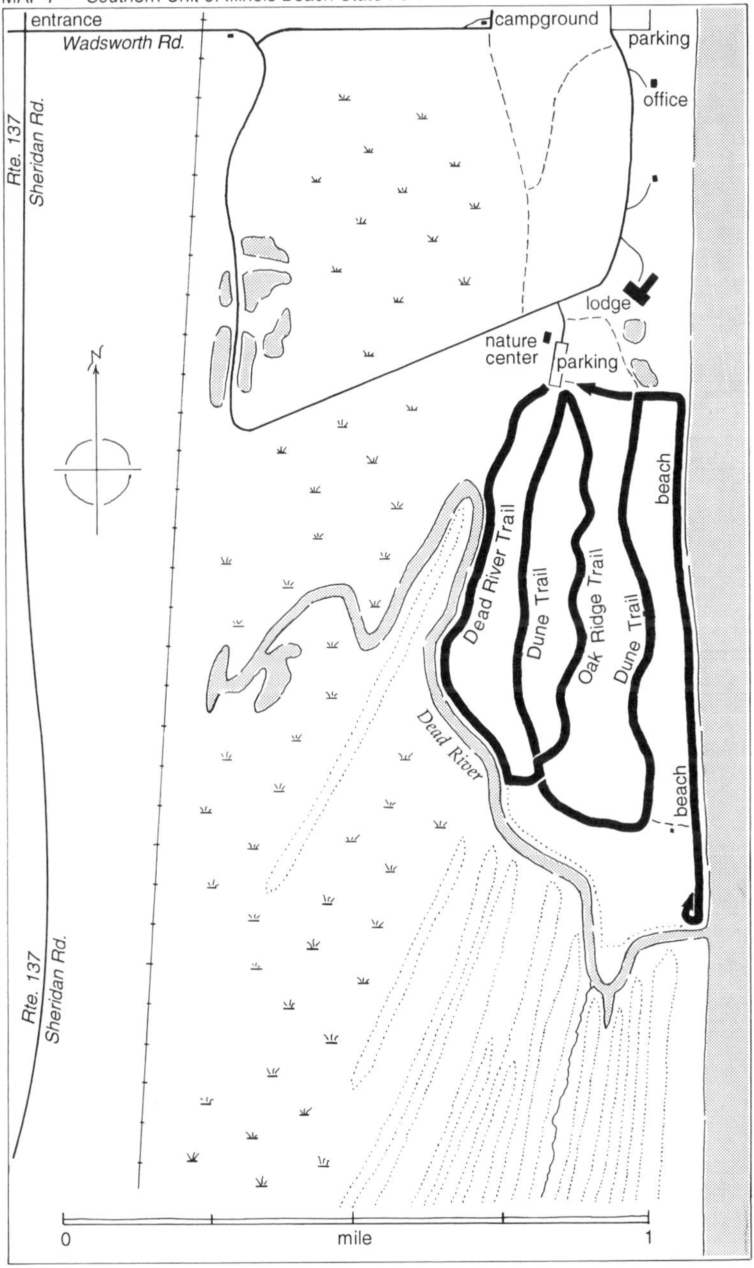

entrance

Wadsworth Rd.

campground

parking

office

Rte. 137
Sheridan Rd.

N

lodge

nature
center

parking

beach

Dead River Trail

Dune Trail

Oak Ridge Trail

Dune Trail

Dead River

beach

Rte. 137
Sheridan Rd.

0   mile   1

31

MAP 8 — Northern Unit of Illinois Beach State Park

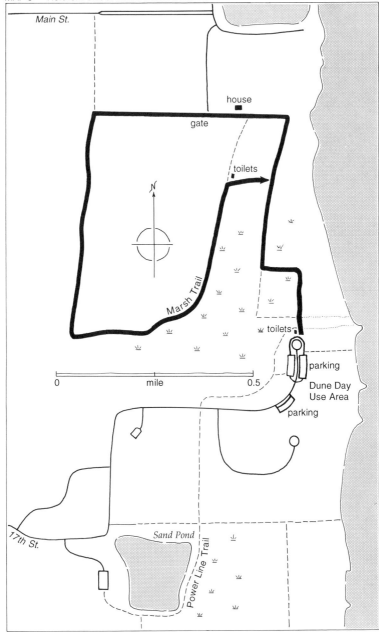

To get started on the walk shown on Map 7, locate the **Dead River trailhead**, which is on the same side of the parking lot as the nature center, but at the other end of the lot. After about a third of a mile, the river comes into view on the right. Continue across a boardwalk and then, after 250 yards, turn left opposite a large block of concrete in the river. At an intersection with a broad path, turn left and then—in just a few yards—turn right onto the Oak Ridge Trail and continue on a footpath along a low ridge covered with scattered, stunted black oak and choke-cherry.

Eventually, within sight of the parking lot, turn very sharply left onto the wide, gravel-paved **Dune Trail**. Follow it in a big U southward through the woods and then back northward through the heath behind the foredunes.

As you again approach the northern limit of the nature preserve, there is a trail junction where you can turn right to the beach. Take a good look at the place where the trail emerges from the dunes so that you will recognize it after walking down the beach to the mouth of the Dead River and then back again. After re-entering the dunes, go straight to reach the parking lot.

≈ ≈ ≈ ≈

WALKING AT THE NORTHERN UNIT OF ILLINOIS BEACH STATE PARK: Map 8 at left shows a circuit of 3 miles through woods and marsh.

To get started, follow a trail to the right of the toilet building and straight into the woods, with Lake Michigan off in the distance to the right. After passing intersecting paths, the trail bears left and arrives at a T-intersection. Turn right. Pass trails intersecting from the left and a house and gate on the right. At another T-intersection, turn left and continue around the loop and along the edge of the marsh. At another toilet building, turn right and then right again back to the parking lot.

3

VOLO BOG STATE NATURAL AREA

Located northwest of Chicago near Fox Lake, Volo Bog includes not only the fascinating bog but also a large area of upland that is explored by several trails.

Map 10 on page 43 shows a floating boardwalk that penetrates to the center of Volo Bog, passing through zones of tamarack, leatherleaf, sphagnum moss, and other unusual bog plants. This intriguing loop is only 0.5 mile long (0.8 kilometer).

Map 11 on page 44 outlines a route of 5.2 miles (8.3 kilometers) that strings together three outlying trails. The route passes through woods and grasslands overlooking Volo Bog and nearby Pistakee Bog.

The Volo Bog area is open daily from 8:00 a.m. to 8:00 p.m. in summer and from 8:00 to 4:00 during the rest of the year. Dogs are prohibited. The visitor center is open Wednesday-Sunday from 9:00 to 3:00. The site is managed by the Illinois Department of Natural Resources; telephone (815) 344-1294 or go to www.dnr.state.il.us/lands/Landmgt/parks/R2/VOLOBOG.htm.

For automobile directions, please turn to page 40. Walking directions start on page 42.

AFTER RETREAT of the last continental ice sheet from the Chicago region about 12,500 years ago, numerous ponds and lakes occupied depressions in the new landscape. Since then these bodies of water have served as catch basins for material eroded from the surrounding upland. Slowly they have become more shallow. Some have been colonized by reeds, cattails, bulrushes, and aquatic plants rooted in the submerged muck, and so have changed into marshes and then into swamps and low, wet woods. There is, however, another route by which ponds and lakes are filled in, not only from the *bottom up*, but also from the *top down*—or that is, by a mat of floating vegetation that covers the water, then slowly thickens and sinks. This is a bog.

In the first stage of bog formation, the water is ringed by cattails and sedges growing from the bank and in the shallows. Next a thin, floating mat of sphagnum moss and leatherleaf (the main bog shrub) spreads from the shore. Because of its vigorous habit of branching, leatherleaf forms a continuous tangle in which separate plants cannot be distinguished. The floating carpet of leatherleaf may be supported in part by logs that have fallen into the water or by rafts of cattails. But for the most part buoyancy is provided by sphagnum moss growing among the vegetation. The sphagnum floats because of gases trapped within the mossy mass. The moss also forms a moist carpet where the branches of leatherleaf, as they spread out and sag under their own weight and the yearly burden of snow, become imbedded and sprout adventitious roots that further bind the mass together and establish a new locus of leatherleaf growth. As branches, leaves, and moss accumulate over the years, the mat of vegetation increases in weight and sinks lower in the water. Although the submerged leatherleaf and sphagnum moss die, the portion of the plant matrix that remains above the surface of the water continues to thrive and to replenish itself, so that the mat slowly thickens and eventually comes to rest at the bottom of the pond or lake.

Long before the floating mat touches bottom, however, it forms a foundation for other shrubs and plants adapted to the bog environment. One common bog shrub is poison sumac, which has compound leaves and off-white berries during the summer and fall. (To be on the safe side, don't handle any unfamiliar shrubs.) A few species of trees appear in areas that once were open water but now are filled with muck and partially-decayed plant debris. In particular, tamarack (also called American larch) often occur in bogs. It is a conifer with clusters of needles that drop in winter. Tamarack roots are shallow so as to avoid the waterlogged substrate and also to support the tree in very unstable soil. Other bog trees are black spruce (rare at Volo Bog) and northern white-cedar (altogether absent here).

Meanwhile, cattails, sedges, and the floating mat of leatherleaf and sphagnum moss continue to close in on the center of the pond or lake. As tamarack in turn advances toward the center, deciduous trees such as red maple, yellow birch, and serviceberry may take over near the shore (but again, not at Volo Bog). Eventually, forest will occupy the entire bog. But until it does, the bog

may show a succession of plant communities in concentric rings, with a small area of open water at the center like the bull's-eye of a target. Such, at any rate, is the idealized, textbook bog.

One peculiarity of bogs is that they are singularly deficient in plant nutrients. The carpet of sphagnum moss tends to retain rainwater, which has a very low mineral content. The sodden sphagnum also seals off the underlying body of water from the air, so that conditions low in oxygen develop. Decay of the vegetable debris below the surface of the water slows down, and so peat accumulates. The type of decay that does occur under these anaerobic bog conditions consumes nitrogen—an essential nutrient —and produces acid, which makes absorption of water difficult for most plants. Acid is also produced directly by the sphagnum, which has the property of absorbing bases and freeing acids. And the fallen needles of tamarack release tannic acid as they steep in the water.

The result is a hostile environment for most plants. Those that survive show special adaptations. For example, the waxy, dry leaves of leatherleaf reflect its need to retain water, even though its roots are immersed in sodden moss. Pitcher plants obtain nitrogen and other nutrients by trapping insects. As shown at left, pitcher plants are so named because of the shape of their leaves. Insects that enter the water-filled pitcher cannot get out because downward-pointing bristles block the way. After the insects drop into the water and decompose, their nutrients are absorbed by the plant. Sundews, which are no longer found at Volo Bog, also trap insects. The disappearance of sundews underscores the injunction that no plant collecting is allowed at Volo Bog.

WHILE YOU'RE ENJOYING the unusual environment at Volo Bog, consider that all too often in Illinois wetlands have been drained for farming or filled for development. Wetlands serve to replenish ground water that ultimately feeds wells for drinking, agriculture, and industry. They are also settling and filtering basins, collecting silt from upland erosion that otherwise would choke streams. Wetlands are often called natural sponges that absorb huge quantities of storm runoff, then release the water slowly over a period of weeks or months. In this way they help to moderate floods and keep streams flowing at normal levels. Often wetlands affect the levels of nearby lakes that have huge recreational value. And apart from their direct value to humans, wetlands provide habitat for many animal and plant species.

≈   ≈   ≈   ≈

AUTOMOBILE DIRECTIONS: Volo Bog is located northwest of Chicago about 3 miles south of Fox Lake. (See **Map 9** at right.) Three approaches—from the **Northwest Tollway**, from **Lake Cook Road**, and from the **Tri-State Tollway**—are described below. All eventually join **Route 12**.

To Volo Bog from the Northwest Tollway (Interstate 90): The Northwest Tollway is the extension of **Kennedy Expressway** out of Chicago.

Leave the Northwest Tollway at the exit for Route 53 north toward Rolling Meadows and the northwest suburbs. (This exit is part of the big interchange where **Interstate 290** joins from the south.) Follow Route 53 north about 7 miles to the exit for Lake Cook Road westbound. Go just 0.8 mile west on Lake Cook Road, then turn right onto Route 12.

Follow Route 12 west 17.4 miles, then turn left onto Brandenburg Road. After 1.2 miles, turn left into the entrance for Volo Bog.

To Volo Bog from Lake Cook Road: Lake Cook Road runs east-west along the boundary between Lake County and Cook County. Linking Highland Park, Deerfield, Buffalo Grove, and Barrington, Lake Cook Road can be reached by exits off **Edens Expressway**, the **Tri-State Tollway**, and **Route 53**.

Once you are on Lake Cook Road, go to the intersection with Route 12 halfway between Buffalo Grove and Barrington. From there take Route 12 west 17.4 miles, then turn left onto Brandenburg Road. After 1.2 miles, turn left into the parking lot for Volo Bog.

To Volo Bog from the Tri-State Tollway near Waukegan: The Tri-State Tollway is designated **Interstate 294** as it circles west of Chicago **but is Interstate 94** where it links with Edens Expressway and continues toward Wisconsin. To reach Volo Bog, there are separate exits off the Tri-State depending on whether you approach from the south or the north.

MAP 9 — Access to Volo Bog State Natural Area

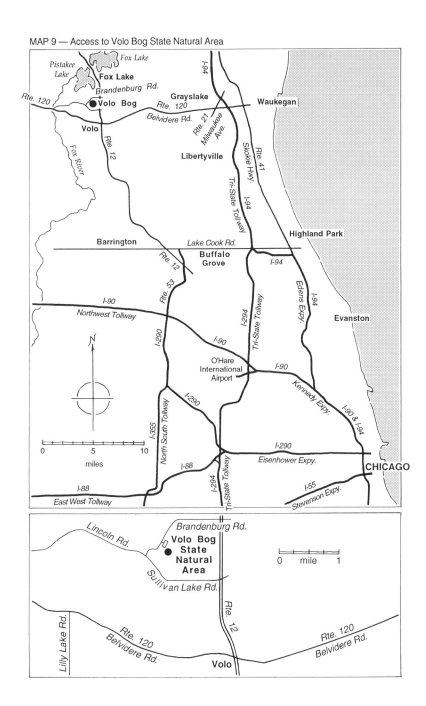

41

From the south: Leave the Tri-State Tollway at the exit for Belvidere Road (Route 120) *westbound.* Go 12.8 miles west through Grayslake to an intersection with Route 12 in the town of Volo. Turn right and follow Route 12 west 2.5 miles, then turn left onto Brandenburg Road. After 1.2 miles, turn left into the parking lot for Volo Bog.

From the north: Leave the Tri-State Tollway at the exit for Milwaukee Avenue (Route 21). Turn right at the top of the exit ramp and go just 0.8 mile, then exit for Route 120 west. From the bottom of the ramp, follow Route 120 west for 11.4 miles to an intersection with Route 12 in the town of Volo. Turn right and follow Route 12 west 2.5 miles, then turn left onto Brandenburg Road. After 1.2 miles, turn left into the parking lot for Volo Bog.

≈   ≈   ≈   ≈

WALKING: The Volo Bog State Natural Area has several trail circuits. Of chief interest is the short loop via boardwalk to the center of Volo Bog itself. Also discussed below are longer loops around the perimeter of the bog and alongside nearby Pistakee Bog. Take time, too, to stop in at the visitor center, housed in a renovated dairy barn and containing some informative exhibits on bog ecology.

Map 10 at right shows the 0.5-mile **Volo Bog Interpretive Trail**.

To get started, follow the path that descends from the visitor center to the edge of the bog, in the process passing a trail intersecting from the left (and by which you will return at the end). At the bottom of the slope, head straight out across the marsh on a boardwalk that leads to a small pond at the center of Volo Bog. Continue around the boardwalk circuit and back to the visitor center.

Map 11 on page 44 shows a route of 4.4 miles through woods, fields, and rolling grassland. You can, of course, take these three loops singly as well as together.

To get started, join the **Tamarack View Trail** (by itself 2.8 miles) at the edge of the bog below the visitor center. With the marshy basin on the left, follow the trail counter-clockwise around the loop. For the first half-mile the trail is near Sullivan Lake Road, but after that it gets much better, passing through

MAP 10 — Volo Bog State Natural Area

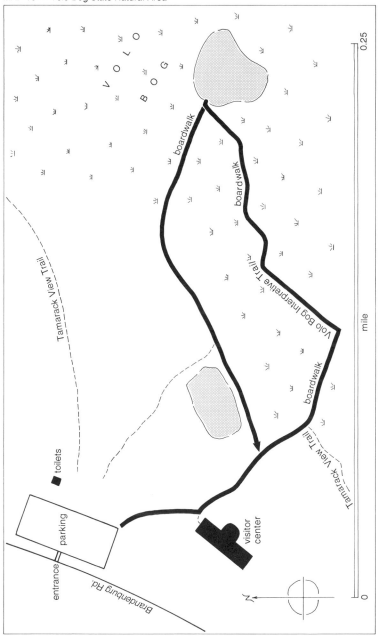

MAP 11 — Volo Bog State Natural Area: outlying trails

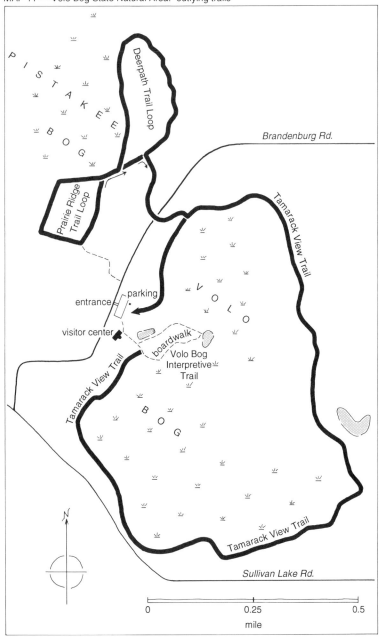

Deepath Trail Loop

P I S T A K E E B O G

Brandenburg Rd.

Prairie Ridge Trail Loop

Tamarack View Trail

parking

entrance

visitor center

boardwalk

V O L O

Volo Bog Interpretive Trail

B O G

Tamarack View Trail

Tamarack View Trail

Sullivan Lake Rd.

N

0   0.25   0.5
mile

woods and rolling prairie overlooking the bog and the forest of tamarack near its center.

Eventually, after nearly completing the circuit, turn right at a trail junction atop a forested ridge above the bog. Descend to and across Brandenburg Road and continue through old fields growing up in brush and thickets. At a T-intersection, turn right for the **Deerpath Trail Loop** and follow it counter-clockwise through young woods and then mature forest alongside Pistakee Bog.

At another T-intersection, turn right for the **Prairie Ridge Trail Loop**. Go a few dozen yards, then fork right to follow the edge of the grassland counter-clockwise in a rectangular circuit. After completing the loop, return to and across Brandenburg Road. Climb to the trail junction overlooking Volo Bog, and there turn right to reach the parking lot.

4

MORAINE HILLS STATE PARK

Map 13 on pages 56 and 57 shows the system of hike-bike paths at Moraine Hills State Park northwest of Chicago. Essentially a triple loop, the route indicated by the bold line is 8.9 miles long (14.2 kilometers), but of course you can do just one or two loops for a shorter outing. The trails meander through a varied landscape of hills, lakes, and marshy basins.

Moraine Hills State Park is open daily for hours that correspond approximately with daylight. Dogs must be leashed. The area is managed by the Illinois Department of Natural Resources; telephone (815) 385-1624 or go to www.dnr.state.il.us and look for the link to state parks.

For automobile directions, please turn to page 54. Walking directions start on page 58.

A NUMBER OF PARKS in the Chicago region could aptly be named "Moraine Hills." In addition to the actual Moraine Hills State Park that is explored in this chapter, there are the Kettle Moraine, Volo Bog, Crabtree Nature Center, and Palos Hills, all featured in this book and all showing the telltale juxtaposition of hillocks and hollows—of abrupt knolls, ridges, marshy basins, and ponds—that are characteristic of glacial moraines.

But what, exactly, is a moraine, and how is one formed? The following is a brief discussion of glacial processes that account for much of the landscape near Chicago.

Glaciers are the result of the accumulation of snow over many years, as frequently occurs at higher elevations and higher latitudes, where the total annual fall of snow exceeds what melts or evaporates. As the snow thaws during the day and refreezes at night, it packs down and becomes granular and then turns to ice. When the ice reaches a thickness of about one hundred feet, it becomes plastic under its own weight and is able to flow, typically only a few inches or feet per day, although sometimes the rate is much faster. The surface, however, remains brittle so that large cracks or *crevasses* develop as the plastic ice below moves under the force of gravity.

Photographs of Alaska, the Alps, and other mountainous regions have made familiar to everyone the image of glaciers flowing like rivers of ice down mountainsides and along broad valleys. As big as they are, these *valley glaciers* are small compared to *continental glaciers*, which develop when snow and ice accumulate over a large area and build to a thickness of one or two miles. For example, even at the present time, the Greenland ice sheet occupies 670,000 square miles and is about 10,000 feet thick at the center; the larger Antarctic ice sheet is about one and a half times as big as the United States and reaches a thickness of 2.5 miles. Spreading from the center, or *zone of accumulation*, a continental glacier flows outward in all directions, like pancake batter spooned onto a griddle. At first tongues of ice advance down valleys and spread out across the lowlands, but as the glacier thickens it overrides hills and even mountains.

At the beginning of the Pleistocene epoch (or Ice Age) in North America about one million years ago, when the world climate was somewhat cooler than at present, snow accumulated in Labrador and in central and western Canada, and from there the ice sheets spread radially until they merged and covered all of Canada and most of the United States north of New Jersey, Pennsylvania, and the Ohio and Missouri Rivers. At the same time, continental glaciers also spread from other, similar zones of accumulation in Scandinavia, Siberia, and Antarctica. In fact, in Europe the first Pleistocene glacier appears to have occurred about two million years ago.

Corresponding to the zone of accumulation at the center of the ice sheet is the *zone of wastage* at the perimeter. The wastage is caused by melting and evaporation (together called *ablation*) and by the *calving* of icebergs where the glacier meets the ocean. If the rate at which the glacier moves forward is greater than the rate of wastage, then on balance the ice sheet advances. If the ice front melts as fast as the glacier moves, the perimeter is stationary. And if the ice front melts faster than the rate of advance, the glacier recedes. The overall balance between advance and reces-

sion is affected by shifts in precipitation, in worldwide climate, and in other factors that are still not altogether understood.

Glaciers act as huge earth scrapers and conveyor belts combined into one ponderous process. As it moves, the ice strips away the soil and grinds down the bedrock of the vast area over which the frozen mass advances. The immense weight of the ice even depresses the crust of the earth, so that the land surface beneath the glacier sinks (but later rises, or *rebounds*, after the ice melts). Boulders, rock fragments, sand, and a huge amount of finely pulverized stone called *rock flour* become imbedded in the bottom few meters of the glacier and constitute its *load*, which is carried forward by the ice sheet and deposited when the glacier melts, if not sooner. Often the bottom layer becomes so overloaded with material that the debris is simply smeared forward for a few miles before dropping out. As boulders are dragged and scraped along the surface beneath the glacier, they sometimes leave scratches or *striations* in the bedrock that show (after the ice sheet melts) the direction from which the glacier advanced.

During the Pleistocene epoch, there were four distinct periods of continental glaciation in North America. The most recent ice sheet is termed the Wisconsin Glacier, but it reached as far south as central Illinois. The Wisconsin Glacier advanced about 70,000 years ago and retreated from the Chicago region only 12,500 years ago. The retreat was spasmodic; periods of steady withdrawal alternated with periods during which the ice front was at a standstill or even advanced again for short distances. In each case the earth material carried by the glacier was deposited to create characteristic landforms. One common assemblage of deposits is that of an *morainic ridge* fronted by an *outwash plain* and backed by a *ground moraine*.

A morainic ridge occurs where the ice front is stationary for a time. The glacier continues to flow forward, carrying its load of debris with it, but the rate of flow is more or less matched by the rate of wastage, so that the earth material is dumped in a line along the ice front. Pushed from behind, the advancing glacier ascends the accumulating debris, heaping the deposits higher and higher as the dirt-laden ice melts. The result is a range of irregular hills composed of clay, sand, small rocks, and boulders mixed together and called *glacial till* or *boulder clay*.

If the glacier advances again after pausing for a period, the morainic ridge is obliterated. But where the ice sheet reaches its furthest extent and comes to a standstill before receding, the ridge will survive and is termed an *end moraine* or *terminal moraine*. And if recession pauses for a period and then resumes, a *recessional moraine* is created, and it too will survive unless overridden by subsequent resurgence of the glacier. Depending on how still the glacial front stood, end moraines and recessional moraines may be many miles wide and scores of miles long, in which case some authorities term them a *morainic system*. The southern end of Lake Michigan is ringed by successive parallel moraines. Some outstanding examples of end moraines in the Midwest and in Europe are many hundreds of miles long. They may be interrupted by gaps carved by subsequent erosion, including erosion from rivers of meltwater pouring out of temporary lakes (called *proglacial lakes*) that were impounded between a morainic ridge and the receding ice front.

In front of a morainic ridge—or that is, in the direction toward which the ice advanced—is the *outwash plain*. Such plains were formed when sediment-laden streams of meltwater flowed out from the glacier and deposited *alluvial fans* or *outwash fans*. Over time the alluvium spread and coalesced to form a continuous apron sloping gently away from the moraine. Because the energy of the meltwater dissipated as the streams fanned out, the deposits are sorted. Gravel and coarse sand were dropped close to the moraine, finer sand farther out, and rock flour (which gives glacial streams their characteristic milky appearance) more distant still. Near the morainic ridge, the outwash plain may be pitted with *kettles*, which are abrupt depressions marking where blocks of ice were buried within the alluvium, either in whole or in part. After the ice melted, the surrounding earth slumped to form the kettles, which may contain lakes and ponds. Kettles can also occur within the moraine itself.

In back of the morainic ridge—that is, on the side from which the ice advanced—is the *ground moraine*. As already noted, the ice at the bottom of a glacier may have become so loaded with clay, sand, and rocks that some of the material dropped out even as the glacier continued to move over it. When the ice sheet receded steadily by melting, additional debris was left behind, so that a vast area was blanketed by till, producing a landscape of gently rolling upland and undrained or poorly-drained flats that may

hold marshes and shallow ponds. In some areas, low, elongated hills called *drumlins* dot the landscape. Drumlins typically occur in areas underlain by bedrock that is relatively soft, like shale, and hence was easily ground into sticky clay. Gradually the ice flowed over these masses, adding still more earth and rock to them and molding them into their elongated, streamlined shape. Drumlins, which may be more than 100 or 150 feet high and more than half a mile long, are common in Wisconsin. Other features occurring in the ground moraine are sinuous ridges of water-sorted sand and gravel sometimes extending for miles, usually in a course more or less parallel with the direction of the ice movement. Such formations are called *eskers* and are thought to have been deposited by meltwater streams that flowed through tunnels beneath the ice.

Although northeastern Illinois shows a remarkable series of morainic ridges, outwash plains, and ground moraines, each with its characteristic features, it is important to keep in mind that these landforms are not always distinct. Frequently they grade into each other and may even obscure one another, overlapping like shingles as the glacier receded spasmodically. Also, successive ridges that in some places are far apart may in other areas merge because the glacier did not retreat at the same rate along the entire ice front.

In North America, the process of withdrawal sometimes followed a scenario called "stagnation zone retreat." The southern margin of the glacier often consisted of a narrow band of stagnant ice. Because of ablation, ice in the stagnation zone was no longer thick enough to flow. Active ice to the north, however, continued to advance, melting as it came and depositing gravel, sand, and silt. Streams pouring out from the glacier carried the material forward and deposited it in thick beds sometimes underlain by the stagnant ice. Of course, after the buried ice melted, the overlying material settled and slumped to form undulating mounds of bedded sand and gravel.

There is also evidence to support another model for glacial retreat: that of *regional* stagnation. As the climate changed and the ice sheet thinned, large units of the glacier may have stopped moving, perhaps because they lay to the south of highlands that were no longer surmountable by the diminished mass of ice flowing from the north. The heights that separate one watershed from another were no obstacle for the waxing ice sheet, but as the glacier waned, even modest ridges may have blocked and redirected the movement of ice. According to this theory, ice to the south of such barriers stagnated in vast units.

≈   ≈   ≈   ≈

AUTOMOBILE DIRECTIONS: Moraine Hills State Park
borders the Fox River northwest of Chicago. (See **Map 12** at right.) Three approaches—from the **Northwest Tollway**, from **Lake Cook Road**, and from the **Tri-State Tollway**—are described below.

To Moraine Hills State Park from the Northwest Tollway (Interstate 90): The Northwest Tollway is the extension of **Kennedy Expressway** out of Chicago.

Leave the Northwest Tollway at the exit for Route 53 north toward Rolling Meadows and the northwest suburbs. (This exit is part of the big interchange where **Interstate 290** joins from the south.) Follow Route 53 north about 7 miles to the exit for Lake Cook Road westbound. Go just 0.8 mile west on Lake Cook Road, then turn right onto Route 12.

Follow Route 12 west 10.2 miles to the exit for Route 176 (Liberty Street). At the bottom of the exit ramp, turn left and follow Route 176 west 3.4 miles, then turn right onto River Road. After 2.1 miles, turn right into Moraine Hills State Park.

There are many parking lots from which you can join the trails shown on **Map 13** on page 56 and 57, but ! suggest that you go 2 miles to the lot for the Northern Woods at the end of the road, which in itself is very scenic.

To Moraine Hills State Park from Lake Cook Road: Lake Cook Road runs east-west along the boundary between Lake County and Cook County. Linking Highland Park, Deerfield, Buffalo Grove, and Barrington, Lake Cook Road can be reached by exits off **Edens Expressway, the Tri-State Tollway,** and **Route 53**.

Once you are on Lake Cook Road, go to the intersection with Route 12 halfway between Buffalo Grove and Barrington. From there take Route 12 west 10.2 miles to the exit for Route 176 (Liberty Street). At the bottom of the exit ramp, turn left and follow Route 176 west 3.4 miles, then turn right onto River Road. After 2.1 miles, turn right into Moraine Hills State Park.

54   *[Directions continue on page 58.]*

MAP 12 — Access to Moraine Hills State Park

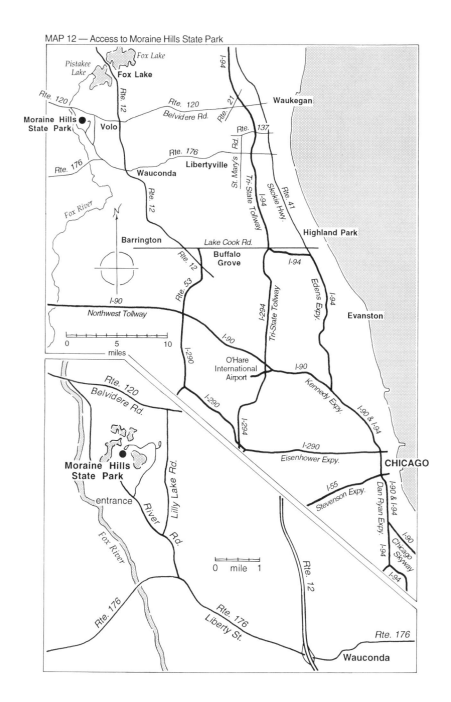

MAP 13 — Moraine Hills State Park

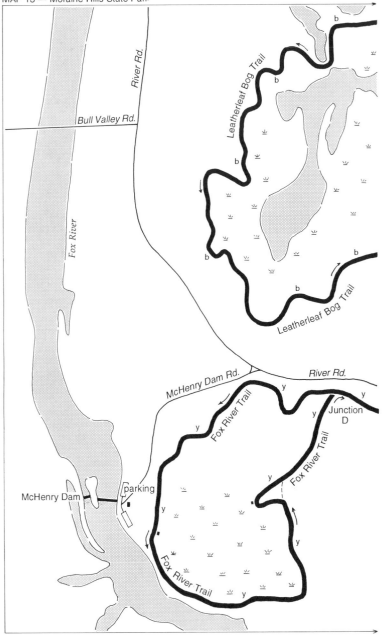

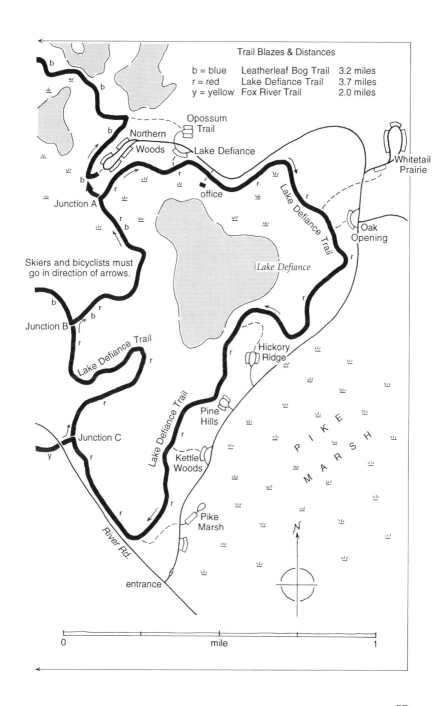

Trail Blazes & Distances

b = blue   Leatherleaf Bog Trail   3.2 miles
r = red   Lake Defiance Trail   3.7 miles
y = yellow   Fox River Trail   2.0 miles

Opossum Trail

Northern Woods

Lake Defiance

Whitetail Prairie

office

Junction A

Oak Opening

Skiers and bicyclists must go in direction of arrows.

Lake Defiance Trail

Junction B

Lake Defiance

Lake Defiance Trail

Hickory Ridge

Junction C

Pine Hills

Lake Defiance Trail

y

Kettle Woods

P I K E   M A R S H

Pike Marsh

River Rd.

entrance

N

0   mile   1

57

There are many parking lots from which you can join the trails shown on **Map 13** on pages 56 and 57, but I suggest that you go 2 miles to the lot for the Northern Woods at the end of the road, which in itself is very scenic.

To Moraine Hills State Park from the Tri-State Tollway near Libertyville: The Tri-State Tollway is designated **Interstate 294** as it circles west of Chicago **but is Interstate 94** where it links with Edens Expressway and continues toward Wisconsin. To reach Moraine Hills, there are separate exits off the Tri-State Tollway depending on whether you approach from the south or the north.

From the south: Leave the Tri-State Tollway at the exit for Route 176 (Rockland Road). Follow Route 176 west 16.6 miles through Libertyville and Wauconda and under Route 12. Eventually, turn right onto River Road and follow it 2.1 miles, then turn right into Moraine Hills State Park.

There are many parking lots from which you can join the trails shown on **Map 13** on pages 56 and 57, but I suggest that you go 2 miles to the lot for the Northern Woods at the end of the road, which in itself is very scenic.

From the north: Leave the Tri-State Tollway at the exit for Buckley Road (Route 137). Follow Buckley Road west 0.8 mile, then turn left onto St. Mary's Road. After 1.8 miles, turn right onto Route 176 and go 16 miles through Libertyville and Wauconda and under Route 12. Eventually, turn right onto River Road and follow it 2.1 miles, then turn right into Moraine Hills State Park.

There are many parking lots from which you can join the trails shown on **Map 13** on pages 56 and 57, but I suggest that you go 2 miles to the lot for the Northern Woods at the end of the road, which in itself is very scenic.

≈   ≈   ≈   ≈

WALKING and BICYCLING: As shown on **Map 13** on pages 56 and 57, there are three main trail loops at **Moraine Hills State Park**. Each loop is blazed with a different color (blue, red, and yellow), and all three loops are joined together by four trail junctions marked A, B, C, and D. (Between A and B the blue and red loops are congruent.)

Depending on where you park, you can, of course, take each of the loops individually, but the bold line on the map shows a grand tour of 8.9 miles through the entire trail system, starting at the Northern Woods parking lot.

To get started from the Northern Woods parking lot, go to the U-turn at the end of the lot. From there, follow a trail past a gate. After 90 yards, turn right at a T-intersection with the blue-blazed **Leatherleaf Bog Trail**, which by itself is 3.2 miles long. Follow the wide hike-bike path counter-clockwise around the circuit to **Junction B**. Turn left to continue on the blue-blazed trail, which in this section is congruent with the red-blazed trail.

At **Junction A** near the Northern Woods parking lot, you can return to your car or—as shown by the bold line on the map— bear right to continue clockwise on the red-blazed **Lake Defiance Trail**, which by itself is 3.7 miles long.

Eventually, after passing alongside River Road, the red loop arrives at **Junction C**. To return to the Northern Woods parking lot, stay on the red trail. But for the yellow-blazed **Fox River Trail**, which is 2 miles long, turn left under the road. At **Junction D**, bear right and go counter-clockwise around the circuit.

After arriving back at Junction D, turn right. At Junction C bear left and follow the red blazes to Junction B. Turn right and follow the blue and red blazes to Junction A at the Northern Woods parking lot.

5

LAKEWOOD FOREST PRESERVE

Lakewood Forest Preserve is located northwest of Chicago near Wauconda. **Map 15** on page 70 shows the preserve's system of bridle paths and foot trails. The best walking is on the bridle paths south of Ivanhoe Road, and I suggest that you start there, as indicated by the bold line on the map. Totaling about 4.5 miles (7.2 kilometers), the wide, well-graded bridle paths explore a rolling landscape of forest, fields, ponds, and marsh. For more walking, you can try the foot trails located north of Ivanhoe Road.

Lakewood Forest Preserve is open daily from 6:30 a.m. to sunset. Dogs must be leashed. The area is managed by Lake County Forest Preserves; telephone (847) 367-6640 or go to www.lcfpd.org.

Lakewood is also the site of the **Lake County Discovery Museum**, which is open Monday through Saturday from 11:00 a.m. to 4:30 p.m. For information telephone (847) 968-3400.

For automobile directions, please turn to page 67. Walking directions start on page 71.

WARNING: This chapter is wholly (some might say, woolly) birdtalk.

Now that I have gotten rid of all but the lunatic fringe (i.e., you, me, and other lovers of birds and words), we can natter happily among ourselves about the rainy-day pastime of bird names. For example, as a word, *titmouse* is worth a little curiosity—isn't it? Although a titmouse is easy to identify, how many birders know what the word means? Why is a petrel so called? And what about *killdeer, nuthatch, knot*, and other peculiar bird names?

Although many American Indian place names (Chicago, for example) were adopted by the Europeans, the settlers and early ornithologists made a clean sweep when it came to naming—or rather renaming—North American birds. In a few cases where the same species (brant, for instance) were found on both sides of the Atlantic, use of the English name was a matter of course. More often, however, the settlers simply reused the names of Old World birds for similar-looking—but actually different—New World species. The English, for example, have given the name *robin* to various red-breasted birds in India, Australia, and North America. More often still, the use of general names like *wren* was extended to American birds, with the addition of qualifying words to identify individual species (house wren, Carolina wren, and so forth). However, scientific classification has sometimes placed whole categories of American birds in entirely different families than their European namesakes, as in the case of American warblers. The only North American birds in the same family as the European warblers are the gnatcatcher and kinglets—not at all what are called warblers here. Finally, in relatively rare instances, American birds have been given unique and colorful new names based on their behavior, appearance, and songs, as, for instance, the yellow-bellied sapsucker, canvasback, and whip-poor-will.

Early American ornithologists seem to have been quite casual about naming birds. Alexander Wilson (1766-1813), author of the nine-volume *American Ornithology,* once shot a bird in a magnolia tree; hence *magnolia warbler* for a bird whose preferred habitat is low, moist conifers. After Wilson's death his work was overshadowed by Audubon's superior, life-sized drawings, but Wilson was in many ways the greater pioneer, depicting 264 species of birds, of which 39 were not previously known. Usually Wilson named birds according to the locality where his specimens were collected. For example, he named the Nashville warbler and the Savannah sparrow, but not the Philadelphia vireo. (It was named by naturalist Charles Lucien Jules Laurent Bonaparte, Prince of Canino and Musignano, a nephew of Napoleon Bonaparte and presumably an authority on names.)

Incidentally, Nashville, Savannah, and Philadelphia are the *only* American cities that share the inestimable honor of having birds named after them. Perhaps Ipswich should be ousted from this select set, inasmuch as the American Ornithologists' Union has determined that the Ipswich bird is merely a pale race of the Savannah breed. And what about the Baltimore oriole? It is *not* named for Baltimore, Maryland. Rather, the bird was named for the Lords Baltimore, colonial proprietors of Maryland. Mark Catesby, an eighteenth-century naturalist from England who traveled in America long before Baltimore Town existed, called the oriole the "Baltimore-Bird" because its colors were the same as those of the Baltimores' heraldic flag.

Not surprisingly, many of the geographic names given to birds by early ornithologists bear no precise relation to the species' breeding territory or winter range. The Savannah sparrow, for example, is found throughout North America and might just as well have been named for Chicago or Seattle or even Anchorage. Among the Tennessee, Connecticut, and Kentucky warblers (all named by Wilson), only the last is at all likely to be found in its nominal state during the breeding season, and none winter north of Mexico. But probably the greatest geographical misnomer among bird names is our native turkey, after the supposed region of its origin. The name was first applied to the guinea cock, which was imported from Africa through Turkey into Europe and with which the American bird was for a time identified when it was first introduced to Europe in about 1530.

Some bird names, although seeming to refer to specific geographic areas, are actually far broader in their historical meaning. The *Louisiana* heron refers to the vast territory of the Louisiana Purchase, even though the bird is usually found only in coastal areas. The species was first collected on the Louis and Clark expedition and was named by Wilson. *Arcadia*, as in Arcadian flycatcher, is an old French name for Nova Scotia, but the term was used generally to suggest a northern clime, as was also *boreal* in boreal chickadee, from the Greek god of the north wind, Boreas.

In addition to birds named *by* early ornithologists and explorers, there are birds named *for* them by contemporary and later admirers of their work. Wilson, for example, is memorialized in the name of a petrel, a phalarope, a plover, a warbler, and also a genus of warblers. Audubon is honored by Audubon's shearwater and Audubon's warbler, a form of the yellow-rumped warbler. There was a measure of reciprocity about this last bird name: In 1837 John Kirk Townsend, a Philadelphia ornithologist and bird collector, named Audubon's warbler, and a year or two later Audubon returned the favor with Townsend's solitaire. Then there are species named for ornithologists' wives, daughters, and relatives, as in Anna's hummingbird and Virginia's,

Country Walks in the Chicago Region

Lucy's, and Grace's warblers. Some birds bear human names connected to no one in particular. Guillemot (French for "little William"), magpie (in part based on Margaret), martin ("little Mars"), and parakeet ("little Peter") are thought to be pet names or affectionate tags that have become attached to various species.

Color is probably the dominant theme in bird names. Plumages cover the spectrum, ranging from the red phalarope through the orange-crowned warbler, yellow rail, green heron, blue goose, indigo bunting, and violet-crowned hummingbird. For stripped-down straightforwardness there are names like bluebird and blackbird. For vividness there are color designations like scarlet tanager, vermilion flycatcher, lazuli bunting, and cerulean warbler. To improve our dictionary skills, there are color-based names like fulvous tree duck, ferruginous hawk, flammulated owl, and parula warbler. For unpoetry, there is hepatic tanager, so called because of the liver-colored, liver-shaped patch on each cheek. For meaninglessness there is the clay-colored sparrow. (What color is that? Answer: buffy brown, at least on the rump.) Some bird names less obviously denote basic hues: vireo (green), oriole (golden), dunlin ("little dull-brown one"), canvasback (for its speckled gray and white back), brant (thought by some to mean "burnt," referring to its black head and neck), and waxwing (whose red-tipped secondary wing feathers recalled to someone the color and substance of sealing wax). A great many bird names pair color with some specific body part, as in redhead, goldeneye, yellowlegs, and so forth.

Shape or other distinctive features often are reflected in bird names. The profile of the bufflehead suggests an American buffalo or bison. The loggerhead shrike has a disproportionately large head. Shovelers have long, broad bills. The word *falcon* is derived from a Latin term for "sickle," suggesting the bird's curved talons. From head to toe, there is a body part that is some bird's nominal identity: tufted titmouse, horned lark, eared grebe (*grebe* itself may come from a Breton word for "crest"), ruffed grouse, pectoral sandpiper (for the air sack under its breast feathers), short-tailed hawk, stilt sandpiper (for its comparatively long legs), rough-legged hawk (for its feathered tarsi), sharp-shinned hawk (it has), semipalmated sandpiper (for its partially webbed feet), and Lapland longspur (for the elongated claw on the hind toe).

Some names indicate size, from *great* and *greater* to *little, lesser,* and *least*. Symmetry would seem to demand a *greatest*, but perhaps that need is filled by *king*, which occasionally refers to stature. The king rail, for example, is the largest of the rails. But sometimes *king* is simply a compliment to a bird's raiment or a reference to distinguishing plumage on its crown, as in the ruby-crowned and golden-crowned kinglets ("little kings"). *Gallinule* itself suggests size, being derived from Latin for "little hen." *Starling* is from the Anglo-Saxon word for bird; with the addition of the diminutive suffix *-ling*, it simply means "little bird." *Titmouse* similarly is a combination of Icelandic and Anglo-Saxon meaning "small bird." The base word *tit* for *bird* also appears in bushtit and wrentit.

A few names, like that of the gull-billed tern, make explicit comparisons with other birds. The hawk owl has a long slender tail that gives this bird a falcon-like appearance. The lark bunting sings on the wing like a skylark, the curlew sandpiper has a downwardly curved, curlew-like bill. The swallow-tailed kite has a deeply forked tail like a barn swallow. The turkey vulture has a head that somewhat resembles that of a turkey. And *cormorant* is derived from French for "sea crow."

Many bird names refer to distinctive behavior. Woodpeckers, sapsuckers, creepers, and wagtails all do what their names suggest. Turnstones do indeed turn over small stones and shells while searching for food. *Black skimmer* describes the bird's technique of sticking its lower bill into the water while flying just above the surface. *Shearwater* similarly suggests the bird's skimming flight. Frigatebirds (also called man-o'-war-birds) were named by sailors for the birds' piratical habit of pursuing and robbing other birds, as do also parasitic jaegers. *Duck* is derived from Anglo-Saxon for "diver." *Nuthatch* is from "nut hack," referring to the bird's technique of wedging a nut into a crevice and then hacking it into small pieces. *Vulture* is akin to Latin *vellere*, "to pluck or tear." The folk name *shitepoke* for various herons is based on these birds' habit of defecating when flushed. Although many people associate *loon* with the bird's lunatic laugh, as in "crazy as a loon," more likely the word is derived from a Norse term for "lame," describing the bird's awkwardness on land—a result of its legs being very near its tail, so that when nesting the loon has to push itself on its stomach. There is, however, at least one North American bird that is named for its mental capacity: the booby. Seamen who raided the isolated colonies thought the birds stupid because they were unaccustomed to predators and inept at protecting themselves. The dotterel (whose name is related to "dolt" and "dotage") is another nominally foolish bird, as is the extinct dodo from Mauritius.

Some birds, such as the whooping crane, clapper rail, piping plover, laughing gull, mourning dove, warbling vireo, and chipping sparrow, are named for how they sound. Similarly, the comparative volume of their vocalizations is the theme that distinguishes between mute, whistling, and trumpeter swans. *Oldsquaw* suggests this duck's noisy, garrulous voice. The catbird mews and the grasshopper sparrow trills and buzzes like the insect. Some dictionaries, however, says that the grasshopper sparrow is named for its diet, as are the goshawk (literally, "goosehawk") and oystercatchers, flycatchers, and gnatcatchers. The saw-whet owl is named for the bird's endlessly repeated note, which suggests a saw being sharpened with a whetstone—a sound now lost to history. The bittern, whose name ultimately is traceable to its call, has a colorful assortment of descriptive folk names, including "bog-bumper," "stake driver," "thunder pumper," and "water belcher." The evening grosbeak and vesper sparrow both tend to sing at dusk. Finally, of course, many birds' songs or calls are also the basis for their names, including the bobolink, bobwhite, bulbul, chachalaca, chickadee, chuck-will's-widow, chukar, crow, cuckoo, curlew, dickcissel, godwit, killdeer, kittiwake, owl, pewee, phoebe, pipits, towhee, veery, whip-poor-will, and willet. *Quail* (like *quack*) is thought originally to have been imitative of bird calls.

Habitat is a major theme of bird names, as with the surf scoter, sandpiper, marsh hawk, meadowlark, and field, swamp, and tree sparrows—and many other birds besides. Then there is the *kind* of tree or shrub, as in spruce and sage grouse, willow ptarmigan, pinyon jay, cedar waxwing, myrtle warbler, pine siskin, and orchard oriole. The barn, cliff, cave, tree, and bank swallows are named for their preferred nesting sites. The *prairie warbler*, however, is a misnomer; the bird is common east of the Mississippi and usually is found in brushy, scrubby areas.

Several bird names are associated with human figures. Knots, which frequent shores and tidal flats, are said to be named for

Canute (or Cnut), King of the Danes. To demonstrate to the sycophants of his court that he was not omnipotent, Canute vainly ordered the tide to stop rising. Petrels are thought to be named for Saint Peter, who walked on the water at Lake Gennesaret. When landing in the water, petrels dangle their feet and hesitate for an instant, thus appearing to stand on the waves. Cardinals, of course, are named for the red robes and hats of the churchmen. Similarly, prothonotory warblers have the golden raiment of ecclesiastical prothonotories. The bizarre and contrasting pattern of the harlequin duck suggests the traditional costume of Italian pantomime.

Finally, there is the ovenbird, almost unique among North American birds for being named after the appearance of its nest, which is built on the forest floor and resembles a miniature, domed brick oven. "Basketbird" and "hangnest" are folk names referring to the pendulous nests of orioles.

≈ ≈ ≈ ≈

AUTOMOBILE DIRECTIONS: Lakewood Forest Preserve is located northwest of Chicago near Wauconda. (See **Map 14** on page 69.) Three approaches—from the **Northwest Tollway**, from **Lake Cook Road**, and from the **Tri-State Tollway**—are described below.

To Lakewood Forest Preserve from the Northwest Tollway (Interstate 90): The Northwest Tollway is the extension of **Kennedy Expressway** out of Chicago.

Leave the Northwest Tollway at the exit for Route 53 north toward Rolling Meadows and the northwest suburbs. (This exit is part of the big interchange where **Interstate 290** joins from the south.) Follow Route 53 north about 7 miles to the exit for Lake Cook Road westbound. Go just 0.8 mile west on Lake Cook Road, then turn right onto Route 12.

Follow Route 12 west 10.2 miles to the exit for Route 176 (Liberty Street). At the bottom of the exit ramp, turn right and go 2.3 miles east on Route 176 to the entrance to Lakewood Forest Preserve on the right.

Follow the entrance drive only 0.1 mile, then turn left and immediately right past the Lake County Discovery Museum. At a T-intersection with Ivanhoe Road, turn left. After just 100 yards, turn right toward the equestrian trails and go 0.1 mile to park.

To Lakewood Forest Preserve from Lake Cook Road: Lake Cook Road runs east-west along the boundary between Lake County and Cook County. Linking Highland Park, Deerfield, Buffalo Grove, and Barrington, Lake Cook Road can be reached by exits off **Edens Expressway, the Tri-State Tollway,** and **Route 53.**

Once you are on Lake Cook Road, go to the intersection with Route 12 halfway between Buffalo Grove and Barrington. From there take Route 12 west 10.2 miles to the exit for Route 176 (Liberty Street). At the bottom of the exit ramp, turn right and go 2.3 miles east on Route 176 to the entrance to Lakewood Forest Preserve on the right.

Follow the entrance drive only 0.1 mile, then turn left and immediately right past the Lake County Discovery Museum. At a T-intersection with Ivanhoe Road, turn left. After 100 yards, turn right toward the equestrian trails and go 0.1 mile to park.

To Lakewood Forest Preserve from the Tri-State Tollway near Libertyville: The Tri-State Tollway is designated **Interstate 294** as it circles west of Chicago **but is Interstate 94** where it links with Edens Expressway and continues toward Wisconsin. To reach Lakewood, there are separate exits off the Tri-State Tollway depending on whether you approach from the south or the north.

From the south: Leave the Tri-State Tollway at the exit for Route 176 (Rockland Road). Follow Route 176 west 10.4 miles through Libertyville toward Wauconda. At an intersection with Fairfield Road, turn left. After just 0.2 mile, turn right onto Ivanhoe Road and go 0.5 mile. After passing the Lakewood Operations Office, turn left toward the equestrian trails and go 0.1 mile to the parking lot.

From the north: Leave the Tri-State Tollway at the exit for Buckley Road (Route 137). Follow Buckley Road west 0.8 mile, then turn left onto St. Mary's Road. After 1.8 mile, turn right onto Route 176 and go 9.7 miles west through Libertyville toward Wauconda. At an intersection with Fairfield Road, turn left. After just 0.2 mile, turn right onto Ivanhoe Road and go 0.5 mile. After passing the Lakewood Operations Office, turn left toward the equestrian trails and go 0.1 mile to the parking lot.

≈   ≈   ≈   ≈

MAP 14 — Access to Lakewood Forest Preserve

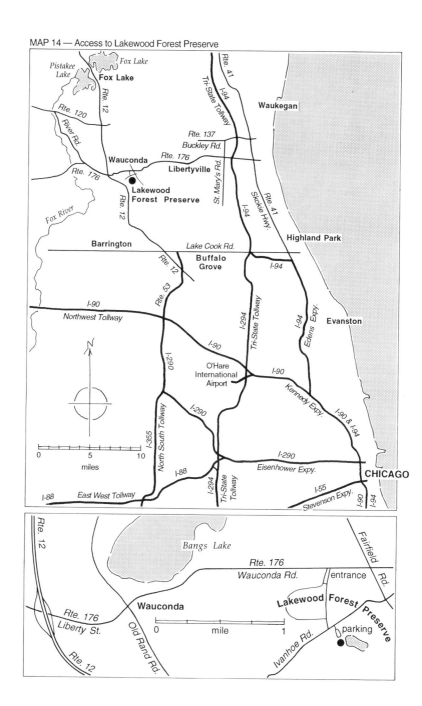

69

MAP 15 — Lakewood Forest Preserve

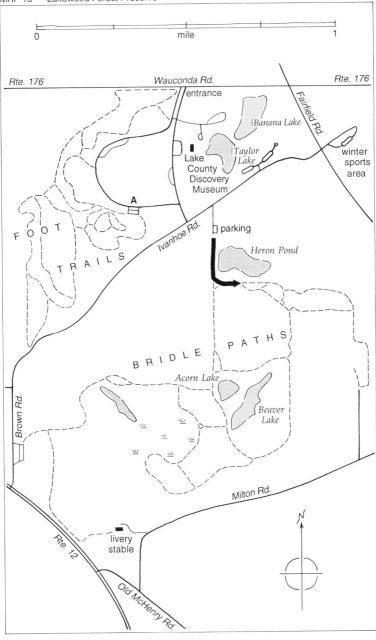

WALKING: Map 15 at left shows the trail system at **Lakewood Forest Preserve**. This is a pleasant place to wander. South of Ivanhoe Road, there are 4.5 miles of wide bridle trails, and it is these that provide the best walking. North of Ivanhoe Road is a system of foot trails totaling 3.3 miles.

To get started, follow the gravel track out the back of the parking lot and past Heron Pond on the left. Bear left at the first opportunity just beyond the pond, and from there use the map to navigate a route of your own choosing through the trail network.

When you are done with your walk, you may want to move your car to the parking lot at point A on the map and from there explore the foot trails. And nearby is the Lake County Discovery Museum.

6

DES PLAINES RIVER TRAIL
including Van Patten Woods, Independence Grove, Old School Forest Preserve, Wright Woods, and the River Trail Nature Center

The Des Plaines River Trail runs north-south through Lake County and part of Cook County, from nearly the boundary with Wisconsin to Golf Road west of Evanston. Except for a short section scheduled for completion in 2004, this outstanding hike-bike path is continuous for nearly 35 miles (56 kilometers). Most of it is very scenic, passing through woods and prairies, often within sight of the river. **Not included** here are yet other disjoined sections of the Des Plaines River Trail near O'Hare International Airport, where the path is interrupted by highways.

Map 16 on page 83 gives an overview of the trail, and **Maps 17-20** on pages 84-87 provide more detail in four overlapping sections that are arranged sequentially from north to south. The other maps in this chapter—**Maps 21-25** on pages 90-94—show several forest preserves through which the trail passes. These places are more than just access points for the river trail; they also have their own trail systems that offer good walking.

The Des Plaines River Trail is open daily from 6:30 a.m. to sunset. Dogs must be leashed. North of Lake Cook Road, the trail is managed by Lake County Forest Preserves; telephone (847) 367-6640 or go to www.lcfpd.org. South of Lake Cook Road, the trail is administered by the Forest Preserve District of Cook County; telephone (847) 824-1900 or go to www.fpdcc.com.

For automobile directions, please turn to page 82. Walking directions start on page 88.

THE DES PLAINES RIVER rises in southeastern Wisconsin and flows south toward Chicago in a course parallel with the shore of Lake Michigan. Ten miles west of the Loop, the elevation of the river is about twenty feet higher than the lake, but the Des Plaines never enters Lake Michigan because the way is barred by a low ridge (reflected in such place names as Park Ridge, Harwood Heights, and Norridge) that is part of the system of glacial moraines that border the lake.

From the suburbs west of Chicago, the Des Plaines turns southwest. Its confluence with the Kankakee River below Joliet forms the Illinois River, which ultimately joins the Mississippi. During the early days of European exploration and fur trading, the proximity of the Chicago River (which empties into Lake Michigan) and the Des Plaines provided an easy portage that made the mouth of the Chicago River an advantageous site for the trading post, fort, and settlement that eventually grew into the nation's largest inland city.

IF BY NOW you have taken some of the walks outlined in this book, you probably have noticed that there is more variety to the local landscape than the region commonly is given credit for. One major variable is the extent to which the different places that are featured here have been affected by our larger rivers, such as the Des Plaines, Fox, and DuPage.

First, there are large areas of confused surface drainage, as is typical in regions across which continental glaciers have advanced and retreated. The clay, sand, pebbles, and cobbles deposited by the ice sheet covered and, in large part, eradicated the old drainage systems. Many small swales, gullies, and minor creeks that are dry or nearly dry between rainfalls carry stormwater runoff to myriad lakes, ponds, and marshes that sometimes have no discernible outlet, as at Volo Bog, Lakewood Forest Preserve, Crabtree Nature Center, and countless other places, especially in northwestern Cook County and in Lake County, so-named because of its numerous small lakes. The irregular hills and broad plains of glacial till are the region's upland, as yet showing only rudimentary stream development.

Other areas show more advanced stream development. Along the stretch of the Des Plaines River featured in this chapter, the river is in places bordered by floodplains and abandoned channels. At Greene Valley the upland slopes down into a wide vale carved by the East Branch of the DuPage River. And at Waterfall

Glen, small, continuously-flowing streams (such as Sawmill Creek) have incised ravines that penetrate to bedrock. These streams drain into the Des Plaines River, which in the vicinity of Lemont and Lockport southwest of Chicago has carved a valley more than a mile wide and a hundred feet lower than the adjacent upland. The Illinois River, in turn, shows the same erosive features on a far larger scale. As you approach from the upland, you drop two hundred feet into a major valley. In the vicinity of Starved Rock State Park, the river is bordered by high cliffs where tributary streams flow into the river through canyons. Considered together, these varied landscapes exemplify some of the stages by which running water cuts into an elevated region—even if only slightly elevated—and works to reduce it to a lower plain.

STREAM EROSION is the dominant force shaping the world's landforms. It works slowly but relentlessly, achieving effects over eons. Although the process of erosion is ceaseless, it of course speeds up during periods of peak flow. Most erosion is attributable to a relatively few heavy rains each year and—even more so—to less frequent but spectacular flood rains. Although these infrequent events may seem freakish, over millions of years they are commonplace and may be said to occur with regularity. In addition, much erosion in the Chicago region is attributable to torrents of meltwater during the period when the last continental ice sheet receded.

   Going hand in hand with erosion—or really as a necessary precursor to it—is the process of weathering, by which a region's rocky foundation is, near the surface, broken down into smaller and smaller pieces that can be carried away by water, which is itself a powerful weathering agent. For example, through *frost action*, water enters cracks in the rocks and splits them apart when the water freezes, eventually reducing rocks near the surface to crumbly fragments. This is the chief form of *physical weathering*, but there are other physical processes, including the penetration into rock fissures by roots of trees and other plants, which as they grow pry the rocks apart. And, significant in the Chicago region, there is the grinding, abrasive action of continental glaciers, which produced a thick blanket of unconsolidated material transported here from farther north.

As rocks are reduced to smaller fragments by physical processes, *chemical weathering* becomes increasingly important, and again water is a major agent. Through *hydrolysis*, water reacts with minerals in the rocks, creating clay and freeing some elements which are carried away in solution. Through *carbonation*, carbon dioxide in soil (where it is produced by bacteria) or in the air combines with water to form a weak acid called carbonic acid, which dissolves limestone. Through *oxidation* some minerals, of which iron is the chief, react with oxygen in air and in water, thus contributing to the disintegration of the parent rock of which the oxidized minerals were formerly part. Acting together, physical and chemical weathering convert bedrock to earthen materials—to clay, sand, and soil—or to an intermediate, crumbly substrate called *saprolite*, on which the process of erosion can then work, as described below.

Wherever rain falls or snow melts, any downward-pitched swale, even though at first shallow or insignificant, is self-aggrandizing, collecting and channeling the water that flows off a broad area of upland. Even in the absence of such troughs, water flowing in sheets down a "smooth" hillside tends to organize itself into runnels that in turn erode little rills, some of which may develop into gullies and eventually into ravines that carry away the runoff. Gradually, the gullies and ravines deepen with erosion, and once they penetrate the water table, they are fed by a steady seepage of groundwater. Now and again steep slopes may simply slump downhill, or a steep embankment may collapse directly into a stream, where the loosened material is easily carried away.

As a stream extends itself by developing tributaries, its erosive power rapidly increases. The larger drainage area concentrates more water in the main channel downstream, where stream energy is swelled by the greater mass of moving water. The increase in energy is more than directly proportional to stream volume. As the volume increases, an ever-smaller fraction of the river's energy is consumed in overcoming friction with the streambed, and in consequence the speed of the river increases and so does its ability to carry fine clay, silt, and sand in suspension, to eat away at the bank, and to wear down rocks.

Lakes constitute a base level below which an inflowing river cannot cut until the lake itself is lowered by erosion where it

drains out. Of course, the ultimate base level is the ocean.*
Nonetheless, even as a river approaches sea level, the current
continues to erode the banks laterally wherever the stream is
deflected by each turn. As the river approaches the ocean,
downward cutting is no longer possible, but sideward cutting can
continue as long as there is flow. Gradually, a meandering course
develops as the river snakes back and forth, eroding first one side
of the valley and then the other. When sinuosity becomes so
extreme that the curves loop back on themselves, the current will
intercept the channel farther downstream, cutting off the looping
meander. Thus, as millennia pass, the river migrates in an ever-
changing course over a broad floodplain, leaving behind abandoned channels here and there.

At the mouth of the river where it empties into a lake or into the
sea, a distinctive geologic feature takes shape. As the current dis-
sipates in the standing water, the capacity of the stream to carry
material in suspension is reduced and then eliminated, so that the
river's load of sand and silt is dropped and forms a delta, as has
occurred where the Fox River empties into Grass Lake in northwestern Lake County. Because the current slows gradually, the
deposits tend to be sorted, with larger, heavier particles dropped
first. After the delta has extended itself a considerable distance in
one direction, a flood may cut a new and shorter channel to open
water, causing the former course to be abandoned, at least for a
period. Large deltas typically have several channels or sets of
channels among which the stream shifts as deposits are concentrated first in one and then in another.

Meanwhile, the countless gullies and ravines at the river's
headwaters continue to fan outward like the branches of a growing tree. As the tributaries extend themselves, the watershed
becomes larger and larger. A growing river may even intercept
and divert to itself (or *capture*) streams that previously took a
different course to the sea. Materials eroded from areas far up a
river's many tributaries are transported downstream, deposited,
re-eroded, and redeposited over and over again as the river's

---

* Submarine canyons, like those along the edge of the Continental Shelf,
are not an exception to this principle. Such canyons were carved by
rivers during the depths of the Ice Age, when so much water was
amassed on land as continental ice that the level of the sea was as much
as three hundred feet lower than it is now.

capacity to carry sand and silt fluctuates with the volume of run-off.

According to one conceptual model of stream erosion proposed in the nineteenth century by William M. Davis, an examination of several variables—including stream gradient, valley depth, valley width, and number of meanders—will indicate the stage of development that has been reached by any stretch of river. In the earliest stage, gullies and ravines eat into the elevated land surface. Because the dominant direction of cutting is downward, the gullies and ravines are steep-sided and V-shaped, and even after they join to form larger valleys, the gradient of the streambed is steep compared to navigable waterways. Rapids are common. There are only minor flats in the valley bottom. The ratio of valley depth relative to width is at its maximum. Such a stream was said by Davis to be in *youth*.

As a stream's elevation approaches base level, the gradient diminishes and downward cutting slows. Bends in the course of the stream become accentuated, meanders start to develop, and the width of the valley increases relative to its depth. Sideward cutting produces a continuous floodplain. Such a stream is said to be in *maturity*.

Finally, when downward cutting has become so slow as virtually to cease and the stream is as close to base level as it can get, sideward cutting may eventually produce a nearly flat and featureless valley, much wider than it is deep, across which the river meanders from side to side. The gradient is low, and the broad bottomland is marked only by the scars, swamps, and lakes left by former channels. Perhaps a few rock hummocks and hills—more resistant to erosion than were their surroundings—are left rising above the low valley floor. This stage of river development is *old age*.

Keep in mind, however, that the inexact terms *youth, maturity,* and *old age* do not describe the actual age of a river but only its stage of erosional development. In reality, the appearance of any stretch of river is determined largely by the durability and structure of the materials through which the stream flows, so that the terrain along even a single river can reflect different stages of erosion in no particular sequence, depending on the underlying materials. It is a common thing for rivers to show a profile passing from youth to maturity to old age (at this last stage,

complete with a wide valley and meandering course), then to reenter a relatively narrow valley with a steep gradient before once again transitioning to an older landscape. This pattern may occur several times along a single river, and in each case the sections characterized by broad floodplains and a meandering course are in areas of relatively unresistant material compared to what is found next downstream.

The terms *youth, maturity,* and *old age* can also be applied to an entire region to describe the extent to which it has been acted upon by stream erosion. As an upland region experiences the headward erosion of streams, more and more of the landscape is given over to a branching system of gullies, ravines, and valleys. Eventually, the upland lying between different branches and watersheds is cut away until the divide changes from a wide plateau to a ridge and then to a low, rounded rise. Meanwhile, the valleys slowly widen and develop broad, flat floodplains. For as long as an area is mostly upland, it is said to be in youth. During the period that valley slopes occupy most of the landscape, the region is said to be in maturity. And when most of the landscape is given over to bottomland, the area is said to be in old age.

In reality, however, regional old age seldom if ever fully develops. Prolonged erosion produces a landscape in which rolling hills occupy much of the region and tend to endure, especially where vegetation protects the land surface. Moreover, tectonic movements in the earth's crust can, for protracted periods, cause the land to rise at rates less than, equal to, or greater than the countervailing rate of erosion, thus retarding or even renewing the sequence of erosion outlined in this discussion. Some such movements may be isostatic adjustments by which pieces of the crust, which are "floating" on softer layers below, rise as the surface is worn away, much as an iceberg would rise if only the part above water were subject to melting. Another factor is that crustal plates, spreading from rifts in the ocean basins, sometimes collide with the continental margins, causing the land to bow, buckle, and rise even as it erodes. Meanwhile, depending of long-term changes in the climate, the level of the sea rises and falls as a varying amount of the earth's water is amassed on land as continental ice. Yet even so, stream erosion continues, shaping and reshaping the land surface in accordance with the trend from youth through maturity into old age.

≈ ≈ ≈ ≈

AUTOMOBILE DIRECTIONS: The Des Plaines River Trail stretches about 35 miles, from nearly the boundary with Wisconsin to Golf Road west of Evanston. The directions below will guide you to a series of parking lots located at intervals along the trail. These access points are indicated by •6-A through •6-G on **Map 16** at right. More detail is provided by **Maps 17-20** on pages 84-87.

The automobile directions start on the **Tri-State Tollway**, which is designated **Interstate 294** as it circles west of Chicago **but is Interstate 94** where it links with Edens Expressway and continues toward Wisconsin.

To the river trail at Van Patten Woods (•6-A): Leave the Tri-State Tollway at the exit for Russell Road just south of the Illinois-Wisconsin boundary. Follow Russell Road east 0.6 mile, then turn right into Van Patten Woods. The trailhead is on the left near the entrance. For a detailed look at Van Patten Woods, see **Map 21** on page 90.

To the river trail at Kilbourne Road (•6-B): Leave the Tri-State Tollway at the exit for Grand Avenue (Route 132) near Waukegan. Follow Grand Avenue east 1.4 miles, then turn left onto Kilbourne Road. Go 0.5 mile to a parking lot on the left. Join the trail where it passes behind the parking lot.

To the river trail at Independence Grove (•6-C): There is a fee to park here, and it is especially hefty for non-residents of Lake County.

Leave the Tri-State Tollway at the exit for Buckley Road (Route 137). Follow Buckley Road west 2.5 miles, then turn right into Independence Grove. After passing the fee station, turn left at the first intersection and continue all the way to the large parking lot at the end of the road. Join the trail where it crosses the river and passes north of the parking lot. For a detailed look at Independence Grove, see **Map 22** on page 91.

To the river trail at Old School Forest Preserve (•6-D): Leave the Tri-State Tollway at the exit for Town Line Road (Route 60). Follow Town Line Road west 1.2 miles, then turn right onto St. Mary's Road. After 2.1 miles, turn right into the forest preserve. Turn right again at a T-intersection and go 0.2

                    [Directions continue on page 88.]

MAP 16 — Overview of Des Plaines River Trail

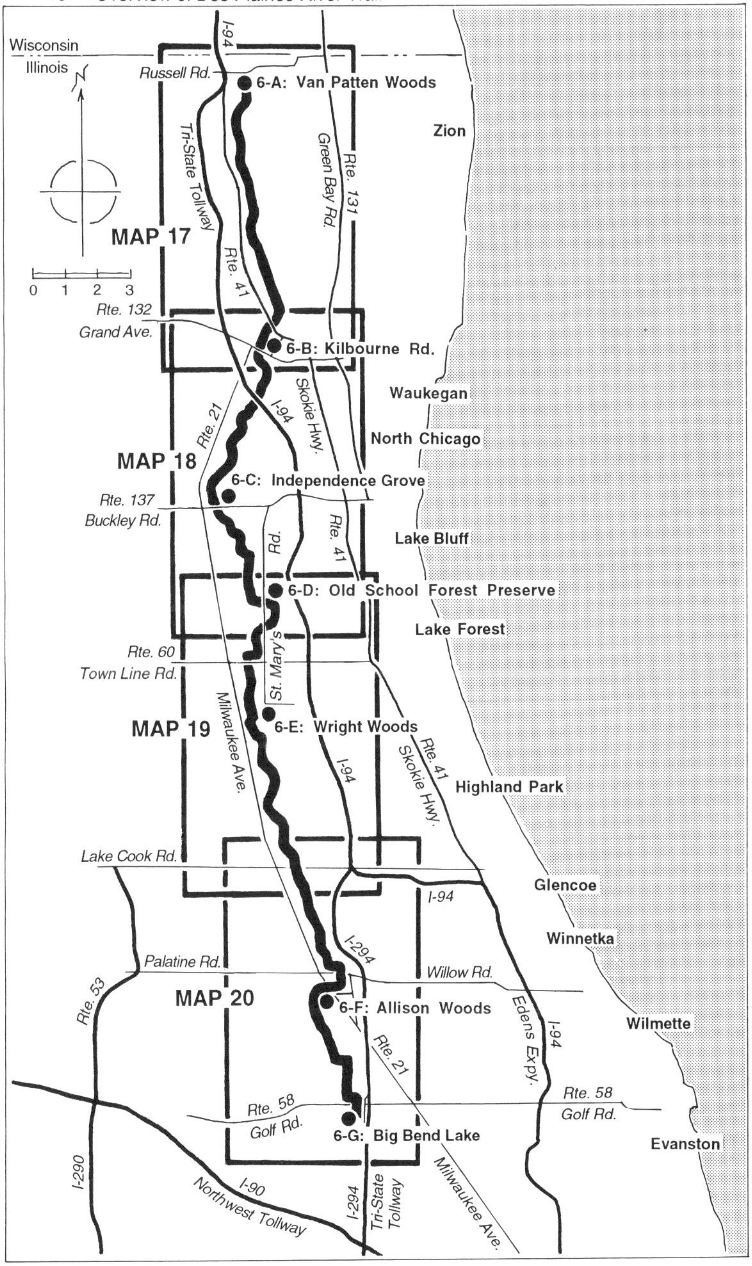

MAP 17 — Des Plaines River Trail

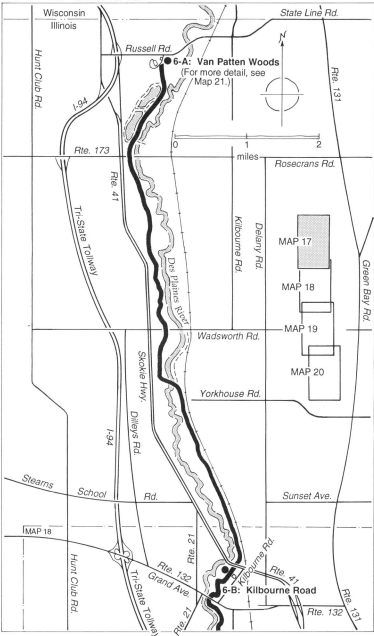

Wisconsin
Illinois

State Line Rd.

Russell Rd.

6-A: Van Patten Woods
(For more detail, see
Map 21.)

N

Hunt Club Rd.

I-94

Rte. 173

Rte. 41

Rte. 131

0   1   2
miles

Rosecrans Rd.

Tri-State Tollway

Des Plaines River

Kilbourne Rd.

Delany Rd.

MAP 17

MAP 18

MAP 19

MAP 20

Green Bay Rd.

Skokie Hwy.

Wadsworth Rd.

Dilleys Rd.

Yorkhouse Rd.

I-94

Stearns   School   Rd.

Sunset Ave.

MAP 18

Hunt Club Rd.

Tri-State Tollway

Rte. 21

Rte. 132

Grand Ave.

Rte. 21

Kilbourne Rd.

6-B: Kilbourne Road

Rte. 41

Rte. 132

Rte. 131

84

MAP 18 — Des Plaines River Trail

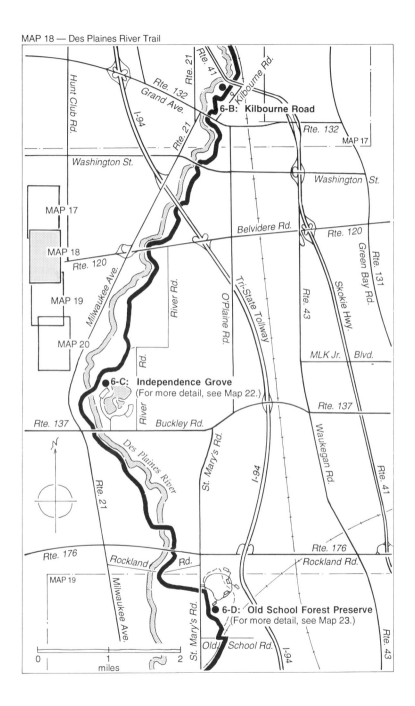

6-B: Kilbourne Road

6-C: Independence Grove
(For more detail, see Map 22.)

6-D: Old School Forest Preserve
(For more detail, see Map 23.)

MAP 19 — Des Plaines River Trail

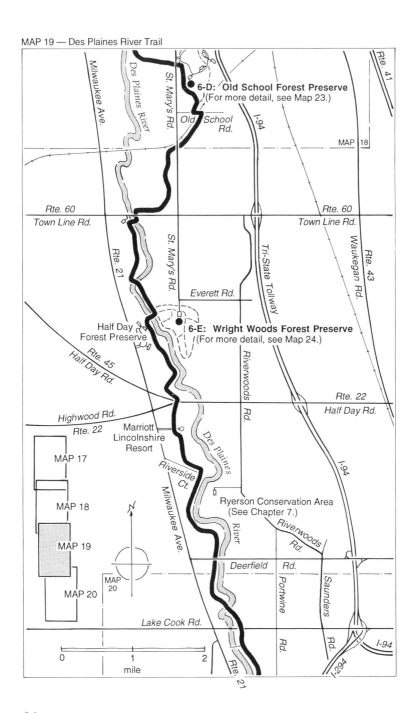

6-D: Old School Forest Preserve
(For more detail, see Map 23.)

Old School Rd.

Rte. 41

Milwaukee Ave.

Des Plaines River

St. Mary's Rd.

I-94

MAP 18

Rte. 60
Town Line Rd.

Rte. 60
Town Line Rd.

Rte. 21

St. Mary's Rd.

Tri-State Tollway

Waukegan Rd.

Rte. 43

Everett Rd.

Half Day Forest Preserve

6-E: Wright Woods Forest Preserve
(For more detail, see Map 24.)

Riverwoods Rd.

Rte. 45
Half Day Rd.

Highwood Rd.

Rte. 22

Rte. 22
Half Day Rd.

Marriott Lincolnshire Resort

Des Plaines

I-94

MAP 17

Riverside Ct.

MAP 18

Milwaukee Ave.

Ryerson Conservation Area
(See Chapter 7.)

River

Riverwoods Rd.

N

MAP 19

MAP 20

MAP 20

Deerfield Rd.

Portwine Rd.

Saunders Rd.

Lake Cook Rd.

I-94

0   1   2
mile

Rte. 21

I-294

86

MAP 20 — Des Plaines River Trail

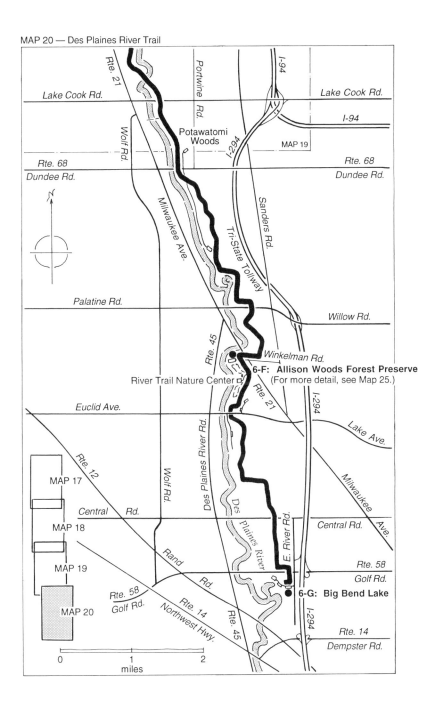

mile to the parking lot for Shelters A and B on the right. Join the trail where it passes near the far end of the lot. For a detailed look at Old School Forest Preserve, see **Map 23** on page 92.

To the river trail at Wright Woods (•6-E): Leave the Tri-State Tollway at the exit for Town Line Road (Route 60). Follow Town Line Road west 1.2 miles, then turn left onto St. Mary's Road. After another 1.2 miles, head straight into Wright Woods at an intersection with Everett Road. Continue 0.2 mile to the parking lot. From there, you can join the Des Plaines River Trail by following a path that starts at a sign board and leads to the right of a pond. For a detailed look at Wright Woods, see **Map 24** on page 93.

To the river trail at Allison Woods (•6-F): Leave the Tri-State Tollway at the exit for Willow Road. Follow Willow Road west 0.5 mile to Sanders (or Saunders) Road. Turn left and follow Sanders Road south 0.6 mile, then turn right onto Winkelman Road. Go 0.4 mile to an intersection with Milwaukee Avenue, and from there continue straight into the parking lot for Allison Woods. Join the trail as it passes through the parking lot. For a detailed look at this area, see **Map 25** on page 94.

To the river trail at Big Bend Lake (•6-G): Leave the Tri-State Tollway at the exit—it is from the southbound lanes only—for Golf Road (Route 58). At a T-intersection, turn left and go 0.2 mile across Golf Road to Big Bend Lake on the right, where the river trail crosses the entrance road.

≈   ≈   ≈   ≈

WALKING and BICYCLING: **Map 16** on page 83 provides an overview of the 35-mile **Des Plaines River Trail**. In turn, **Maps 17-20** on pages 84-87 give more detail in four overlapping sections arranged in sequence from north to south, as indicated by the diagram on each map. The dots on the maps (•6-A, •6-B, •6-C, and so forth) are the seven access points discussed in the automobile directions. Most of these access points are at major forest preserves that have their own trail systems—in addition to the Des Plaines River Trail—and are therefore in themselves good places to walk, per **Maps 21-25** on pages 90-94.

   Please note that the trail is sometimes flooded during spring thaw and after heavy rain. Under these circumstances, turn back. Don't risk a serious accident by trying to wade through. Also, the trail occasionally crosses roads and parking lots, so use caution at all places where cars may be present.

As this book goes to press, a short section of the Des Plaines River Trail south of the Marriott Lincolnshire Resort and north of Lake Cook Road is still unfinished. Perhaps by the time you get there, it will have been completed.

To start at Van Patten Woods (•6-A on the maps), join the Des Plaines River Trail only a few dozen yards from the Russell Road entrance. As shown on **Map 21** on page 90, there are many other trails at Van Patten Woods, including an attractive loop around Sterling Lake and also circuits east of the Des Plaines River.

To start at Kilbourne Road (•6-B on the maps), join the Des Plaines River Trail where it passes behind the parking lot.

To start at Independence Grove (•6-C on the maps), join the Des Plaines River Trail where it crosses the river and passes north of the lake. As shown on **Map 22** on page 91, there are other trails at Independence Grove, including a loop of 2 miles around the lake.

To start at Old School Forest Preserve (•6-D on the maps), join the Des Plaines River Trail where it passes near the parking lot at Shelters A and B and under St. Mary's Road just south of the entrance. As shown on **Map 23** on page 92, there are also several circuit trails at Old School.

To start at Wright Woods (•6-E on the maps), join the Des Plaines River Trail by following a path that leads from the parking lot to the right of a pond. Go to a four-way intersection in front of the river. To head north on the river trail, turn right. To go south, continue straight across the bridge. As shown on **Map 24** on page 93, there are also other trails at Wright Woods, including an attractive circuit of 3 miles downstream along the river and then around through the woods.

To start at Allison Woods (•6-F on the maps), join the Des Plaines River Trail where it passes through the parking lot. As

[Directions continue on page 95.]   89

MAP 21 — Van Patten Woods Forest Preserve

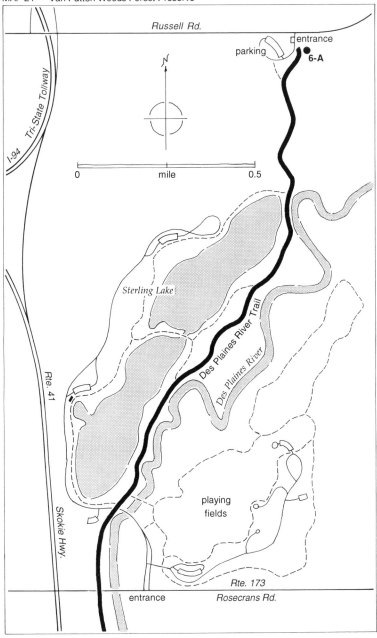

MAP 22 — Independence Grove Forest Preserve

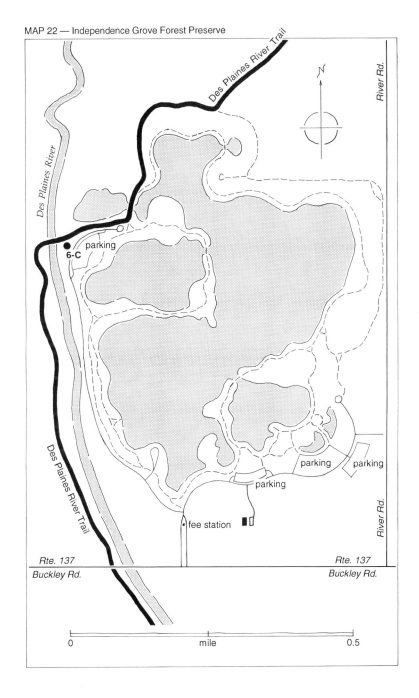

MAP 23 — Old School Forest Preserve

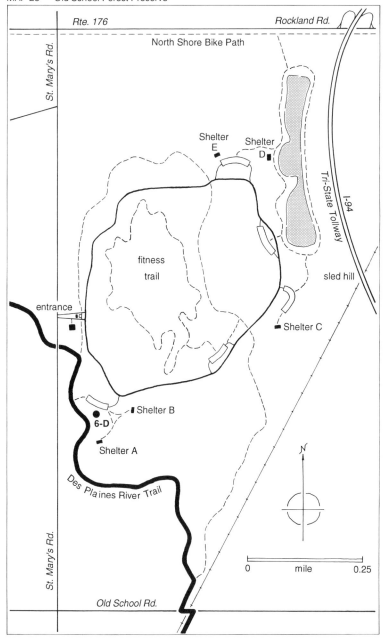

MAP 24 — Wright Woods Forest Preserve

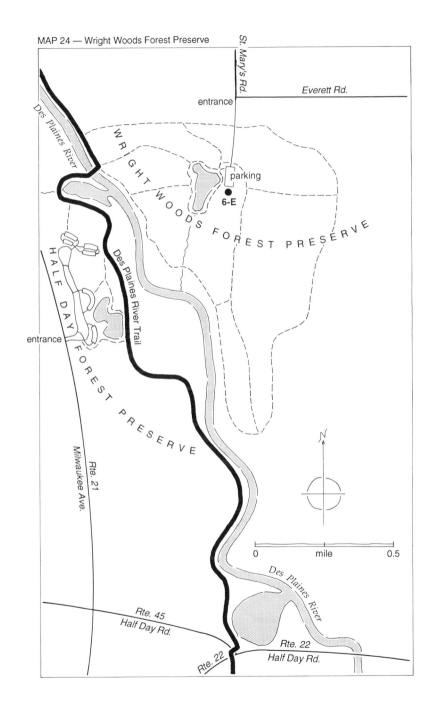

St. Mary's Rd.

Everett Rd.

entrance

Des Plaines River

WRIGHT WOODS FOREST PRESERVE

parking

6-E

Des Plaines River Trail

HALF DAY FOREST PRESERVE

entrance

N

Milwaukee Ave.

Rte. 21

0   mile   0.5

Des Plaines River

Rte. 45
Half Day Rd.

Rte. 22

Rte. 22

Half Day Rd.

MAP 25 — Allison Woods Forest Preserve and the River Trail Nature Center

parking

6-F:
Allison
Woods

Winkelman Rd.

Rte. 21
Milwaukee Ave.

Green Bay Trail

vernal
pond

Des Plaines River Trail

Little Fort Trail

gate

exhibits

parking

RIVER TRAIL NATURE CENTER

Des Plaines River

Grove Portage Trail

N

Lake Avenue Woods

0   mile   0.25

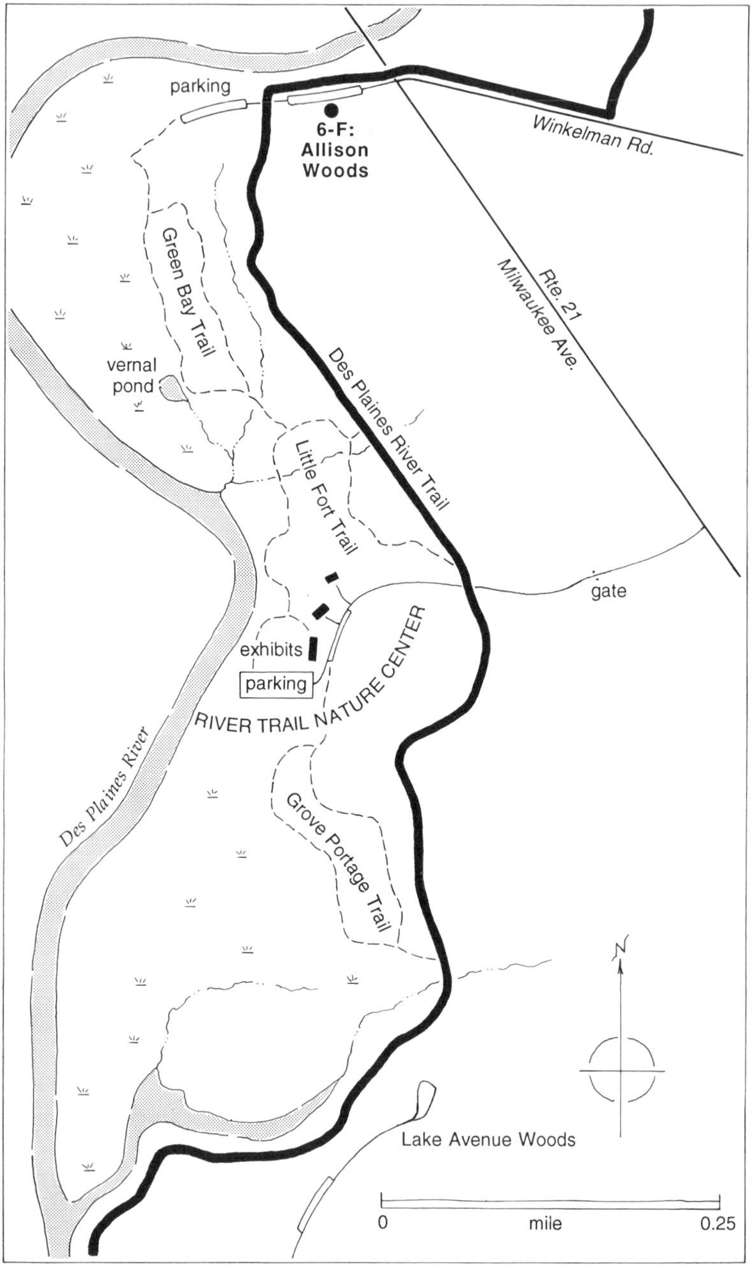

shown on **Map 25** at left, just south of Allison Woods is the
River Trail Nature Center, which is a great place to take
children.

At the entrance of Allison Woods, the river trail crosses
Milwaukee Avenue and follows the shoulder of Winkelman
Road for 280 yards before continuing north through the woods.

To start at Big Bend Lake (•6-G on the maps), join the Des
Plaines River Trail where it crosses the entrance road only a
few yards from East River Road. With the parking lot behind
you, turn left onto the narrow path and follow it to Golf Road.
After crossing at the traffic light, turn left and continue alongside
Golf Road until the river trail veers right into the woods.

7

RYERSON CONSERVATION AREA

Located north of Chicago in Deerfield, the Edward L. Ryerson Conservation Area consists of meadows and forested floodplain bordering the Des Plaines River. The flat terrain and lofty woods combine to create a sense of sanctuary. **Map 27** on page 102 shows the trail network, which altogether totals about 6.5 miles (10 kilometers).

The trails are open daily from 6:30 a.m. to sunset. Dogs, horses, and off-road bicycling are prohibited. Cross-country skiing is permitted only when the snow is at least four inches deep. The visitor center is open from 9:00 a.m. to 5:00 p.m. Monday through Saturday and from 11:00 to 4:00 on Sunday. The site is managed by Lake County Forest Preserves. For information call the visitor center at (847) 968-3321 or go to www.lcfpd.org.

For automobile directions, please turn to page 100. Walking directions start on page 103.

THE RYERSON CONSERVATION AREA is a large tract of mature forest and farmland bordering the Des Plaines River. This property, so valuable from an aesthetic and environmental perspective, obviously also has great worth in terms of its potential for residential development, yet most of the land was given to Lake County in the late 1960s by owners who had grown to love the area as it was and who wished to see it preserved in a natural state.

The result might easily have been very different. In the mid-1920s, the land that now forms the southern part of the Ryerson Area was acquired by a group of investors interested in land speculation. Their plan was to sell their entire holding of several hundred acres to subdividers. Among the first sales, however, were some parcels of fifteen acres purchased by individuals who had no immediate plans for development and who, in at least one or two cases, were simply looking for a place to build weekend cabins. The idea caught on, and instead of subdividing their property into houselots, the original partners saved large parcels for their own recreational use and sold the rest to a few like-minded buyers. Although most built cabins, none of the owners at first thought of anything but eventual sale to subdividers for conventional housing.

At about the same time, Edward and Nora Ryerson (Mr. Ryerson was heir to a fortune derived from Inland Steel) bought land nearby, and in 1928 they built a small log cabin on the banks of the Des Plaines River. In 1939 the Ryersons purchased a large tract to the north of their cabin from an elderly resident of the area named Whigham, who was a descendant of Daniel Wright, the first recorded settler in Lake County. After the Ryersons acquired the Whigham property, they built the farm buildings seen today and hired a farmer to run the operation, which they called Brushwood Farm. Later the Ryersons built a handsome house, finished in 1942, using old, weathered bricks and other material salvaged from the demolition of a woolen mill in Hanover, Illinois. After completion of the house, the Ryersons made Brushwood Farm their summer home for the rest of their lives.

During the 1950s and '60s, the area remained essentially un-changed, even as suburban development in the region accelerated after World War II. Eventually, Mr. Ryerson and some of the neighboring landowners began to talk informally among them-selves about the future of their land and the possibility of preserving it in a natural state by giving or selling it to the Lake County Forest Preserve District, which Mr. Ryerson had helped to form in 1958. Inclusion of the large Ryerson property was clearly necessary to the project, and so as years passed the other owners looked to the Ryersons to take the first step. This the Ryersons did starting in 1966, when they sold eighty-five acres to the Lake County Forest Preserve District and established a schedule to give, both during their lives and by bequest, the rest of their land to the county.

During the following three years, several neighboring landowners also gave their land to the county, and others proved to be willing to sell, in some cases at prices substantially below

full market value. In this manner, without there ever having been any formal arrangement among the Ryersons and the other owners, the county eventually acquired a preserve that now totals 552 acres. Of this the Ryersons gave more than half.

After you have visited the Ryerson Conservation Area, you may want to consider joining the Friends of Ryerson Woods, a group whose modest annual membership fee helps to support various activities held at the conservation area. Members receive a newsletter of activities and discounts on programs.

≈   ≈   ≈   ≈

AUTOMOBILE DIRECTIONS: The Ryerson Conservation Area is located north of Chicago in Deerfield a few miles west of Highland Park. (See **Map 26** at right.) Four approaches—from **Edens Expressway**, the **Tri-State Tollway**, **Route 53**, and **Deerfield Road**—are described below.

To the Ryerson Conservation Area from Edens Expressway *northbound:* Edens originates at the **Kennedy Expressway** out of Chicago and runs north to Highland Park. For most of its length, Edens is part of **Interstate 94**, but Edens and I-94 eventually split at Exit 29. Leave Edens in order to follow Interstate 94 west to join the Tri-State Tollway toward Milwaukee. Once you are on the Tri-State Tollway, follow the directions in the next paragraph.

To the Ryerson Conservation Area from the Tri-State Tollway: The tollway is designated **Interstate 294** as it circles west of Chicago **but is Interstate 94** north of Lake Cook Road and the link with Edens Expressway.

Leave the Tri-State Tollway at the exit for Half Day Road (Route 22). Go west 0.8 mile, then turn left onto Riverwoods Road. After 1.2 miles, turn right into the Ryerson Conservation Area. Follow the entrance road 0.4 mile to the parking area at the end.

To the Ryerson Conservation Area from Route 53: Built to the specifications of an interstate highway, Route 53 is the northward extension of **I-290** and **I-355**. Together these expressways provide easy access to the Ryerson Conservation Area from the suburbs west of O'Hare International Airport.

MAP 26 — Access to Ryerson Conservation Area

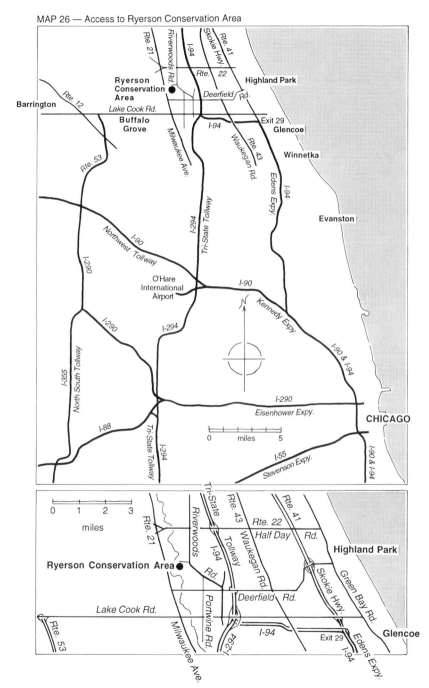

101

MAP 27 — Ryerson Conservation Area

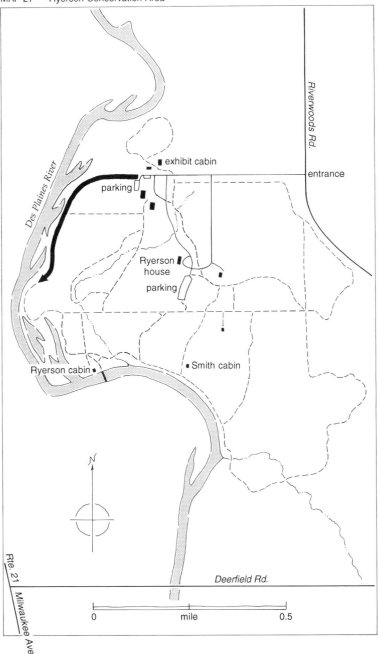

Riverwoods Rd.

Des Plaines River

■ exhibit cabin

parking

entrance

Ryerson ■
house

parking

Ryerson cabin ■

■ Smith cabin

N

Rte. 21

Milwaukee Ave.

Deerfield Rd.

0   mile   0.5

Follow Route 53 north to the exit for Lake Cook Road east-bound. From the top of the exit ramp, follow Lake Cook Road east 6 miles, then turn left onto Portwine Road. Go 1.5 miles (in the process crossing Deerfield Road), then turn left onto River-woods Road. After just 0.7 mile, turn left into the Ryerson Conservation Area. Follow the entrance road 0.4 mile to the parking area at the end.

To the Ryerson Conservation Area from Deerfield Road:
Running east-west, Deerfield Road links Skokie Highway (Route 41) in Highland Park with Milwaukee Avenue (Route 21).
At the intersection of Deerfield Road and Riverwoods Road 0.5 mile west of the Tri-State Tollway, turn north and go 1.7 miles to the Ryerson Conservation Area on the left. Follow the entrance road 0.4 mile to the parking area at the end.

≈   ≈   ≈   ≈

WALKING: Map 27 at left shows the trail system at the **Ryerson Conservation Area**. This is an attractive and quiet place to wander through the bottomland woods and fields bordering the Des Plaines River. Altogether there are about 6.5 miles of footpaths.

To get started, I suggest that you go first to the Des Plaines River. From the parking lots at the end of the entrance road, leave the farm buildings behind by following a trail with woods on the right and a field on the left. Eventually the river and its bordering bayous come into view on the right. Continue downstream and around one or another circuit on the trail network.

8

CHICAGO BOTANIC GARDEN

Located in Glencoe north of the city, the Chicago Botanic Garden is a marvel. **Map 29** on page 111 shows the paths and outstanding display gardens of the main area, where you can stroll and browse for hours. In addition, **Map 30** on page 112 outlines a route of 1.2 miles (1.9 kilometers) around the lagoons through a re-created prairie and past several outlying gardens. With views across the water to the principal islands, this is a good way to conclude your visit.

The Chicago Botanic Garden is open daily except Christmas from 8:00 a.m. to sunset. Dogs are prohibited. A parking fee is charged. For information call (847) 835-5440 or go to www.chicago-botanic.org.

For automobile directions, please turn to page 108. Walking directions start on page 110.

SCIENTIFIC BOTANIC GARDENS are an outgrowth of interest in the medicinal properties of plants. Theophrastus, who succeeded Aristotle as head of the Lyceum in 323 B.C., described in his voluminous writings approximately 300 species used for the treatment of disease. Upon his death, he bequeathed his garden, house, and colonnades to the school as a permanent place of instruction. Dioscorides, a Greek botanist of the first century, A.D., similarly emphasized the medicinal value of plants, and Pliny the Elder detailed the natural history of about a thousand species, many of them famous for their curative qualities. During the Middle Ages, these ancient texts survived in monasteries and in Middle Eastern libraries. With the coming of the Renaissance, they were often cited by herbalists—that is, men who wrote books (called herbals) containing descriptions and illustrations of herbs and other plants, together with discussions of their various "virtues" that made them useful as medicines. Most herbals were written between the late 1400s and late 1600s, and they contain a blend of painstakingly accurate observation and fantastic superstition, including, for example, the "doctrine of signatures" by which a plant's medicinal powers were based on the superficial resemblance of certain plant parts to specific human organs. Thus various heart-shaped leaves were thought to relieve heart disease, and the walnut, which has a shell with a convoluted surface like the cerebral cortex, was prescribed for headaches and brain disorders.

The herbalists and their herbals stimulated the founding of botanic gardens or "physic gardens" in association with early medical schools at various universities. For example, the circular design of the Heritage Garden at the Chicago Botanic Garden is based on Europe's first scientific botanic garden, started in 1545 at the University of Padua in Italy, followed by others at Pisa, Florence, and Bologna. Professors of medicine were the principal botanists of that time, and their physic gardens provided training for students as well as sources of plants for medicines. During the next two hundred years, interest in botanic gardens spread northward throughout the Continent and Great Britain, and by the late 1700s there were 1,600 botanic gardens in Europe, including gardens belonging to wealthy individuals for whom botanizing was a fashionable hobby. The botanists of the seventeenth and eighteenth centuries, however, turned away from medical botany and instead sought to describe all plants, including the many new ones that were being introduced to Europe from Asia, Africa, and the Americas by explorers and settlers. Botanic gardens affiliated with medical schools declined and were replaced by gardens devoted to plant collecting, to research in plant culture, and to the display of ornamental and exotic plants, as at London's Royal Botanic Gardens at Kew (founded about 1730) and now at the Chicago Botanic Garden.

The circular Heritage Garden at the Chicago Botanic Garden is also a tribute to Carolus Linnaeus, and a large statue representing Linnaeus dominates one quadrant of the circle. Linnaeus was a Swedish botanist and taxonomist (or classifier) who lived from 1707 to 1778. Extremely prolific, he wrote more than 180 works. In 1753 he published *Species Plantarum*, which contains careful descriptions of six thousand species of plants from all parts of the world known at that time. In this work, Linnaeus established the practice of binomial nomenclature—that is, the denomination of each kind of plant by two words, the genus name and the species name, as in *Quercus alba*, or white oak. Binomial nomenclature had been introduced much earlier by some of the herbalists, but it was not generally accepted until Linnaeus devised a comprehensive taxonomic methodology.

The Heritage Garden itself is organized according to Linnaeus' system of plant classification. But before discussing the basis for that system, here is a question: How would you, if confronted with the task of classifying and cataloguing the hundreds of thousands of varieties of known plants, go about the job? Theophrastus classified plants merely as trees, shrubs, and herbs. Dioscorides also grouped plants under only three headings: aromatic, culinary, and medicinal. Until the invention of the compound microscope in about 1590, the classification of plants was for the most part based on their external appearance and their uses to man.

And what was the basis of Linnaeus' system? In 1737 he published *Genera Plantarum*, in which he explained his method of classifying plants in accordance with their sexual characteristics. This approach examines the number and forms of flower parts— especially stamens, which produce male sex cells, and styles, which are prolongations of plant ovaries that receive pollen grains. For non-flowering plants, other reproductive features form the basis of classification. By focusing on only a few marked characteristics, the sexual system of plant classification serves as a convenient index by which a botanist can take an unfamiliar species, quickly narrow down choices, and thus identify the specimen.

Linnaeus's system of plant classification introduced order, consistency, and precision where previously there had been a huge mishmash of unorganized information. However, Linnaeus himself acknowledged that his approach was artificial, inasmuch as it excluded many non-sexual features from consideration, and so he also promulgated fragments of a system for arranging plants in classes according to a broader range of affinities. Since Linnaeus's time, increasingly refined studies of plant anatomy, embryology, cell structure, and other factors have led to the development of a "natural" system of plant classification that recognizes more than

500,000 species. However, there is still an element of speculation because the fossil record for plants is relatively poor compared to that for animals. In consequence, paleobotanists have been unable so far to determine clear evolutionary relationships among plants.

From high-school biology you may remember some of the basic distinctions used for classifying plants. Skipping over algae, fungi, bacteria, mold, liverworts, and mosses (aren't you glad?), we will start with the phylum Tracheophyta, named for the vascular structures that visually (not functionally) resemble miniature animal tracheas. These vascular tubes distribute water and nourishment throughout the plants—even very large ones—and thus enable them to live on land. All but a few of the tracheophytes fall into one of three groups: (1) the ferns, which reproduce by making spores, (2) the gymnosperms, most of which are conifers that reproduce by means of naked seeds, and (3) the angiosperms, which have true flowers and reproduce via seeds that are enclosed within a vessel, often fleshy. Showing amazing variety in size and form, angiosperms in turn consist of two groups, depending on the number of seed leaves (aka cotyledons) that emerge when the seeds first sprout. Plants with one seed leaf are called monocotyledons, and those with two seed leaves are dicotyledons. Monocotyledons have scattered vascular bundles in the stems, little or no cambium (a tissue that enables plants to grow in diameter), and parallel veins in the leaves. They include all the grasses (including bamboo and grains), reeds, rushes, lilies, bananas, palms, and orchids. Dicotyledons have cylindrical vascular bundles in regular patterns, cambium that grows seasonally and thus produces annual rings, and leaves with net-like veins. Most are deciduous, but some, such as laurels and hollies, are not. Altogether, dicotyledons account for nearly a third of all plant species, including most of those cultivated as ornamentals or for their vegetables, fruits, and nuts.

≈   ≈   ≈   ≈

AUTOMOBILE DIRECTIONS: The Chicago Botanic Garden is located north of Chicago in Glencoe. (See **Map 28** at right.) The entrance to the Botanic Garden is on **Lake Cook Road**, which runs east-west along the boundary between Lake County

MAP 28 — Access to the Chicago Botanic Garden

Barrington

Rte. 12

Milwaukee Ave.
Rte. 21
Tri-State Tollway
I-94
Waukegan Rd.
Skokie Hwy.
Rte. 41

Highland Park

Lake Cook Rd.

Buffalo
Grove

I-94

Exit 29

Chicago Botanic Garden

Glencoe

Rte. 53

Rte. 43

Edens Expy.

I-94

Winnetka

Evanston

I-294
Tri-State Tollway

Northwest Tollway
I-90

I-290

O'Hare
International
Airport

I-90

N

Kennedy Expy.

I-90 & I-94

I-290

I-294

North South Tollway

I-355

I-88
Tri-State Tollway
I-294

I-290
Eisenhower Expy.

0   miles   5

CHICAGO

I-55
Stevenson Expy.

I-90 & I-94

0   1   2   3
miles

Tri-State
Half Day   Rd.   Rte. 22
Skokie
Green Bay

Rte. 21

I-94
Tollway
Waukegan Rd.
Hwy.

Highland Park

Deerfield Rd.

Rte. 41
Rd.

Lake Cook Rd.

Rte. 53

Milwaukee Ave.

I-294

I-94

Rte. 43

Exit 29

Chicago Botanic
Garden

Glencoe

Edens Expy.
I-94

109

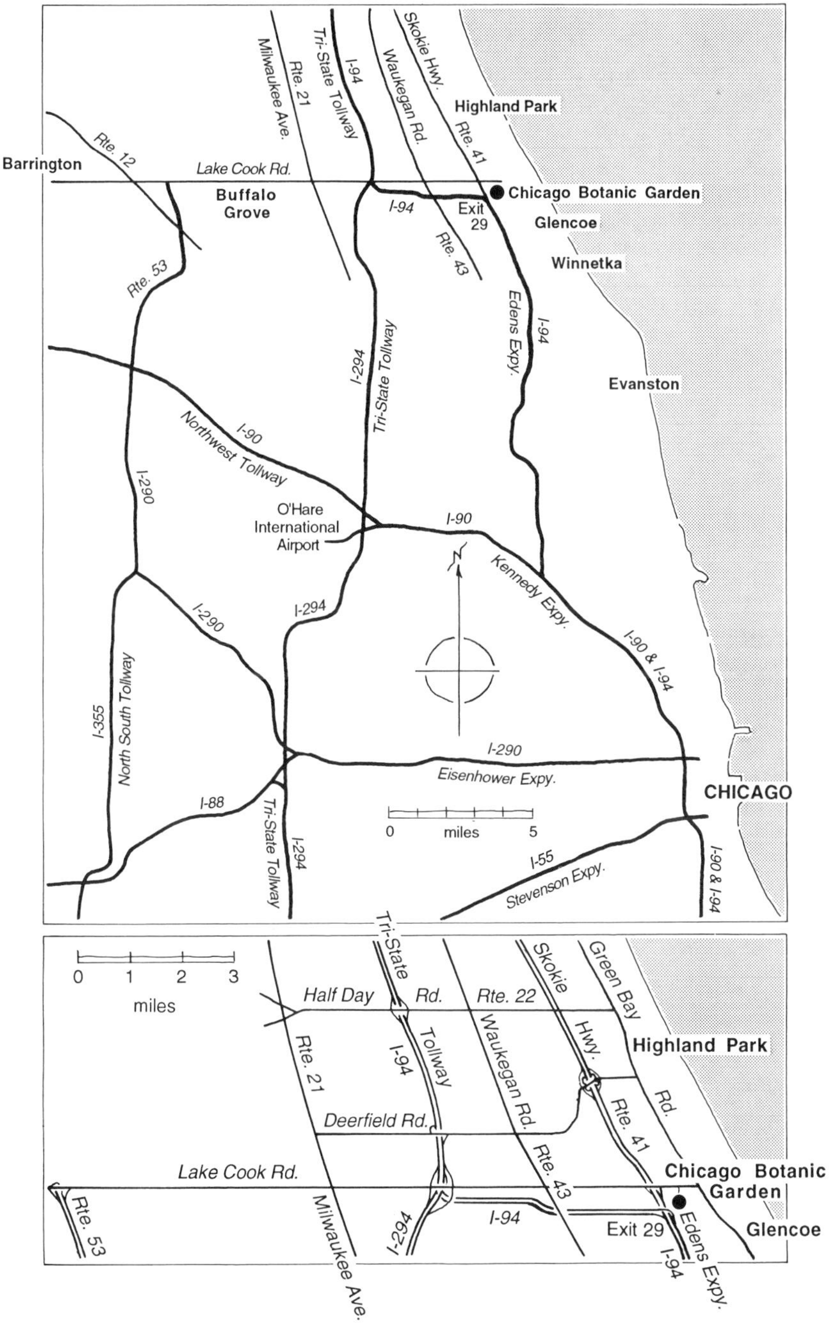

and Cook County. Linking Highland Park, Deerfield, Buffalo Grove, and Barrington, Lake Cook Road can be reached by exits off **Edens Expressway**, the **Tri-State Tollway**, and **Route 53**, as described below.

To the Chicago Botanic Garden from Edens Expressway *northbound:* Edens originates at the **Kennedy Expressway** out of Chicago and runs north to Highland Park. For most of its length, Edens is part of **Interstate 94**, but Edens and I-94 eventually split at Exit 29. Remain on Edens (now Route 41) at Exit 29, then take the next exit for Lake Cook Road. At the top of the exit ramp, turn right. Follow Lake Cook Road east 0.6 mile, then turn right into the Chicago Botanic Garden. From the fee station, follow the drive to the parking lots on the left.

To the Chicago Botanic Garden from the Tri-State Tollway: The tollway is designated **Interstate 294** as it circles west of Chicago **but is Interstate 94** north of Lake Cook Road and the link with Edens Expressway.

Leave the Tri-State Tollway at the exit for Lake Cook Road. Follow Lake Cook Road east 4.4 miles, then turn right into the Chicago Botanic Garden. From the fee station, follow the drive to the parking lots on the left.

To the Chicago Botanic Garden from Route 53: Built to the specifications of an interstate highway, Route 53 is the northward extension of **I-290** and **I-355**. Together these expressways provide easy access to Lake Cook Road and the Botanic Garden from the suburbs west of O'Hare International Airport.

Follow Route 53 north to the exit for Lake Cook Road eastbound. From the top of the exit ramp, follow Lake Cook Road east 11.7 miles, then turn right into the Chicago Botanic Garden. From the fee station, follow the drive to the parking lots on the left.

≈   ≈   ≈   ≈

WALKING: Map 29 at right shows the main islands at the **Chicago Botanic Garden**.

After touring the outstanding demonstration gardens and conservatory on the islands, you may want to end your visit with a pleasant 1.2-mile loop to the south, as shown by the bold line

MAP 29 — Chicago Botanic Garden

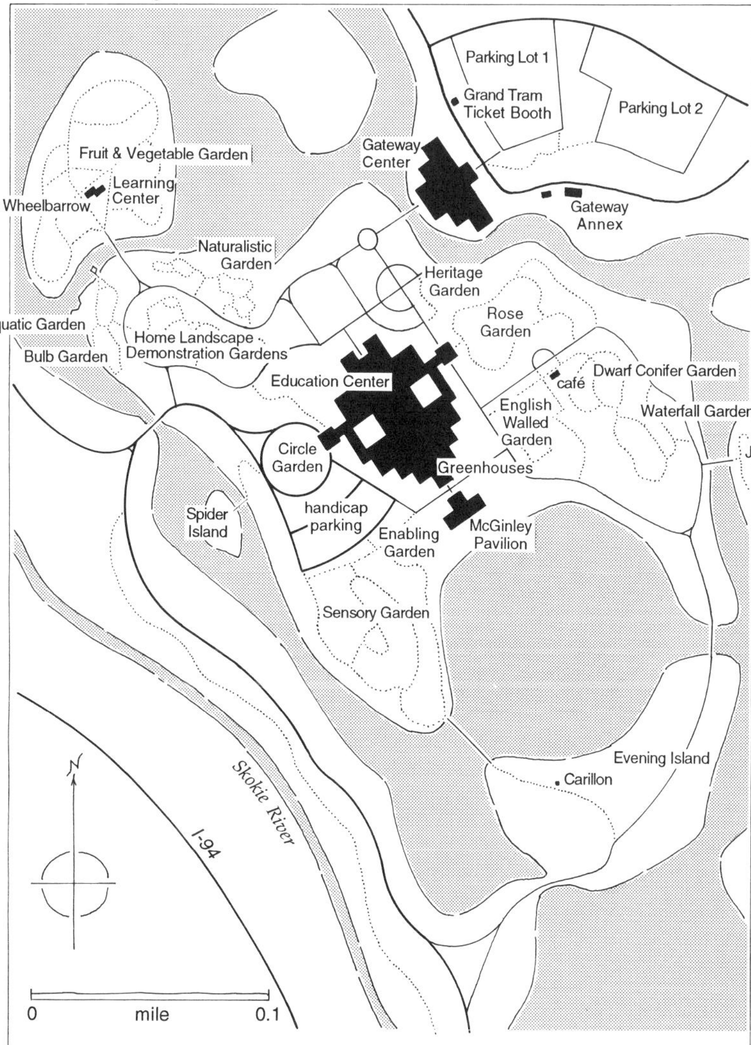

Parking Lot 1

Grand Tram
Ticket Booth

Parking Lot 2

Fruit & Vegetable Garden

Gateway
Center

Learning
Center

The Wheelbarrow

Gateway
Annex

Naturalistic
Garden

Heritage
Garden

Rose
Garden

Aquatic Garden

Home Landscape
Demonstration Gardens

Bulb Garden

Education Center

café

Dwarf Conifer Garden

Waterfall Garden

English
Walled
Garden

Circle
Garden

Japanese
Garden

Greenhouses

handicap
parking

Spider
Island

Enabling
Garden

McGinley
Pavilion

Sensory Garden

Evening Island

Carillon

Skokie River

I-94

N

0   mile   0.1

GARDEN ETIQUETTE

Help preserve the Garden's serene atmosphere and maintain its unique and beautiful collections. Please refrain from climbing on trees and shrubs, picking fruits and vegetables, walking in garden beds and collecting plants, flowers or labels.

No pets are permitted except support animals.

Bicycle riding is allowed on designated bike routes only. The Forest Preserve speed limit is 8 mph.

No active sports or games (inline skating, Frisbee, skiing, swimming, fishing, skating, etc.) are permitted.

Picnicking is allowed in designated areas only. Campfires and outdoor cooking are prohibited. Laying blankets on the grass is permitted for Garden performances only.

No alcohol is permitted on the grounds.

MAP 30 — Chicago Botanic Garden

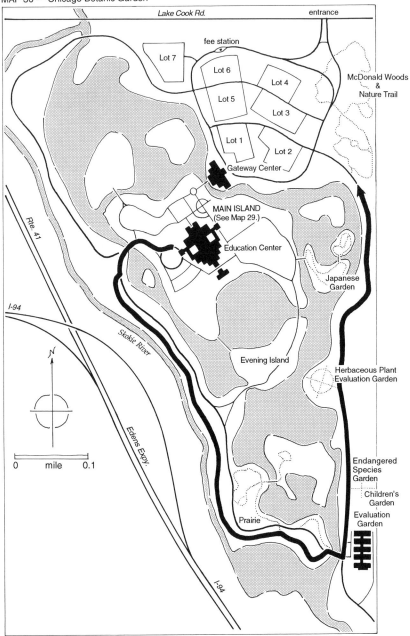

Lake Cook Rd.   entrance

fee station

Lot 7

Lot 6

Lot 4

Lot 5

Lot 3

Lot 1

Lot 2

McDonald Woods
&
Nature Trail

Gateway Center

MAIN ISLAND
(See Map 29.)

Education Center

Japanese
Garden

Rte. 41

I-94

Skokie River

Evening Island

Herbaceous Plant
Evaluation Garden

N

Edens Expy.

0   mile   0.1

Endangered
Species
Garden

Children's
Garden

Evaluation
Garden

Prairie

I-94

on **Map 30** at left. This route overlooks the lagoons and prairie and ends at the parking lots.

To get started, follow the automobile road that leaves the main island toward the west—or that is, toward Edens Expressway—then fork left on the tram road. Before long, join a footpath on the right that parallels the tram road. Eventually, rejoin the road, cross a bridge, then turn left to head north to the parking lots, perhaps stopping in at the evaluation and endangered species gardens along the way. If you want to extend your walk, there is an opportunity just before the parking lots to bear right off the road and onto a nature trail through the McDonald Woods.

9

CRABTREE NATURE CENTER

The lower panel of **Map 31** on page 120 shows a route of 2.8 miles (4.5 kilometers) at the Crabtree Nature Center northwest of Chicago near Barrington Hills. The trails pass through woods and prairie and by marshes and ponds. Although not large, the prairie here is one of the most attractive in the region because trees around the perimeter of the preserve block views of extraneous development.

The parking lot and trails at Crabtree Nature Center are open daily year-round (except Thanksgiving, Christmas, and New Year's Day) starting at 8:00 a.m. During the period March through October, the gates close at 5:00 on weekdays and at 5:30 on weekends. During the rest of the year, the gates close an hour earlier. There is also an exhibit building that has somewhat shorter hours and is closed each Friday. Dogs are prohibited. Crabtree is managed by the Forest Preserve District of Cook County; telephone (847) 381-6592 or go to www.fpdcc.com.

For automobile directions, please turn to page 121. Walking directions also start on page 121.

IN WHAT SORT OF SETTING would you expect to find a bur oak? Sycamore? Jack pine? Elm? Field guides contain this sort of information, but far more fun is simply to see for yourself. Every outing is an opportunity to practice the visual habit of relating different species of trees to the settings where they typically grow.

In the deciduous hardwood forest of the Chicago region, most trees are mesophytes, meaning that they occur under medium conditions of moisture. *Medium* in this context should be interpreted broadly, since many trees can grow almost anywhere that is not excessively wet or dry. In particular, white and red oaks and shagbark hickory are broadly adaptable and broadly distributed. Nonetheless, many mesophytic species prefer—although they do not necessary require—a narrower range of moisture and soil conditions. For example, in mature forests on well-drained uplands, sugar maple and white ash occur with greater frequency than they do elsewhere. Dry conditions (which often means high ground and gravelly soils in the region's many glacial moraines) favor black, chinquapin, and jack oaks, perhaps mixed with pignut hickory, blue ash, and rock elm. Moist, rich lowlands are a typical setting for pin and shingle oaks, bitternut hickory, red maple, green ash, and American basswood (aka linden). The name *swamp white oak* speaks for itself, but swamp conditions are also tolerated by red maple and black ash. Beech, which has a widespread, shallow root system, favors sites with ample moisture at the surface, but not standing water. Beech trees are rare on dry hilltops and sodden bottomlands; they are common on slopes and in loamy, level woods, where they sometimes form pure stands because their shade is so dense that oak and hickory seedlings cannot survive. All of the species mentioned here—and also many others—can occupy both the canopy and the understory in different combinations or associations.

Some small trees, including witch-hazel (usually found near streams), sassafras, redbud, and dogwood, rarely escape the understory. Allegheny serviceberry (or shadbush) occurs in forest borders, where its five-petaled flowers are conspicuous early in spring.

Floodplains and riverbanks are a typical setting for some species of trees, including silver maple (commonly with shaggy bark and several trunks), boxelder (a maple with pinnately compound leaves), American elm (with branches spreading like the mouth of a trumpet), and sycamore (showing white blotches on the trunk). From a hilltop or highway in winter, you can sometimes trace a nearby watercourse simply by the broad swath of white-branched sycamores occupying the floodplain. Willows too are moisture loving; three common species are black willow (often with several trunks and very narrow leaves), peachleaf willow (somewhat broader leaves), and the small sandbar willow (forming thickets on low embankments and islands of alluvium). Eastern cottonwood often occurs in rich bottomlands and along streams—and also in lakefront dunes, where its peculiar adaptability enables it to survive having its trunk buried by drifting sand. On some of your walks, you may have noticed the unusual-looking American hornbeam (aka ironwood or blue beech or water beech), which is a small riverside tree with a fluted, muscular-looking trunk and smooth gray bark.

Some species of trees—mainly oaks and hickories—are resistant to fire, which has helped them to survive on the edge of the Illinois prairie. For centuries prior to being forced out by white settlers, the Indians set the prairie ablaze each fall to drive game and also to improve forage when the grass sprouted back in the spring. Because its thick bark and corky twigs provide particularly good protection from fire, bur oak often occurs in open groves or savannas that stand like islands of timber in what was once prairie and is now farmland and suburbia. (See the photograph on page 80.) Some of these large savannas were the basis for place-names—Downers Grove, for instance—that go back to the 1820s and '30s. There is a small oak savanna at the Crabtree Nature Center and a bigger one at Greene Valley Forest Preserve—and also in many other places described in this book or visible from the region's highways. However, nowadays the savannas are threatened by the growth of other species that formerly were killed by fires. In particular, if invasive hawthorns are not burned or cut periodically, the savannas develop a congested understory that shades out wildflowers and kills the lower boughs of the oaks.

The ability of some trees to sprout back from cutting favors their survival in certain settings. For example, oaks, hickories, and ash (sometimes termed sprout hardwoods) are often seen in former woodlots with two, three, or even four trunks, indicating that they grew from suckers emerging from the stumps or roots of older trees that were cut down.

Most evergreens in the Chicago region are confined to particular niches. Sun-loving and fast-growing, white pine occurs at the Indiana Dunes and also in stands where farm fields—especially in areas of sandy loam—have been abandoned and colonized by seedlings. Pine forests, however, are not self-sustaining; the canopy of full-grown pines prevents light from reaching the shade-intolerant pine seedlings. Instead, it is hardwood saplings that establish themselves in the understory, then make a spurt of growth in the sun when the mature pines die or are cut or blown down. Some evergreens, including jack pine, red pine, and

Eastern redcedar, find a place in dry, meager soils where other trees cannot survive. For example, jack pine—a quintessentially northern tree with stubby needles covered by a thick cuticle to withstand drought—occurs atop the windy, dry ridges of sand at the Indiana Dunes. In sharp contrast, cool, shady ravines and canyons (especially the moist, north-facing slopes) provide a suitable environment for hemlock, which otherwise is characteristic of northern Wisconsin and the Upper Peninsula of Michigan. Black spruce and northern white-cedar, occurring near Chicago at the southern limit of their range, occupy cool, wet hollows, swamps, and bogs, as does also the deciduous tamarack (aka American larch).

Some species of trees are especially opportunistic. Quaking aspen, pin cherry, paper birch, and yellow birch quickly re-seed burned areas. Eastern redcedar, chokecherry, staghorn sumac, sassafras, and prickly-ash are among the first trees and shrubs, along with pines, to grow in abandoned fields. Redcedars often spring up at the base of fences where berry-eating birds perch and pass seeds; sometimes a line of scraggly redcedars is seen in the shade of resurgent hardwoods long after the fence has disappeared. In the absence of fire, hawthorn and buckthorn invade grasslands, as seen at the Crabtree Nature Center, where much prairie was lost during the 1990s when nearby residents successfully lobbied against burning. As this book goes to press, efforts are underway to restore the Crabtree prairie by fire and cutting.

Acting over long periods of time, the tendency of each species to thrive in certain settings and to fail or lag in others gives rise to more or less stable associations of trees. The associations blend into one another where the terrain changes gradually, but show sharp demarcations where conditions change abruptly. However, even as the forest organizes itself along broadly predictable lines, it is often visited with reversals. Ice storms, insect infestations, blights, floods, fires, and other such events can undo many decades of maturation and provide the opportunity for a new mix of trees and shrubs to establish themselves. These then begin again the process of natural succession that leads eventually to stable plant associations adapted to local conditions and the prevailing climate.

≈ ≈ ≈ ≈

MAP 31 — Crabtree Nature Center

Barrington Hills
Rte. 59 & Rte. 68
Crabtree Nature Center
Algonquin Rd.
Rte. 62
Palatine
Lake Cook Rd.
Rte. 12
I-94
Palatine Rd.
Willow Rd.
Winnetka
Rte. 53
Arlington Heights
Tri-State Tollway
Northfield
I-94
I-90
Northwest Tollway
I-294
Evanston
Edens Expy.
I-290
O'Hare International Airport
I-90
Rte. 59
I-290
I-294
Kennedy Expy.
I-365
North South Tollway
I-90 & I-94
0 miles 5
I-290
Eisenhower Expy.
CHICAGO

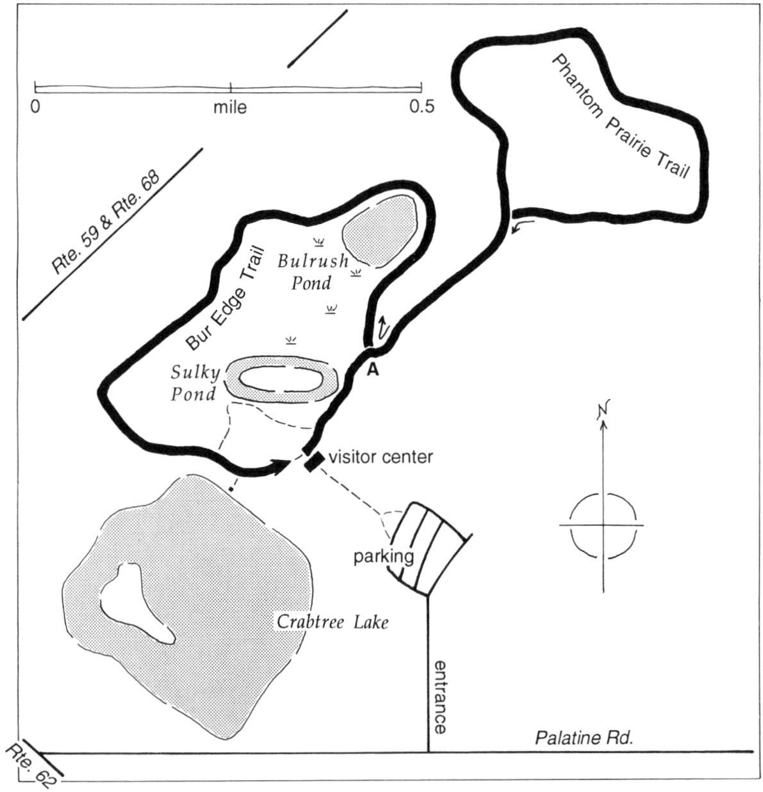

Phantom Prairie Trail
0 mile 0.5
Rte. 59 & Rte. 68
Bur Edge Trail
Bulrush Pond
Sulky Pond
A
N
visitor center
parking
Crabtree Lake
entrance
Palatine Rd.
Rte. 62

120

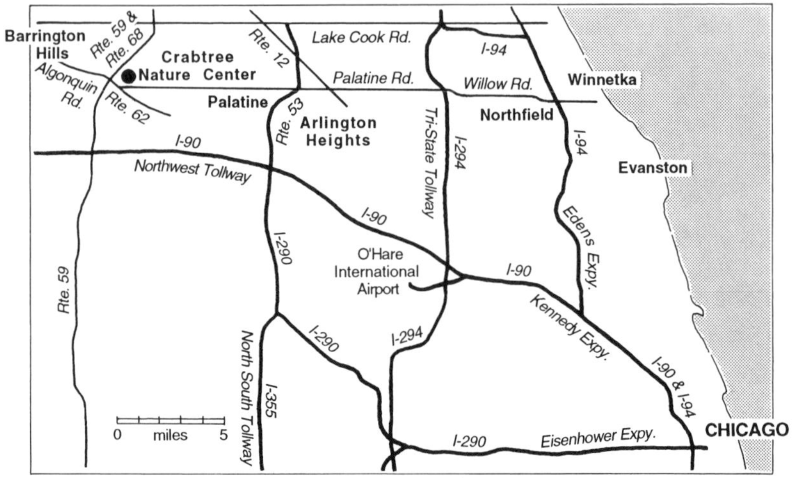

AUTOMOBILE DIRECTIONS: Crabtree Nature Center is located northwest of Chicago near Barrington. (See the upper panel of **Map 31** at left.)

The entrance to the nature center is on **Palatine Road**, which is the westward extension of **Willow Road**, linking Winnetka, Northfield, Palatine, and Barrington Hills. Two approaches to Crabtree—from the **Northwest Tollway** and the **Tri-State Tollway**—are described below.

To Crabtree Nature Center from the Northwest Tollway (Interstate 90): The Northwest Tollway is the extension of **Kennedy Expressway** out of Chicago.

Leave the Northwest Tollway at the exit for Route 59. Follow Route 59 north toward Barrington for 3.4 miles, then turn right onto Route 62 (Algonquin Road). After just 0.4 mile, turn left onto Palatine Road and go 0.5 mile to the entrance to Crabtree Nature Center on the left.

To Crabtree Nature Center from the Tri-State Tollway: The Tri-State Tollway is designated **Interstate 294** as it circles west of Chicago.

Leave the Tri-State Tollway at the exit for Willow Road. From the top of the exit ramp, follow Willow Road—it soon becomes Palatine Road—west 15 miles to the entrance to Crabtree Nature Center on the right.

≈   ≈   ≈   ≈

WALKING: The lower panel of **Map 31** at left shows a route of 2.8 miles through woods and prairie at the **Crabtree Nature Center**.

To get started, go to the terrace behind the visitor center. From there, follow a path that heads off to the right. Fork right and continue past Sulky Pond. At a fork in the trail (marked A on the map), bear right for the **Phantom Prairie Trail** circuit, about 1.7 miles in length.

After completing the Phantom Prairie loop, return to the trail junction at point A on the map, then turn right to continue around the **Bur Edge Trail** circuit (1.3 miles) and back to the visitor center. Toward the end the trail passes an intersection with a spur that leads a short distance to a bird blind overlooking Crabtree Lake.

10

ILLINOIS PRAIRIE PATH

Map 32 on pages 128 and 129 shows the Illinois Prairie Path west of Chicago. Altogether totaling 45 miles (72 kilometers), this hike-bike trail follows an old trolley bed. From Wheaton, branches run to Elgin and Aurora on the Fox River, and off these branches there are spurs to Geneva and Batavia (also on the Fox River). The Main Stem stretches eastward from Wheaton to Maywood on the Des Plaines River.

The most attractive section of the trail system is the Elgin Branch, outlined in greater detail on **Map 33** on page 131. I strongly recommend doing it first. Unlike nearly all other rails-to-trails conversions in the Chicago region, the Elgin Branch is little impacted by development. For the most part, it passes through woods, fields, and marsh. The round-trip distance is 32 miles (51 kilometers), so presumably hikers will want to take it in two or more pieces. In Elgin the trail arrives at the huge, ersatz riverboat of the Grand Victoria Casino, which if nothing else provides a strong sense of destination.

Managed by a non-profit corporation of the same name, the Illinois Prairie Path is open daily from dawn to dusk. Dogs must be leashed. For information go to www.ipp.org or write to Illinois Prairie Path, P.O. Box 1086, Wheaton, Illinois 60189-1086.

For automobile directions, please turn to page 127. Walking directions start on page 130.

THE ILLINOIS PRAIRIE PATH follows the former roadbed of the Chicago, Aurora and Elgin Railroad, an electric interurban line which contributed to the rapid suburbanization of the region west of Chicago. The railroad corporation was chartered in 1899, but construction did not begin until 1901. The Aurora Branch opened in 1902, and nine months later the line from Wheaton to Elgin was completed, as well as a spur off the Aurora Branch to Batavia.

At first the eastern terminus was at Laramie Avenue just inside the Chicago boundary, but starting in 1905 the trains continued into town all the way to the Loop on the Metropolitan West Side Elevated. In 1909 yet another western spur was added, branching off the Elgin line a little northwest of Wheaton and running through the town of West Chicago to Geneva and St. Charles on the Fox River. The headquarters, railroad yard, and repair shops were in Wheaton at the junction of the Aurora and Elgin Branches with the Main Stem, as the line into Chicago was called. Although the trains operated as trolleys through the city streets of Aurora and some other towns, along most of the right-of-way they drew current from a 600-volt third rail, earning for the line the nickname Great Third Rail.

In its early years the Great Third Rail prospered. This was the heyday of the interurban trolley. In 1910, for example, Illinois had nearly eight hundred miles of such lines. The electric coaches were fast and also cleaner and cheaper to ride than the sooty, coal-fired trains of the competing steam railroads. By 1914 the Great Third Rail had seventy wooden coaches and even two parlor-buffet cars named Carolyn and Florence, where for an extra twenty-five cents—which also could be applied toward an order of food—passengers sat in individual plush leather chairs.

Following World War I, however, the Great Third Rail began to lose money. The physical plant deteriorated, and because of inflation during the post-war years, costs exceeded revenues. Creditors successfully petitioned to have the railroad placed in receivership. In 1922 the company was reorganized and equipped with new steel passenger coaches. Using electric locomotives, the revivified C. A. & E. also inaugurated freight service.

In 1926 Samuel Insull's Middle West Utilities purchased control of the railroad. A protégé of Thomas Edison, Insull by 1907 had already gained control of Chicago's electrified public transit system (which like the Great Third Rail was a privately run, for-profit affair). After numerous mergers, Insull expanded his operations throughout Illinois and into neighboring states. In 1912 he formed a complex of companies with interlocking directorates that operated over three hundred steam plants, almost two hundred hydroelectric generating plants, and numerous other power plants throughout the United States. Under Insull's regime, the C. A. & E. prospered for a few years, but in 1932, as the nation plunged into the Great Depression and business activity declined, Insull's electric utilities empire collapsed. Accused of embezzlement and of using the mail to defraud investors, Insull fled to Greece and later to Turkey. Eventually, he was extradited to the United States. His trial in Chicago lasted several weeks, but it took the jury only three hours to acquit him. It was apparent that Insull was guilty not of deceit but of hubris and over-leveraged finance. He had fully (and perhaps correctly) believed in the limitless future of electricity, and he had used—and lost—his own fortune in attempting to stem the red ink after the Depression hit. Meanwhile the Great Third Rail again failed and entered receivership.

As World War II got underway and the nation emerged from the Great Depression, the number of riders on the Great Third Rail increased, largely because gasoline rationing curtailed automobile travel. The railroad's freight business also prospered. In 1946 the line finally emerged from its protracted receivership as suburban development boomed and rush-hour commuter traffic grew. Weekend traffic, however, declined abruptly as people turned to cars for leisure-time excursions and as the five-day work week eliminated the commuter rush on Saturday.

In 1952 the C. A. & E. management petitioned the Illinois Commerce Commission to be allowed to replace its trains with buses because the elevated tracks west from Chicago were scheduled to be torn down to make room for the Congress Street Expressway (now the Eisenhower Expressway). Although the Illinois Commerce Commission refused to allow the C. A. & E. to discontinue its commuter rail service altogether, it authorized the company to terminate its trains at Forest Park. There passengers could transfer to and from the trains of the Chicago Transit Authority, by now a public agency. Operating on temporary, ground-level tracks during the period of highway construction, the Chicago transit trains were forced to stop at every grade crossing between Forest Park and the Loop. During the first week after the new system went into effect, thousands of Third Rail riders switched to automobiles or to the competing Chicago and North Western Railroad. Soon the Great Third Rail was losing nearly a million dollars per year. In mid-1957 the company successfully petitioned to suspend passenger service temporarily, and at midday on July 3, the commuter trains stopped running and returned (for the last time, as matters developed) to the Wheaton yard. Chicago's afternoon newspapers carried banner headlines advising C. A. & E. passengers to find other transportation home.

For the next three years a series of commuter committees sought ways to restart passenger service. Freight operations continued for two years, then ceased. In 1960 a proposal to form a governmental agency to purchase and run the defunct line was rejected by voters after vigorous opposition from the Chicago and North Western Railroad and a local bus company. Finally, the C. A. & E. applied for permission to abandon the line, and the request was approved effective July 10, 1961. During the same period, many hundreds of other small railroads and trolley lines, with histories similar to the Great Third Rail, were going out of business throughout the United States.

The transformation of the abandoned roadbed into a public path is yet another story—one that helped spark the national rails-to-trails movement of recent years. In 1963 May Theilgaard Watts, a naturalist at the Morton Arboretum and author of *Reading the Landscape of America*, proposed converting the abandoned right-of-way to a public trail. A small corps of backers generated public support for the railroad path by giving hundreds of illustrated talks and leading dozens of field trips. They also sought and received the necessary cooperation of state, county, and local officials, and also of utility companies that used part of the roadbed for their transmission lines. In 1965 the group formed the nonprofit Illinois Prairie Path Corporation, which the following year leased the railroad right-of-way in DuPage County from the county government, its new owner. In 1972 the Illinois Department of Conservation acquired the Kane County segments of the right-of-way and then leased the property to the county forest preserve district for use as part of the hike-bike path. And in 1979 the state acquired 4.5 miles of right-of-way in Cook County to be managed by the trail corporation.

The Illinois Prairie Path is administered by an all volunteer board of directors elected annually by the membership. Similarly, volunteers perform basic maintenance, such as picking up litter—so please be sure not to leave any. The many improvements that have been made along the trail, including the planting of trees, recreation of prairies, and construction of new bridges, have been paid for by members' dues, corporate donations, county contributions, and state grants. If you would like to join the Prairie Path or simply want more information, send a letter enclosing a self-addressed stamped envelop to the Illinois Prairie Path, P.O. Box 1086, Wheaton, Illinois 60189-1086, or go to www.ipp.org.

≈   ≈   ≈   ≈

AUTOMOBILE DIRECTIONS: The main trailhead for the **Illinois Prairie Path** is in Wheaton west of Chicago. (See **Map 32** on pages 128 and 129, where Wheaton is located at the juncture of the branches heading east to Chicago, northwest to Elgin, and southwest to Aurora. For greater detail, find •10-A on **Map 33** on page 131.)

Two approaches to Wheaton—from the **East-West Tollway** and the **North-South Tollway**—are described below. There are also directions to the Elgin trailhead (•10-B on Map 33) from the **Northwest Tollway**.

To the Wheaton trailhead from the East-West Tollway (Interstate 88): Leave I-88 at the exit for Naperville Road. After paying the toll, turn left at a T-intersection and follow Naperville Road north 3.7 miles to an intersection with Roosevelt Road (Route 38). Turn left and follow Roosevelt Road west 0.7 mile, then turn right onto Carlton Avenue. Follow Carlton Avenue north 0.3 mile to a T-intersection with Liberty Street. This intersection is the zero-mile point on the Prairie Path. Park in the nearby garage or on the street, where some of the meters are good for 12 hours.

To the Wheaton trailhead from the North-South Tollway (Interstate 355): Leave I-355 at the exit for Roosevelt Road (Route 38). Follow Roosevelt Road west 3.8 miles, then turn right onto Carlton Avenue. Follow Carlton Avenue north 0.3 mile to Liberty Street. This intersection is the zero-mile point on the Prairie Path. Park in the nearby garage or on the street, where some of the meters are good for 12 hours.

To the Elgin trailhead from the Northwest Tollway (Interstate 90): The Northwest Tollway is the extension of **Kennedy Expressway** out of Chicago.

Leave the Northwest Tollway at the exit for Route 25 south toward Elgin. After paying the toll, turn left at a T-intersection

[Directions continue on page 130.]   127

MAP 32 — Illinois Prairie Path

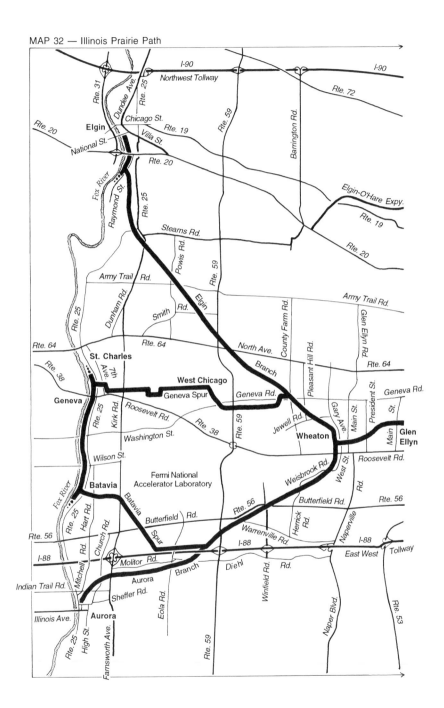

128

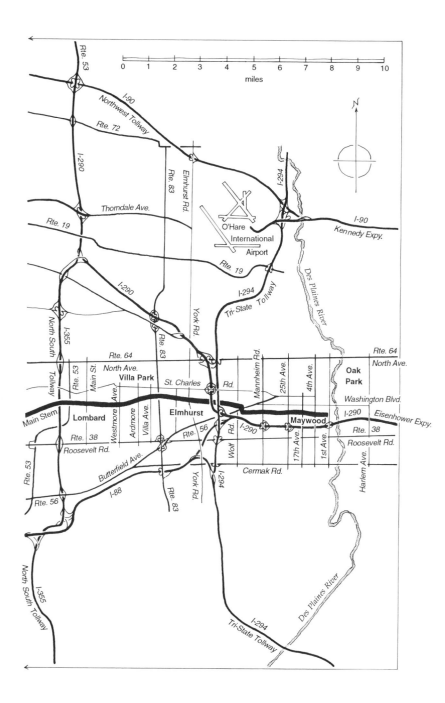

and follow Dundee Avenue south for 2.7 miles (ignoring Route 25 where it forks to the left). Continue as Dundee Avenue becomes Villa Street, then turn right at a traffic light onto National Street. Go 0.2 mile, then turn right onto Grove Street and right again into the public parking lot.

≈   ≈   ≈   ≈

WALKING and BICYCLING: Map 32 on pages 128 and 129 provides an overview of the entire **Illinois Prairie Path**. Formerly the Chicago, Aurora and Elgin Railroad, the 45-mile trail system is centered at Wheaton. It crosses many roads where caution is required.

While fine for exercise, the **Main Stem** runs through suburban neighborhoods. Foliage shields much of the trail from nearby development, but east of Interstate 294 the path's visual appeal diminishes and one section simply follows local streets past warehouses and business establishments.

The Aurora Branch is more attractive. Even so, much of it is bordered by roads and the pylons of electric transmission lines.

The Elgin Branch is first-rate by any standard, so do it first. This 16-mile section is shown in greater detail on **Map 33** at right and is discussed below.

On a bicycle, you can of course easily do the entire Elgin Branch for a round-trip of 32 miles. For hikers, the easiest approach is to divide the trip in two. On one day start at Wheaton and on another at Elgin, and on each occasion walk to the approximate midpoint at Smith Road and back.

To start from the Wheaton trailhead at the intersection of Carlton Avenue and Liberty Street, follow the Prairie Path uphill and across a railroad bridge. Continue all the way to the out-skirts of Elgin, where the Prairie Path meets the Fox River Trail just after crossing Raymond Road. Bear right on the Fox River Trail and follow it to National Street in Elgin within view of the Grand Victoria Casino.

To start from the Elgin trailhead, join the Fox River Trail where National Street crosses the Fox River just south of the Grand Victoria Casino. Follow the Fox River Trail downstream 1.2 miles to the junction with the Prairie Path, then fork left and continue all the way to the intersection of Carlton Avenue and Liberty Street in Wheaton.

MAP 33 — Illinois Prairie Path: Elgin Branch

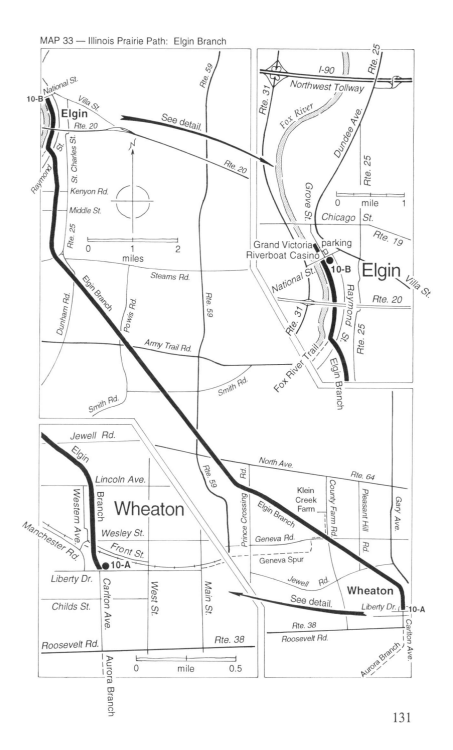

131

Please note that 2.5 miles northwest of Wheaton, the Prairie Path passes diagonally through the intersection of Geneva Road and County Farm Road. Also converging at this crossroads is the **Timber Ridge Trail**, which leads north 0.6 mile to DuPage County's **Klein Creek Farm**, open daily except Tuesday, Wednesday, and major holidays from 9:00 a.m. to 5:00 p.m.; telephone (630) 876-5900. Finally, at this same crossroads there is the junction with the Prairie Path's **Geneva Spur**.

The Fox River Trail is sometimes touted as a good connector with the westernmost extremities of the Prairie Path at Elgin, Geneva, Batavia, and Aurora. The Prairie Path's own literature suggests the possibility of a triangular 48-mile bicycle ride via the Elgin Branch, the Fox River Trail, and the Aurora Branch. I have done this, and it was a disappointment. The Fox River Trail is often merely one or another road. However, between Geneva and Batavia, there is a real trail along the Fox River, as indicated on Map 32. The circuit from Wheaton to Geneva to Batavia to Wheaton is 30 miles long; it entails some on-road biking on the Geneva Spur.

11

DANADA FOREST PRESERVE and HERRICK LAKE FOREST PRESERVE

Map 35 on pages 146 and 147 shows the system of hike-bike paths at Danada and Herrick Lake Forest Preserves west of Chicago near Wheaton and Naperville. The route indicated by the bold line is 6.3 miles long (10 kilometers), but of course you can omit one or two loops for a shorter outing. (But why would you want to do that? This is a beautiful place, especially the big circuit around Herrick Marsh.) The trails wind through woods and rolling prairie, occasionally passing ponds and reedy sloughs.

The trails at Danada and Herrick Lake are open from an hour after sunrise to an hour after sunset. Dogs must be leashed. The area is managed by the Forest Preserve District of DuPage County—in fact, the trail starts at the district headquarters. For information call (630) 933-7200 or go to www.dupageforest.com.

For automobile directions, please turn to page 144. Walking directions start on page 149.

WITH THEIR VARIED HABITATS—deciduous woods, thickets, marshes, prairie, and several ponds and lakes—Danada and Herrick Lake Forest Preserves are excellent places to see a wide assortment of birds. Of course, to spot the greatest number of species, spring and fall migration are the best seasons of the year and dawn is the best time of day.

Even for fledgling birders, identifying the many species that occur in northern Illinois is easier than might at first be thought. Shape, size, plumage, and other physical characteristics are distinguishing field marks. Range, season, habitat, song, and behavior are other useful keys, as discussed below.

Range is of primary importance for the simple reason that many birds are not found throughout North America or even the Midwest, but only in certain regions such as the Atlantic and Gulf coasts. For example, cedar waxwings and Bohemian waxwings closely resemble each other, so it helps to know that cedar waxwings are fairly common near Chicago, whereas Bohemian waxwings are rare here. Good field guides provide range maps based on years of reported sightings and bird counts. Of course, bird ranges are not static; some pioneering species, such as the glossy ibis and house finch, have extended their ranges during recent decades. Other birds, such as the ivory-billed woodpecker, have lost ground and may have died out.

Season is related to range, since migratory birds appear in different parts of their ranges during different times of year. To use again the example of rarely-seen Bohemian waxwings, they occur in our region (if at all) only during winter. Similarly, the five species of spot-breasted thrushes are sometimes difficult to distinguish from each other; all are common in the Chicago area during spring and fall migration, yet all but the wood thrush are rare during summer. Again, the maps in most field guides reflect this sort of information, and a detailed account of seasonal occurrence often is contained in local bird lists maintained and disseminated at some of the parks and forest preserves discussed in this book.

Habitat, too, is important in identifying birds. Even before you spot a bird, the surroundings can tell you what species you are likely to see. Within its range a species usually appears only in certain preferred habitats, although during migration some species are less particular. (In many cases, birds show a degree of physical adaptation to their preferred environment.) As their names imply, the marsh wren and sedge wren are seldom found far from cattails, rushes, or tall marsh grasses; if a wrenlike bird is spotted in such a setting, it is unlikely to be a house wren or Carolina wren or one of the other species commonly found in thick underbrush or shrubbery. Ducks can be difficult to identify unless you tote a telescope; but even if all you can see is a silhouette, you can start with the knowledge that shallow marshes, ponds, and streams normally attract few diving ducks (such as redheads, canvasbacks, ring-necked ducks, scaup, goldeneye, and buffleheads) and that large, deep bodies of water are not the usual setting for surface-feeding puddle ducks (mallards, black ducks, pintails, widgeons, shovelers, teals, and wood ducks). The area where two habitats join, called an *ecotone*, is an especially good place to look for birds because species peculiar to either environment might be present. For example, both meadowlarks and wood warblers might be found where a hay field abuts a forest. All good field guides provide information on habitat preference that can help to locate a species or to assess the likelihood of a tentative identification.

Songs announce the identity (or at least the location) of birds even before they are seen. Although some species, such as the red-winged blackbird, have only a few songs, others, such as the mockingbird, have an infinite variety. Some birds, most notably thrushes, sing different songs in the morning and evening. In many species the basic songs vary among individuals and also from one part of the country to another, giving rise to regional "dialects." Nonetheless, the vocal repertory of most songbirds is sufficiently constant in timbre and pattern to identify each species simply by its songs.

Bird songs, as distinguished from calls, can be very complex. They are sung only by the male of most species, usually in spring and summer. The male arrives first at the breeding and nesting area after migration. He stakes out a territory for courting, mating, and nesting by singing at prominent points around the area's perimeter. This wards off other males of his species and simultaneously attracts females. On the basis of the male's display and the desirability of his territory, the female selects her mate. Experiments suggest that female birds build nests faster and lay more eggs when exposed to the songs of males with a larger vocal repertory than others of their species, and the relative volume of their songs appears to be a way for males to establish status among themselves.

In a few species, including eastern bluebirds, Baltimore orioles, and cardinals, both sexes sing, although the males are more active in defending their breeding territory. Among mockingbirds, both sexes sing in fall and winter, but only males do in spring and summer. Some birds, such as canaries, have different songs for different seasons.

Birds tend to heed the songs of their own kind and to ignore the songs of other species, which, after all, do not compete for females nor, in many cases, for the same type of nesting materials or food. In consequence, a single area usually includes the overlapping breeding territories of several species. From year to year such territories are bigger or smaller, depending on the food supply. Typically, most small songbirds require about half an acre from which others of their species are excluded.

Bird calls (as distinguished from songs) are short, simple, sometimes harsh, and used by both males and females at all times of year to communicate alarm, aggression, location, and existence of food. Nearly all birds have some form of call. Warning calls are often heeded by species other than the caller's. Some warning calls are thin, high-pitched whistles that are difficult to locate and so do not reveal the bird's location to predators. Birds also use mobbing calls to summon other birds, as chickadees and crows do when scolding and harassing owls and other unwanted visitors. Birds flying in flocks, like cedar waxwings, often call continuously. Such calls help birds migrating by night to stay together.

The study of bird dialects and experiments with birds that have been deafened or raised in isolation indicate that songs are genetically inherited only to a very crude extent. Although a few species, such as doves, sing well even when raised in isolation, most birds raised alone produce inferior, simplified songs. Generally, young songbirds learn their songs by listening to adult birds and by practice singing, called *subsong.* Yet birds raised in isolation and exposed to many tape-recorded songs show an innate preference for the songs of their own species. Probably the easiest way to learn bird songs is to listen repeatedly to recordings and to refer at the same time to a standard field guide. Most guides describe bird vocalizations with such terms as *harsh, nasal, flutelike, piercing, plaintive, wavering, twittering, buzzing, sneezy,* and *sputtering.* Although these terms are somewhat descriptive, they do not take on real meaning until you have heard the songs. Incidentally, bird recordings that are played slowly demonstrate that the songs contain many more notes than the human ear ordinarily hears.

Shape is one of the first and most important aspects to notice once you actually see a bird. Most birds can at least be placed in the proper family and many species can be identified by shape or silhouette, without reference to other field marks. Some birds, such as meadowlarks, are chunky and short-tailed, while others, such as catbirds and cuckoos, are elegantly long and slender.

Kingfishers, blue jays, tufted titmice, waxwings, and cardinals are among the few birds with crests.

Bird bills frequently have distinctive shapes and, more than any other body part, show adaptation to food supply. The beak can be chunky, like that of a grosbeak, to crack seeds; thin and curved, like that of a creeper, to probe bark for insects; hooked, like that of a shrike, to tear at flesh; long and slender, like that of a hummingbird, to sip nectar from tubular flowers; or some other characteristic shape depending on the bird's food. Goatsuckers, swifts, flycatchers, and swallows, all of which catch flying insects, have widely hinged bills and gaping mouths. The long, thin bills of starlings and meadowlarks are suited to probing the ground. In the Galapagos Islands west of Ecuador, Charles Darwin noted fourteen species of finches, each of which had evolved a different type of beak or style of feeding that gave it a competitive advantage for a particular type of food. Many birds are nonetheless flexible about their diet, especially from season to season when food sources change or become scarce. For example, Tennessee warblers, which ordinarily glean insects from foliage, also take large amounts of nectar from tropical flowers when wintering in South and Central America.

In addition to beaks, nearly every other part of a bird's body is adapted to help exploit its environment. Feet of passerines, or songbirds, are adapted to perching, with three toes in front and one long toe behind; waterfowl have webbed or lobed feet for swimming; and raptors have talons for grasping prey.

Other key elements of body shape are the length and form of wings, tails, and legs. The wings may be long, pointed, and developed for swift, sustained flight, like those of falcons. Or the wings may be short and rounded for abrupt bursts of speed, like those of accipiters. The tail may have a deep fork like that of a barn swallow, a shallow notch like that of a tree swallow, a square tip like that of a cliff swallow, or a rounded tip like that of a blue jay.

Size is difficult to estimate and therefore not very useful in identifying birds. The best approach is to bear in mind the relative sizes of different species and to use a few well-known birds, like the chickadee, sparrow, robin, kingfisher, and, crow as standards for mental comparison. For example, if a bird resembles a song sparrow but looks unusually large, it may be a fox sparrow.

Plumage, whether plain or princely, muted or magnificent, is one of the most obvious keys to identification. Color can occur in remarkable combinations of spots, stripes, streaks, patches, and other patterns that make even supposedly drab birds a pleasure to see. In some instances, like the brown streaks of American bitterns and many other species, the plumage provides camouflage. Most vireos and warblers are various shades and combinations of yellow, green, brown, gray, and black, as one would expect from their forest environment. The black and white backs of woodpeckers help them to blend in with bark dappled with sunlight. The bold patterns of killdeers and some other plovers break up their outlines in much the same manner that warships used to be camouflaged before the invention of radar. Many shorebirds display countershading: They are dark above and light below, a pattern that reduces the effect of shadows and makes them appear an inconspicuous monotone. Even some brightly colored birds have camouflaging plumages when they are young and least able to avoid predators.

For some species, it is important *not* to be camouflaged. Many seabirds are mostly white, which in all light conditions enables them to be seen at great distances against the water. Because flocks of seabirds spread out from their colonies to search for food, it is vital that a bird that has located food be visible to others after it has landed on the water to feed.

To organize the immense variation in plumage, focus on different basic elements and ask the following types of questions. Starting with the head, is it uniformly colored like that of the red-headed woodpecker? Is there a small patch on the crown, like that of Wilson's warbler and the ruby-crowned kinglet, or a larger cap on the front and top of the head, like that of the common redpoll and American goldfinch? Is the crown striped like the ovenbird's? Does a ring surround the eye, as with a Connecticut warbler, or are the eye rings perhaps even joined across the top of the bill to form spectacles, like those of a yellow-breasted chat? Is there a stripe over or through the eyes, like the red-breasted nuthatch's, or a conspicuous black mask across the eyes, like that of a common yellowthroat or loggerhead shrike? From the head go on to the rest of the body, where distinctive colors and patterns can also mark a bird's bill, throat, breast, belly, back, sides, wings, rump, tail, and legs.

Finally, what a bird *does* is an important clue to its identity. Certain habits, postures, ways of searching for food, and other behavior characterize different species. Some passerines, such as meadowlarks, juncos, and towhees, are strictly ground feeders; other birds, including flycatchers and swallows, nab insects on the wing; and others, such as nuthatches and creepers, glean insects from the crevices in bark. Woodpeckers peck into the bark. Vireos and most warblers pick insects from the foliage of trees and brush.

All of these birds may be further distinguished by other habits of eating. For example, towhees scratch for insects and seeds by kicking backward with both feet together, whereas juncos rarely do, although both hop to move along the ground. Other ground feeders, such as meadowlarks, walk rather than hop. Despite the children's song, robins often run, not hop. Swallows catch insects while swooping and skimming in continuous flight, but flycatchers dart out from a limb, grab an insect (sometimes with an audible smack), and then return to their perch. Brown creepers have the curious habit of systematically searching for food by climbing trees in spirals, then flying back to the ground to climb again. Woodpeckers tend to hop upward, bracing themselves against the tree with their stiff tails. Nuthatches walk up and down trees and branches head first, seemingly without regard for gravity. Vireos are sluggish compared to the hyperactive, flitting warblers.

Many birds divide a food source into zones, an arrangement that apparently evolved to ensure each species its own food supply. The short-legged green heron sits at the edge of the water or on a low overhanging branch, waiting for its prey to come close to shore. Medium-sized black-crowned and yellow-crowned night herons hunt in shallow water. The long-legged great blue heron stalks fish in water up to two feet deep. Swans, geese, and many ducks graze underwater on the stems and tubers of grassy plants, but the longer necks of swans and geese enable them to reach deeper plants. Similarly, different species of shorebirds take food from the same mud flat by probing with their varied bills to different depths. Various species of warblers that feed in the same tree are reported to concentrate in separate areas, such as the trunk, twig tips, and tree top. Starlings and cowbirds feeding in flocks on the ground show another arrangement that provides an

even distribution of food: Those in the rear fly ahead to the front, so that the entire flock rolls slowly across the field.

Different species also have different styles of flight. Soaring is typical of some big birds. Gulls float nearly motionless in the wind. Buteos and vultures soar on updrafts in wide circles, although turkey vultures may be further distinguished by wings held in a shallow V. Some other large birds, such as accipiters, rarely soar but instead interrupt their wing beats with glides. Ospreys, kestrels, terns, and kingfishers can hover in one spot. Hummingbirds, like oversized dragonflies, can also hover and even fly backward. Slightly more erratic than the swooping, effortless flight of swallows is that of swifts, flitting with wing beats that appear to alternate (but do not). Still other birds, such as the American goldfinch and flickers, dip up and down in wavelike flight. Some species, including jays and grackles, fly dead straight. Among ducks, the surface-feeding species launch themselves directly upward into flight, seeming to jump from the water, but the heavy diving ducks typically patter along the surface before becoming airborne.

Various idiosyncrasies distinguish yet other species. The spotted sandpiper and northern waterthrush walk with a teetering, bobbing motion. Coots pump their heads back and forth as they swim. The eastern phoebe regularly jerks its tail downward while perching, but wrens often cock their tails vertically. Herons and egrets fly with their necks folded back; ibises and cranes fly with their necks outstretched. Still other birds have characteristic postures while sitting or flying or other unique habits that provide a reliable basis for identification.

AND NOW for a few practice puzzlers to illustrate and apply some of the points discussed above.

Standing at the edge of thickets early in May, you hear a distinctive song: about eight buzzy notes rising in a series of half tones. This song is enough to identify—what? Finally, you spot a small warbler with an olive back and yellow underparts, streaked black along the sides. The bird bobs its tail. It is the misnamed prairie warbler, which is common in bushy pastures, saplings, and low pines. The palm warbler also bobs its tail, but it is brown above and in spring has a chestnut cap.

At the wooded edge of a pond in spring or fall you observe a small bird that is all brown above and streaked with brown below. A long, pale-yellow stripe runs above each eye. As it walks the bird teeters and bobs. This is a . . . (I'm waiting for you to answer first) . . . a northern waterthrush, which migrates through the Chicago region and whose peculiar gait is shared by the somewhat larger spotted sandpiper, also seen near water.

Soaring overhead in big circles in summer is a bird with broad wings and a wide unbanded tail. It is probably a buteo, but which? Referring to your field guide, you see that there are only four buteos that occur in northern Illinois in summer, and all but one have banded tails. More specifically, red-winged hawks have wide white tail bands (i.e., equal in width to the intervening black bands); red-shouldered hawks have narrow white tail bands; Swainson's hawk (a bird of the prairies that sometimes nests near Chicago) has a long, finely barred tail with a dark terminal band; and finally, mature red-tailed hawks have no tail bands, so this is your bird. Your identification is confirmed by a glimpse of red on the upper surface of the tail as the hawk banks in its flight. At prairie preserves near Chicago, you might also see a harrier (or marsh hawk), flying low over the meadows with wings held in a shallow V as it veers from side to side, showing a white spot at the rump just above its long tail. Also present sometimes—but usually only during migration—are ospreys, soaring like buteos above lakes and ponds. From time to time, they hover and then plunge feet first into the water, from which they immediately emerge and fly off, interrupting their wing beats to shudder in mid-flight, like a dog shaking itself.

≈   ≈   ≈   ≈

AUTOMOBILE DIRECTIONS: Danada and Herrick Lake Forest Preserves are located west of Chicago near Wheaton and Naperville. (See **Map 34** at right.) Two approaches—from the **East-West Tollway** and the **North-South Tollway**—are described below. Both lead to the Danada trailhead, from which the trail stretches west to Herrick Lake.

To the Danada trailhead from the East-West Tollway (Interstate 88): Leave I-88 at the exit for Naperville Road. After paying the toll, turn left at a T-intersection and follow

     [Directions continue on page 149.]

MAP 34 — Access to Danada and Herrick Lake Forest Preserves

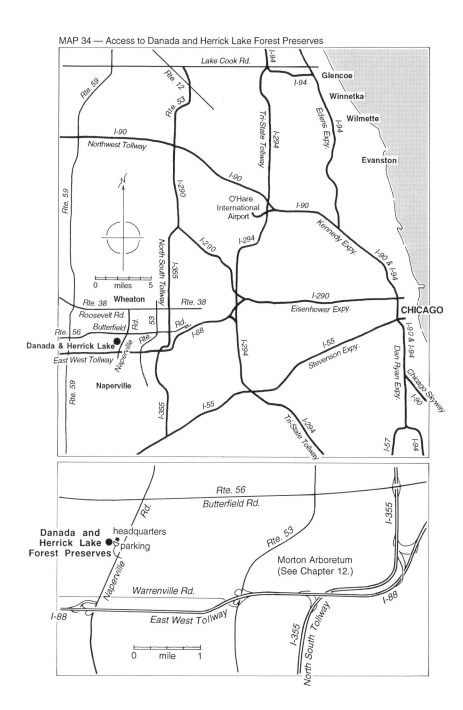

145

MAP 35 — Danada and Herrick Lake Forest Preserves

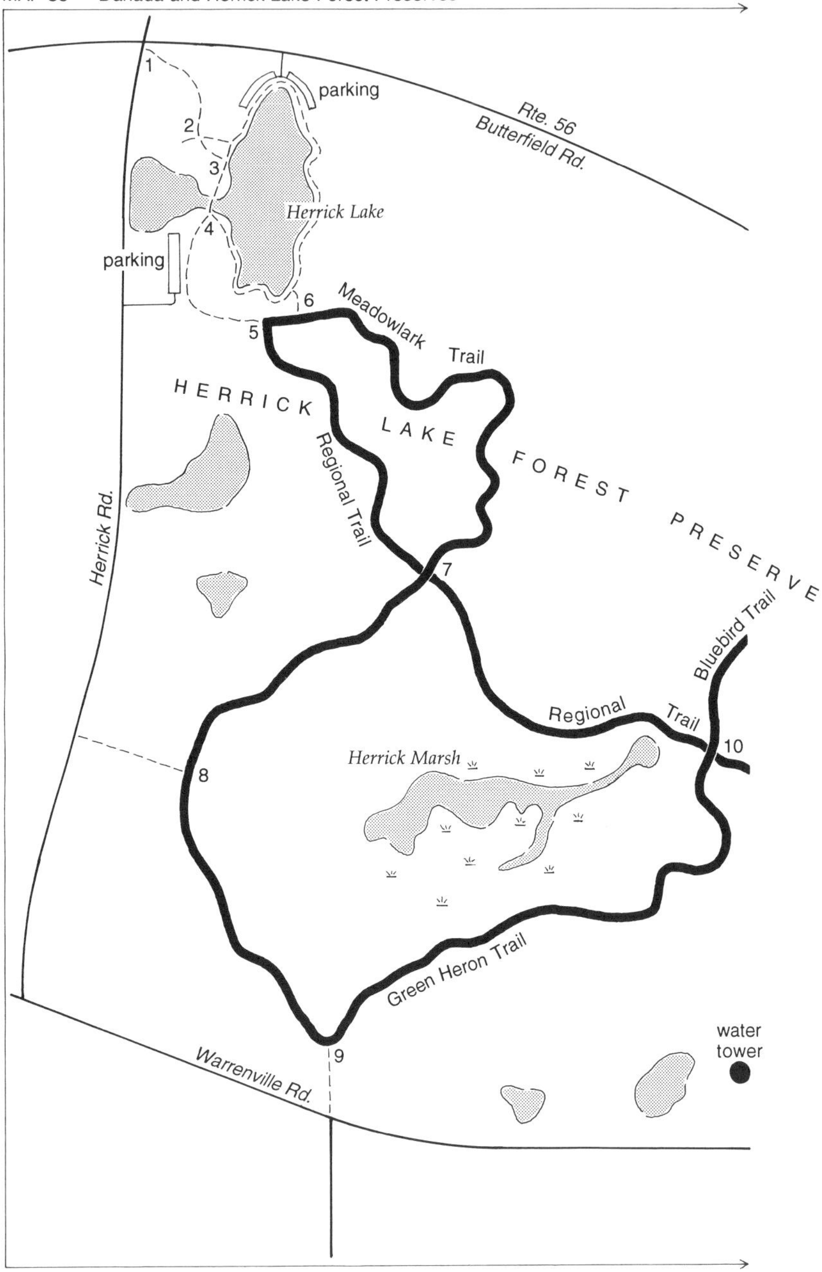

1

2

3

parking

Rte. 56
Butterfield Rd.

Herrick Lake

parking

4

6

Meadowlark

Trail

5

H E R R I C K

L A K E

F O R E S T

Regional Trail

P R E S E R V E

Herrick Rd.

7

Bluebird Trail

Regional Trail

10

8

Herrick Marsh

Green Heron Trail

water
tower

9

Warrenville Rd.

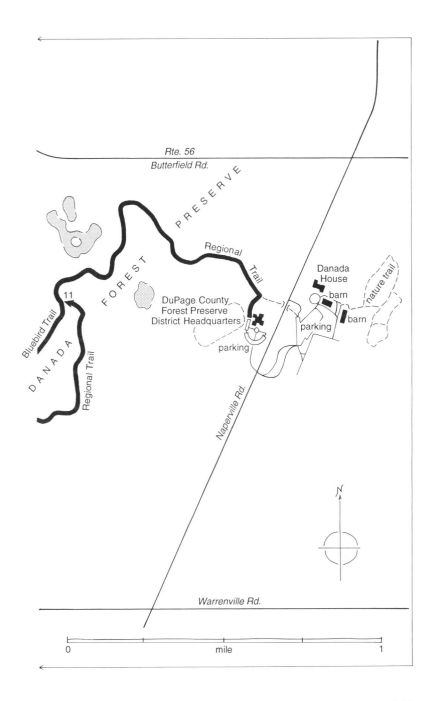

Rte. 56
Butterfield Rd.

P R E S E R V E

F O R E S T

Regional Trail

11

Bluebird Trail

Regional Trail

D A N A D A

DuPage County
Forest Preserve
District Headquarters

parking

Danada
House

barn

barn

nature trail

parking

Naperville Rd.

Warrenville Rd.

N

0   mile   1

Naperville Road north 0.7 mile, then turn left into the entrance for the headquarters of the Forest Preserve District of DuPage County. Park as far to the left of the building as you can.

To the Danada trailhead from the North-South Tollway (Interstate 355): Leave I-355 at the exit for Butterfield Road (Route 56). Follow Butterfield Road west 4 miles, then turn left onto Naperville Road. After 0.9 mile, turn right into the entrance for the headquarters of the Forest Preserve District of DuPage County. Park as far to the left of the building as you can.

≈ ≈ ≈ ≈

WALKING and BICYCLING: Map 35 on pages 146 and 147 shows a route of 6.3 miles through **Danada and Herrick Lake Forest Preserves**. Obviously, a shorter outing can be had by cutting off one or another loop (just as the path around Herrick Lake has been omitted). Navigation is made easy by the fact that trail junctions are unequivocally identified by numbers—an approach that in my opinion should be used universally.

To get started from the forest preserve district headquarters, follow a trail to the left of the building. At a T-intersection, turn left to follow the wide and winding **Regional Trail** to **junction 11**, and there fork right onto the **Bluebird Trail**.

Continue straight though **junction 10** in order to follow the **Green Heron Trail**. Pass side trails on the left at **junctions 9 and 8**.

Pass straight through **junction 7** and follow the **Meadowlark Trail** past **junction 6** to **junction 5**, where the route shown on the map turns left to follow the **Regional Trail** back through **junctions 7, 10, and 11** to the forest preserve district head-quarters. As you near the building, turn right to the parking lot.

12

THE MORTON ARBORETUM

Located west of Chicago, The Morton Arboretum features groves of specimen trees and shrubs, as well as gardens, meadows, and native woods—all interconnected by an extensive trail network. You could easily walk here all day if you wanted to. **Map 37** on pages 160 and 161 outlines a route of 5.6 miles (9 kilometers). There are still more trails west of Route 53.

The grounds at The Morton Arboretum open every day at 7:00 a.m. When daylight saving time is in effect, the grounds close at 7:00 p.m., and during the rest of the year they close at 5:00 p.m. Dogs are prohibited. An admission fee is charged. For recorded information call (630) 719-2400 or go to www.mortonarb.org. The telephone number for the main office is (630) 968-0074. The Bloom and Color Hotline is (630) 719-7955.

For automobile directions, please turn to page 158. Walking directions start on page 162.

THE MORTON ARBORETUM comprises 1,700 acres of rolling meadows, woods, lakes, and scattered marshes. Joy Morton, one of the early partners in a firm that eventually became the Morton Salt Company under his leadership, started buying land here in 1909 for a country estate, which he called Lisle Farms. Already in 1902 he and his brothers had established a small arboretum at their family home in Nebraska as a memorial to their father, J. Sterling Morton, who was the territorial governor of Nebraska before statehood and later the Secretary of Agriculture under President Glover Cleveland. J. Sterling Morton was also the originator of Arbor Day (now April 22), which grew out of his efforts to encourage Nebraska's farmers to plant trees.

In 1921 Joy Morton hired Charles Sargent, director of the Arnold Arboretum in Boston, to advise him on the development of a major arboretum at Lisle Farms. The aim was to collect from around the world specimens of trees and shrubs that can tolerate the Chicago climate. Sargent thought that Lisle Farms was a suitable site, and accordingly, in 1922 Morton founded the arboretum by placing four hundred acres under the authority of a board of trustees, which he headed until his death in 1934. During the first year of development, Lake Marmo was excavated (all of the arboretum's lakes are man-made) and 138,000 trees and shrubs were planted. During the following years, Joy Morton and his heirs gave other large tracts to the arboretum, and some adjoining areas were purchased.

The arboretum functions as a research center, school, and park rolled together. One of its chief purposes is to conduct research on tree and shrub culture. The arboretum also sponsors educational programs ranging from nature walks for school children and adults to courses for college credit. For information about the various lectures, shows, field trips, courses, and other special events offered by the arboretum, call the visitor center or go to the Web site listed on page 151.

The Morton Arboretum is the perfect place to learn native and foreign trees or just to walk in a pleasant setting. In the vicinity of the visitor center, the grounds have been attractively landscaped; small signs provide the names of trees and shrubs and other pertinent information. Farther afield, a system of footpaths weaves through woods and meadows.

LEARNING TO IDENTIFY TREES is not difficult. Every walk, bicycle ride, or automobile trip is an opportunity for practice. Notice the overall forms and branching habits of the trees, and also the distinctive qualities of their twigs, buds, bark, leaves, flowers, and fruits or seeds. These factors are the key identification features that distinguish one species from another. Finally, when referring to a field guide, check the maps or descriptions that delineate the geographic range within which a tentatively identified tree or shrub is likely to be found. Near Chicago, however, geographic considerations are not always useful because the region lies where the central hardwood forest, the northern forest, and the central plains all adjoin and blend together.

Some trees, of course, have very distinctive and reliable forms. Familiar evergreens like balsam fir and Eastern redcedar have a conical shape, like a dunce cap, although in dense stands the red-cedar tapers very little and assumes the columnar form of the Italian cypress, which it somewhat resembles. The deciduous littleleaf linden, imported from Europe and used as a street tree, is also more or less conical in shape, but with wider-spreading lower branches than the evergreens mentioned above. The American elm displays a spreading form like a head of broccoli. A full-bodied egg-shape is characteristic of sugar maple and beech, although both will develop long, branchless trunks in crowded woods, as do most forest trees competing for light. The vertically exaggerated cigar shape of Lombardy poplar—a form called *fastigiate*—and the pendulous, trailing quality of weeping willow are unmistakable. (Both Lombardy poplar and weeping willow have been introduced to North America from abroad.)

Branching habit is an important clue to some trees. White pine, for example, has markedly horizontal branches with a slight upward tilt at the tips, like a hand turned with its palm up. Norway spruce (another imported species) is a very tall evergreen—sometimes reminding me of a pagoda—with long, evenly-spaced, festoon-like branches. The slender lower branches of pin oak slant downward, while those of white oak and red oak are often massive and horizontal, especially on mature trees growing in the open. The lower branches of the horse chestnut (yet another European import) also droop but then curl up at the tips in chunky twigs. The branches of American elm spread up and out like the mouth of a trumpet. The trunk of the mature honeylocust diverges into large branches somewhat in the manner of an elm. Even the reviled *ailanthus* or tree of heaven, which in many urban areas springs up in dense groves of spindly, spiky saplings wherever earth has been disturbed, eventually develops a spreading form somewhat like an elm or honeylocust.

A good botanist or forester can identify trees by their twigs alone—or that is, by the end portion of the branch that constitutes the newest growth. During winter the shape, color, size, position, and sheathing of buds are important. For instance, beech buds are long and pointed, tan, and sheathed with overlapping scales like shingles. Sycamore and magnolia buds are wrapped in a single scale. The twigs of horse chestnut are tipped with big, sticky, brown buds, while those of silver maple and to a lesser extent red maple end with large clusters of red buds. Some oaks, such as white oak, have hairless terminal buds, while other species, such as black oak, have hairy end buds.

Aside from buds, other characteristics of twigs are the size, shape, and position of leaf scars marking where the leaf stems were attached. The scars can be circular, polygonal, crescent, or even heart-shaped, and they also show different numbers of bundle scars or vascular dots. One fundamental factor is the distinction between *opposite* and *alternate* scars. The location of leaf scars in opposite pairs along the twigs (as with maples) distinguishes a wide variety of trees and shrubs from those with leaf scars arranged alternately, first on one side and then on the other (as with oaks).

Yet other twig characteristics are color, thorns, odor, hair, flanges, and pith. For example, most maple twigs are reddish brown, but the twigs of striped maple and mountain maple are greenish. Thorns and spines are significant because relatively few trees have them, notably honeylocust, black locust, Hercules club, prickly ash, buckthorn bumelia, devil's walking stick, Osage-orange, American plum, some crabapples, and the many varieties of hawthorn. *Ailanthus* twigs, which show huge heart-shaped leaf scars, have a rank odor when broken open, and the twigs of black birch (also called sweet birch) have a strong wintergreen odor. Most oaks have hairless twigs, although some species such as blackjack oak are distinctly hairy. Bur oak and sweetgum often have peculiar flanges growing from the twigs. As for pith, it can be chambered, solid, spongy, or of different colors, depending on the species. Oak and hickory are common forest species in the Chicago region, but only the pith of white oak in cross section forms a star. All of these distinguishing features can best be appreciated simply by examining the twigs of different species.

Bark is not always a reliable clue for identifying trees, as the color and texture of bark change with age or from trunk to branches to twigs. Often the distinctive character of bark is seen only in the trunks of large, mature trees. Bark can be smooth, furrowed, scaly, plated, shaggy, fibrous, crisscrossed, or papery. Some trees, of course, may be clearly identified by their bark. The names *shagbark hickory* and *paper birch* speak for themselves. Striped maple has longitudinal, whitish stripes in the smooth green bark of the younger trees. The crisscrossed ridges of white ash, the light blotches on sycamores, and the smooth gray skin of

beech are equally distinctive. Birches and some cherries are characterized by horizontal lenticels like random dashes.

Most people notice leaves, particularly their shape. The leaves of gray birch and Eastern cottonwood are triangular; ginkgo, fan-shaped; catalpa, heart-shaped; sweetgum, star-shaped; beech, elliptical (or actually pointed at each end); and willow narrower still and thus *lanceolate*. Notice also the leaf margin or edge. Is it smooth like rhododendron, serrated like basswood, or deeply lobed like most maples? And how many lobes are there? For example, tulip trees (also called yellow-poplar) have easily recognized four-lobed leaves; maples have three- or five-lobed leaves. Also, are the lobe tips rounded like white oak or pointed like red oak? Or maybe, as with sassafras and red mulberry, the same tree has leaves that are shaped differently, the most distinctive being those with a single asymmetrical lobe creating a leaf outline like a mitten. In some trees, such as the large-leaf magnolia with its tobacco-like foliage, the sheer size of the leaves is significant. Sycamores have leaves resembling sugar maples or red maples, but usually bigger and coarser.

Some leaves such as those of the Japanese maple, horse chestnut, and Ohio buckeye are *palmately* compound, meaning that they are actually composed of leaflets radiating from the end of the stem. In the fall the whole compound leaf may drop off the tree as a unit, or the leaflets may fall off individually, and then finally the stem. Other leaves, such as ash, hickory, and sumac, are *pinnately* compound, being composed of leaflets arranged in opposite pairs along a central stalk. With pinnately compound leaves growing from the top of a branchless trunk, the saplings of *ailanthus* resemble little palm trees. Still other leaves are *bipinnately* compound, somewhat like a fern. The leaflets grow from stalks that, in turn, spread from a central stalk. Honeylocust, Kentucky coffeetree, and the ornamental imported silktree are examples.

Although the needles of evergreens are not as varied as the leaves of deciduous plants, there are still several major points to look for, such as the number of needles grouped together. White pine has fascicles of five; pitch pine and loblolly pine have fascicles of three; and jack pine, red pine, Virginia pine, and Austrian pine have fascicles of two. Needles of spruce, hemlock, and fir grow singly, but are joined to the twig in distinctive ways.

Spruce needles grow from little woody pegs, hemlock needles from smaller bumps, and fir needles directly from the twig, leaving a rounded pit when pulled off. Spruce needles tend to be four-sided, hemlock flat, and fir somewhere in-between. The needles of tamarack (also called American larch) grow in dense clusters and all drop off in winter. The needles of bald cypress (not that you would ever see one near Chicago) also drop off—hence its name. Finally, northern white-cedar has scalelike foliage, and—except for the prickly tips of the branches—so does Eastern redcedar.

Flowers are a spectacular, though short-lived, feature of some trees and shrubs. Three variables are color, form, and (less reliably) time of bloom. Shadbush (also called Allegheny serviceberry), with small, white, five-petaled flowers, is among the first of our native trees to bloom, usually in mid- or late April. Redbud, with red-purple clusters, also typically blooms in April. As members of the rose family, cherries, peaches, plums, pears, crabapples, and hawthorns all have flowers with five petals (usually pink or white) in loose, white clusters, typically blooming from late April through late May. The blossoms of flowering dogwood, which also appear in early or mid-May, consist of four white, petal-like bracts, each with a brown notch at the tip, while the flowers of alternate-leaf dogwood consist of loose, white clusters. These are a few of our native species commonly thought of as flowering trees, but the blossoms of other native species are equally distinctive, such as the small but numerous flowers of red maples, appearing with forsythia early in April, or the tuliplike flowers and durable husks of tulip trees, appearing in mid-June. Unlike most trees, witch-hazel—which produces small, yellow, scraggly flowers—blooms in fall or winter.

Finally, the seeds or fruit of a tree are a conspicuous element in summer and fall, sometimes lasting into winter and spring. Even if a tree is bare, the fruits and seeds (or for that matter, the leaves) can often be found littered on the ground around the trunk. Nobody who sees a tree with acorns could fail to know that it is an oak, although some varieties, such as willow oak and shingle oak (also known as northern laurel oak) are deceptive. Distinctive nuts are also produced by beech trees, horse chestnuts, hickories, and walnuts. Some seeds, like ash and maple, have wings; such winged seeds are termed *samaras*. Others, such as honey locust, Kentucky coffeetree, and redbud, come in pods like beans and in fact are members of the same general legume family. The seeds of birches and alders hang in catkins that in some species develop into conelike strobiles. Sweetgum and sycamore form prickle-balls (as do the shells of horse chestnut and buckeye). Eastern cottonwood and quaking aspen produce seeds that are wind-borne by cottonlike fluff. And, of course, brightly colored berries and fruits are produced by many species, such as crab-apples, dogwood, holly, hawthorn, and hackberry. The female ginkgo has pale pink, globular, and remarkably foul-smelling fruit. Among needle evergreens, spruce and pine cones hang from the twigs, while fir cones stand upright like stubby candles, and the small hemlock cones grow from the twig tips.

In conclusion, the trick to tree identification is to consider, either simultaneously or in rapid succession, a variety of features of which the ones discussed here—form and branching habit, twigs, buds, bark, leaves, flowers, and fruits or seeds—are the most obvious. Don't get hung up pondering any single ambiguous or inconclusive feature; move on to consider other clues.

≈   ≈   ≈   ≈

AUTOMOBILE DIRECTIONS: The Morton Arboretum is located west of Chicago and south of Wheaton. (See **Map 36** at right.) Two approaches—from the **East-West Tollway** and the **North-South Tollway**—are described below.

To the Morton Arboretum from the East-West Tollway (Interstate 88): There are separate exits depending on whether you approach from the east or the west.
  From the east: Leave I-88 at the exit for Route 53 north. Follow Route 53 north just 0.2 mile, then bear right into the arboretum's main entrance. Curve left past the visitor center and continue to the fee booth and visitor center parking lot.
  From the west: Leave I-88 at the exit for Naperville Road. After paying the toll, turn left at a T-intersection and follow Naperville Road north just 0.2 mile. Turn right onto Warrenville Road and go 2.1 miles, then turn left onto Route 53. Follow Route 53 north 0.2 mile, then bear right into the arboretum's main entrance. Curve left past the visitor center and continue to the fee booth and visitor center parking lot.

     [Directions continue on page 162.]

MAP 36 — Access to the Morton Arboretum

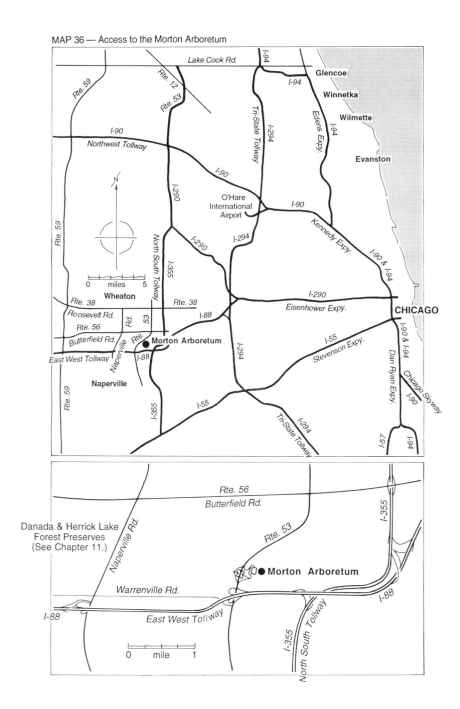

MAP 37 — The Morton Arboretum

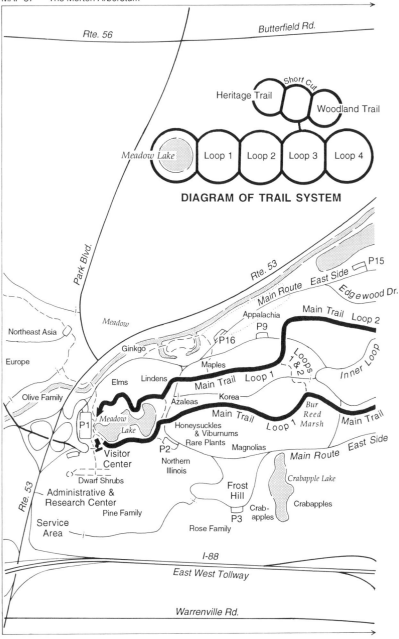

Rte. 56

Butterfield Rd.

Short Cut

Heritage Trail

Woodland Trail

Meadow Lake

Loop 1 | Loop 2 | Loop 3 | Loop 4

DIAGRAM OF TRAIL SYSTEM

Park Blvd.

Rte. 53

Main Route East Side

Edgewood Dr.

P15

Meadow

Appalachia

P9

Main Trail Loop 2

Northeast Asia

Ginkgo

P16

Loops 1 & 2

Inner Loop

Europe

Maples

Main Trail Loop 1

Elms

Lindens

Olive Family

Azaleas

Korea

Bur Reed Marsh

P1

Meadow Lake

Main Trail Loop 1

Main Trail East Side

Honeysuckles & Viburnums

Rare Plants

Visitor Center

P2

Magnolias

Main Route East Side

Northern Illinois

Dwarf Shrubs

Crabapple Lake

Administrative & Research Center

Frost Hill

Pine Family

Crabapples

Rte. 53

Service Area

Rose Family

Crab-apples

P3

I-88

East West Tollway

Warrenville Rd.

160

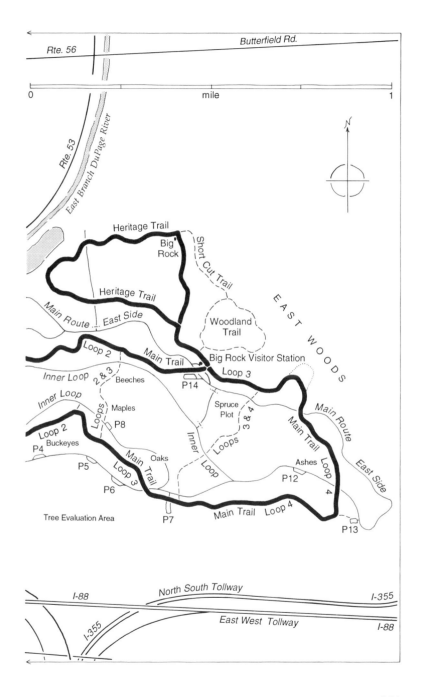

Rte. 56

Butterfield Rd.

0   mile   1

Rte. 53

East Branch DuPage River

N

Heritage Trail

Big Rock

Short Cut Trail

Heritage Trail

E A S T   W O O D S

Main Route   East Side

Woodland Trail

Loop 2

Main Trail

Inner Loop

Big Rock Visitor Station

Loops 2 & 3   Beeches

Loop 3

P14

Inner Loop

Maples

Spruce Plot

Loops 3 & 4

Main Route   East Side

Loop 2

P8

Main Trail

Loop 4

P4   Buckeyes

P5

Loop 3

Oaks

Inner Loop

Ashes

P12

P6

Main Trail

P13

Tree Evaluation Area

P7

Main Trail   Loop 4

I-88

North South Tollway

I-355

I-355

East West Tollway

I-88

To the Morton Arboretum from the North-South Tollway (Interstate 355): Leave the tollway at the exit for Butterfield Road (Route 56). Follow Butterfield Road west 1.3 miles, then turn left onto Route 53 southbound. After 1.7 miles, curve right into the arboretum's main entrance and under Route 53. Continue past the visitor center and the fee booth to the visitor center parking lot.

$$\approx \qquad \approx \qquad \approx \qquad \approx$$

WALKING: Map 37 on pages 160 and 161 shows a route of 5.6 miles through the **Morton Arboretum**. Obviously, a shorter outing can be had by simply omitting one or more of the loops at the eastern end of the arboretum.

Before you start, take a moment to understand the structure of the trail system. Essentially, it is a sequence of loops, each one pressed against the next and sharing a trail segment, as shown by the diagram on the map. The first loop around Meadow Lake is un-numbered, but the next four are designated Loops 1 through 4. Finally, at the arboretum's northeast corner, there are more circuit trails joined to Loop 3 by a spur.

To get started from the Visitor Center, descend the steps at the back leading to the edge of Meadow Lake. With the water on the left, follow a path about a third of the way around the lake, then fork right across a road onto **Loop 1** of the East Side Main Trail.

At a T-intersection, turn right to continue on **Loop 2** of the Main Trail. Cross a road and then eventually fork right across a boardwalk through a marsh.

At another trail junction, bear right via **Loop 3**, which leads through an oak savanna toward Loop 4 and parking lot 7. After crossing a road and lot 7, re-enter the woods and immediately fork right to join **Loop 4**. Continue past a side trail for parking lot 13, across a road, and through the woods. After again crossing the road, follow the main trail as it curves left and then passes a trail on the left shared by Loops 3 and 4. Continue to the **Big Rock Visitor Station**.

From the rear of the pavilion at the Big Rock Visitor Station, enter the woods. Soon, fork left for the Heritage Trail, then left again. Eventually, the trail emerges from the oak forest and crosses a prairie to the **Big Rock** (a glacial erratic).* Turn right to go back to the Big Rock Visitor Station.

Leaving the Big Rock Visitor Station behind, cross the road and pass through parking lot 14. Follow **Loop 3** of the East Side Main Trail to the junction with **Loop 2**. Bear right and continue, eventually crossing another road and reaching a T-intersection with **Loop 1**—and there turn right. After once again crossing a road, continue across the grass to a paved path. Follow the paved path to the right back to the main parking lot and the visitor center where you started.

---

*Boulders are a common occurrence throughout glaciated regions. They were plucked from their original bedrock ledges by the ponderous ice sheet that four times advanced from Canada during the last million years, retreating most recently about 12,500 years ago. Dislodged from their parent ledges, the boulders were dragged along the surface of the ground beneath the ice. Sometimes bigger than a house an d weighing thousands of tons, the largest rocks were rarely transported more than a mile or two. Smaller ones may have been carried hundreds of miles before coming to rest as the ice melted and left them strewn over the landscape or buried in glacial till. Big and small, the boulders invariably lie to the south of their place of origin, indicating that the ice advanced from the north. Transported far enough, the rocks may be composed of material unlike anything in their vicinity, and so they are called *erratics*. For example, boulders of red jasper are found in Kentucky, six hundred miles from the nearest bedrock ledge of that type north of Lake Superior.

13

GREENE VALLEY FOREST PRESERVE

Greene Valley is located west of Chicago near Naperville. The route outlined on **Map 39** on page 175 is 8 miles long (12.8 kilometers). Passing through meadows, overgrown fields, scrubby wood, and mature forest (including an excellent example of an oak savanna), the trail links the upland and the floodplain along the East Branch of the DuPage River.

Greene Valley Forest Preserve is open daily from an hour after sunrise to an hour after sunset. Dogs must be leashed. The area is managed by the Forest Preserve District of DuPage County; telephone (630) 933-7200 or go to www.dupageforest.com.

For automobile directions, please turn to page 172. Walking directions start on page 174.

HOW COME GREENE is this valley? Because a large section of the present-day forest preserve was purchased from the Greene family, whose name in this vicinity goes back to the early period of settlement in DuPage County. In 1835, only two years after Chicago was incorporated as a town, Daniel Moon Greene bought a quarter section (160 acres) on the East Branch of the DuPage River in Lisle Township. The site was desirable because it included water and some timber—although settlers were beginning to understand that the best soils were on the open grasslands and that ample well water could be tapped anywhere. Greene purchased his tract for three dollars per acre from the federal government, which had established a land office in Chicago in 1834, thus facilitating a land rush as settlers fanned out into the prairie. Some settlers had squatted on the land earlier, but to keep their claims they had to record them and pay for their tracts once the land office opened.

Under the Northwest Ordinance, the federal government had

the power of "primary disposal" of all land to which title was obtained from the Indians by a series of dubious treaties. Many of these compacts were negotiated with local chiefs who were said by the whites to speak for much larger groups of Native Americans than was actually the case. One land cession was a swath ten miles wide from Chicago along the Des Plaines River to the Illinois River. The federal government—looking forward to the construction of a canal linking Lake Michigan and the Mississippi River—obtained the valley of the Des Plaines in 1816 from representatives of the Ottawa, Chippewa, and Potawatomi. The northwestern boundary of this cession runs through present-day Greene Valley Forest Preserve. Another contemporaneous treaty called for the Indians to vacate all of Illinois south of a line connecting the tip of Lake Michigan with the Mississippi. In 1828 and '29, leaders of the Winnebago and other tribes signed three treaties that relinquished 4.5 million acres in northern Illinois in exchange for annual payments of cash and goods, the provision of services (such as blacksmithing), and other promises.

After leaving the state and starving for two years in Iowa Territory, approximately 1,500 Sauk and Fox under Chief Black Hawk crossed back into Illinois in 1832 in the hope of joining with the Winnebago at Prophet's Town on the Rock River—perhaps for war, or perhaps merely to live and cultivate corn, as Black Hawk said. About two-thirds of his people were women and children, but the rest were armed warriors. In response, Governor John Reynolds called out the militia. (Among them was Abraham Lincoln, who was elected Captain by his company.) Rebuffed by the Winnebago, Black Hawk withdrew toward Iowa. Along the way he was attacked by militiamen, whom he routed. Encouraged, the Indians took the offensive in a few small raids that incited huge alarm among settlers. Several thousand militia volunteers and regular army troops assembled to find and destroy Black Hawk and his band. The brief war ended in disaster for Black Hawk's people when most of them were slaughtered despite efforts to surrender. Summoned to Chicago the following year, seventy-seven Indian chiefs representing all Native Americans still living in Illinois signed away their last lands, then left the state with the remnants of their tribes. So thorough was their subjugation and expulsion that Illinois today, unlike the states to the north and west, has no Indian reservations nor federally recognized tribes. With the elimination of the Indian threat, the pace of white settlement in northern Illinois accelerated.

As already noted, Daniel Moon Greene was a part of this land rush, and in 1841 he was joined by his twenty-three-year-old nephew, William Briggs Greene, a school teacher from Wallingford, Vermont. William worked on his uncle's farm and taught at the nearby one-room Goodrich School. Eventually, he saved enough money to buy land for himself from the widow of Deacon Goodrich, one of the first settlers in DuPage County. The property adjoined his uncle's farm and cost $5 per acre. William could have taken up better, cheaper land from the government a dozen miles southwest at Plainfield, but he preferred to stay in the vicinity of the East Branch, where not only his uncle but also a number of other educated New Englanders had settled—and which therefore would make a more congenial home for the woman he hoped to marry. This was Harriet Meeker, also of Wallingford, with whom William carried on an expensive correspondence. Letters then cost fifty cents each, and custom expected the gentleman to enclose the postage for a reply. A minister's daughter, delicate in health, and accustomed to a comfortable home, Harriet nonetheless agreed to marry William, despite her parents' lack of enthusiasm for her move to the far distant west, as Illinois was regarded.

In 1845 William returned to Wallingford, married Harriet, and headed back with her to Illinois. First they traveled to Troy, New York, then to Buffalo via packet boat on the Erie Canal. From Buffalo they continued by steamboat through the Great Lakes to Chicago, as did tens of thousands of other people moving to the frontier during the 1830s and '40s. Easy and inexpensive compared to overland transport, the water route greatly facilitated the settlement of northern Illinois by New Englanders, New Yorkers, and immigrants from Europe after the Erie Canal opened in 1825. And for the out-shipment of farm products, water transport reduced freight rates to a small fraction of the cost of moving goods by land to the East Coast. Before completion of the Erie Canal and the establishment of steamboat service through the Great Lakes, most settlers in Illinois came from southern Indiana, Kentucky (again, like Abraham Lincoln), Tennessee, and even Virginia. Some brought slaves with them. They arrived in Illinois via the Ohio and Mississippi Rivers, took up land in the southern

part of the state, and usually sent their farm products downstream to New Orleans. In fact, the first federal land office in
Illinois opened at Kaskaskia on the Mississippi River in 1804,
thirty years before Chicago.

In a letter to her family in Vermont, Harriet Greene described
the countryside as she approached her new home west of
Chicago.*

Stop a moment, picture to yourself a lumber wagon well loaded
with our boxes and as many more, nicely packed in—a Hoosier
lady and her husband—with your son and daughter. Twenty-
six miles before us—quite a pretty drive, and some dust too.
We passed the first sandy prairie, meeting the greatest variety
of Western teams, visages of their drivers most delightfully
painted with black dust—and the new habitations as various as
they were numerous. . . .

There were woods before us, yet it seemed as though we
never should reach them—while passing through the woods, I
observed the beautiful flowers of the West—well may they be
famed—their colors are brilliant, many are fragrant to great
degree, and so curious in their formation—was surprised to see
the sweet briar in bloom. My favorite flowers opened their blue
eyes even under the feet of the horses—the second prairie was
more fertile, yet quite vivid.

Passing through another thicket, we came to a rolling prairie.
This was indeed pretty. . . . 'Twas now dark and were glad to
find ourselves in the last wood and soon turning from the main
road to see a light at Uncle Daniel's. Met with a cordial
reception, and after some warm tea, and quite tired, we were
glad about eleven to indulge in the luxury of a feather bed.

Since then, we have been quite domesticated—like my new
aunt, uncle, and cousins much—attended church last Sabbath at
Naperville, quite a little place. The [meeting] house is new, not
finished, the hearers seated on rough boards, and Mr. Lyman,
the preacher, behind a table or desk. Something of a contrast to

---

* The letters of Harriet Elizabeth Meeker Greene quoted here, and also
other material on the Greene family, are taken from *God Bless Our Home*,
a memoir published in 1977 by Harriet's grandson William Bertram
Greene.

our neat church. Have been about as usual in regard to my health. Some days even better than the two past years. Think the climate is favorable to restore me some future day. . . .

For a few weeks the young couple stayed with the family of Daniel Moon Greene, then they moved onto their own farm and lived in an old long cabin, which they occupied for five years. "Come, lay aside your work awhile and look into your daughter's home," Harriet wrote to her mother in June 1845:

"[I]s not this a nice yard, larger than yours. Notice the large oak trees—twelve—what a nice shady place. But come on, since the outer part is ragged to behold—naught but logs, their natural form and color, walk in. . . . What a nice room 15x16. . . . My walls are white, although rough. My table stands on the west side and over it my glass and Wm's watch. Shall have just an hour to write.

In the corner is our stand—on it my lamp, work basket and Bible. We read every evening—commenced the book of Psalms. My chairs are on each side, and our spit box [i.e., spittoon] by the rocking chair. My curtains are up at the windows. . . .

Look into our bedroom, window faces the East, bed stands South, wash bowl and pitcher in a chair. Have not brought home our wash stand yet. . . . Can you climb above—I guess not. I'll tell you how it looks. A bed is on the floor—could not bring the other bedstead. . . . We go down cellar from the bedroom through a trap door. Nothing there now but a half barrel of salt mackerel. Come a moment longer out the South door into my back room. See my stove, a Premium stove—two ovens, a low one and an elevated one, four griddles. . . . Let me look into the oven lest my Indian pudding be burning. Wm. bought me a cookbook, could not do without it. . . .

We breakfast at six, dine at twelve, and sup at five or half after. I wake every morning now, the first one, and route my household. . . . Mother, Wm. is as good as a girl about the house. He grinds my coffee, and on the whole have quite an easy time. I begin to see what you find to do from morning to night—when I think my work done, something else comes along. We are very happy. I am quite contented, now I can sit

under my own oak tree, and this is *our* home. Do come this fall and stay all winter. . . . I think of you every day and every hour. . . . [T]ell grandma and grandpa every time I open the cupboard door our old-fashioned china plate looks me in the face—love to them all—I wish they would all write me. . . . Will not my mother write me now—now I am away off in Illinois—that land of exile, as you are pleased to call it. Nevertheless, it is pleasant, and I do not repent or even regret coming.

In 1850 William and Harriet moved into a new frame and clapboard house that they called the Oak Cottage. Enlarged over the years with four additions, it grew into a substantial home that still stands at the corner of Greene and Hobson Roads north of 75th Street. (The main section is shown at left.) Here the Greenes raised three children. Another three died in infancy. In their old age, William and Harriet lived in just one wing of the house, while a son, William Spencer Greene, occupied the rest with his family.

After completing a business course at North Central College in Naperville, the younger William took over management of the farm, bought more land to the south, and built up a substantial dairy operation. Each day, milk was taken to Lisle by wagon and from there shipped to Chicago by train. William's wife Jessie, a Chicago girl of high Episcopal background, ran the Greene household, which included six children (all eventually went to college) plus three or four farm hands and one or two hired girls, some of them recent immigrants who ate in the kitchen and slept in an annex to the house. Friends and relatives were frequent guests. William Bertram Greene, one of Jessie's sons, remarked in his memoirs that the family occupied both the world of farmers who labored with their hands and that of respected and prosperous landowners and gentle folk who observed all the amenities. Late in his life, after a distinguished and very successful business career manufacturing construction equipment and after the death of his wife in 1973, this William—a grandson of William Briggs Greene—returned to live in Oak Cottage with his sister.

Eventually, the Greene family sold about half their property for residential development and the rest to the Forest Preserve District of DuPage County at a below-market price. Together with other land, Greene Valley Forest Preserve now totals more than

1,400 acres. The management program for the area specifies periodic controlled burns to re-establish and maintain the kind of plant communities, including upland prairie and oak savannas, that characterized DuPage County more than a hundred and fifty years ago.

One anomalous feature at Greene Valley is the giant landfill at the southern edge of the forest preserve. Constructed of nonhazardous waste, this huge mound was started in 1974 and is now in a "post-closure" phase while the mass settles and vegetation is established. A circumferential trail and a road to the top have been built. Although not yet open as this book goes to press, perhaps they will be by the time you go there.

≈   ≈   ≈   ≈

AUTOMOBILE DIRECTIONS: Greene Valley Forest Preserve is located west of Chicago near Naperville. (See **Map 38** at right.) Three approaches—from the **East-West Tollway**, the **North-South Tollway**, and **Interstate 55**—are described below.

To Greene Valley from the East-West Tollway (Interstate 88): There are separate exits depending on whether you approach from the east or the west.

From the east: Leave I-88 at the exit for Route 53 south. Follow Route 53 south 4.3 miles, then turn right onto 75th Street. After 0.5 mile, turn left onto Greene Road. Go 0.4 mile, then turn right onto 79th Street. After 0.5 mile turn left into the West Area of Greene Valley Forest Preserve. Follow the road 0.5 mile to a parking lot.

From the west: Leave I-88 at the exit for Naperville Road. After paying the toll, turn right at a T-intersection and go south 4.3 miles, during which Naperville Road becomes Naper Boulevard. Turn left onto 75th Street. After 2.1 miles, turn right onto Greene Road. Go 0.4 mile, then turn right onto 79th Street. After 0.5 mile turn left into the West Area of Greene Valley Forest Preserve. Follow the road 0.5 mile to a parking lot.

To Greene Valley from the North-South Tollway (Interstate 355): Leave the tollway at the exit for 75th Street. Follow 75th Street west 2 miles, then turn left onto Greene Road. Go 0.4 mile, then turn right onto 79th Street. After 0.5 mile turn left into

MAP 38 — Access to Greene Valley Forest Preserve

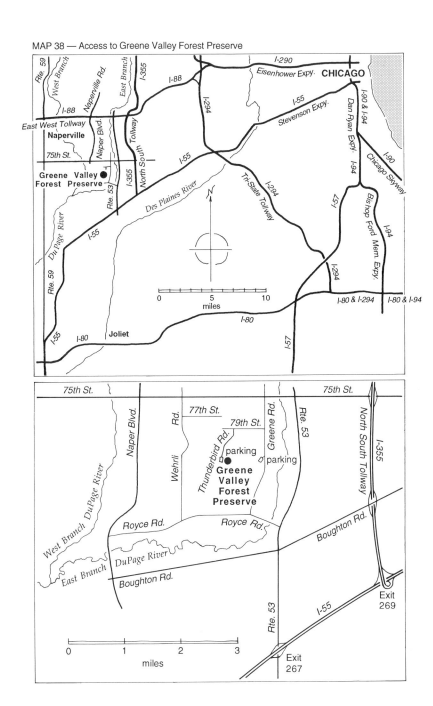

the West Area of Greene Valley Forest Preserve. Follow the road 0.5 mile to a parking lot.

To Greene Valley from Interstate 55: This highway is the extension of **Stevenson Expressway** southwest toward Joliet. Leave the expressway at Exit 267 for Route 53 and follow it north 2.2 miles. Not long after crossing Boughton Road, turn left onto Royce Road. After 0.5 mile, turn right onto Greene Road and go 1.7 miles, in the process passing a large parking lot on the left. You can park here if you want, but the walk outlined on **Map 39** at right starts at a different lot, so I suggest that you continue to 79th Street and turn left there. After 0.5 mile turn left into the West Area of Greene Valley Forest Preserve. Follow the road 0.5 mile to a parking lot.

≈   ≈   ≈   ≈

WALKING and BICYCLING: Map 39 at right shows a route of 8 miles at **Greene Valley Forest Preserve** bordering the East Branch of the DuPage River.

To get started from the information board at the Thunderbird Road parking lot, bear right where two paths diverge. Follow the wide track through an area that is fast growing up in brush and trees. At a trail junction, fork right and continue into the woods and downhill.

Eventually, after crossing tiny Anderson Creek, turn right at a trail junction. Pass to the left of a parking lot. With caution, cross Greene Road and continue downhill. At the bottom, bear right across Anderson Creek, then bear right again in order to head obliquely uphill toward the big mound of a former landfill. Wind through the prairie and along the edge of the woods. At a fork in the trail, bear left and continue clockwise around the oak savanna, then return to the trail juncture just beyond Anderson Creek. Tun right in order to follow a trail that runs parallel with the East Branch of the DuPage River, which is concealed from view behind the riverside brush).

Eventually, the trail bends left uphill. At a trail junction near the intersection of 75th Street and Greene Road, bear right. With caution, cross 75th Street at the traffic light and follow the path to the Greene Farm and Oak Cottage at the end of the trail. From there, return by the way you came across 75th Street. With Greene Road uphill to the right, continue to a T-

MAP 39 — Greene Valley Forest Preserve

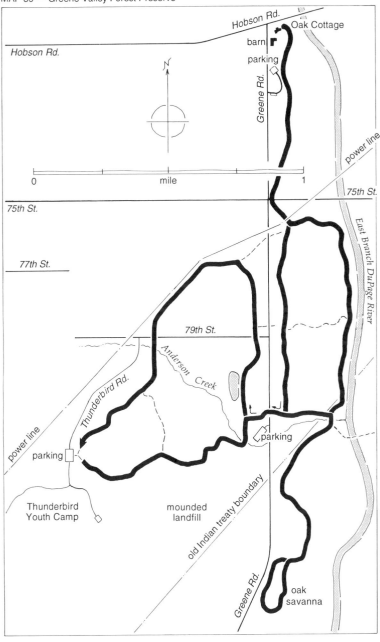

Hobson Rd.

Oak Cottage

barn

parking

Greene Rd.

power line

75th St.

Hobson Rd.

N

0   mile   1

75th St.

East Branch DuPage River

77th St.

79th St.

Anderson Creek

Thunderbird Rd.

power line

parking

parking

Thunderbird
Youth Camp

mounded
landfill

old Indian treaty boundary

Greene Rd.

oak
savanna

175

intersection, and there turn right in order to cross Greene Road at the same place you did before.

After crossing Greene Road and re-entering the woods, turn right at a T-intersection. Eventually, after crossing 79th Street, continue to a T-intersection near high electric transmission lines.

With the transmission lines on the right, follow the trail along the edge of the woods and across a scrubby prairie. Pass a trail intersecting from the left and—with the transmission lines in the distance on the right—continue to the parking lot.

14

WATERFALL GLEN FOREST PRESERVE

Waterfall Glen completely surrounds Argonne National Laboratory southwest of Chicago. Neither the research complex at the center nor the surrounding highways and residential development at the periphery can be seen from the circular hike-bike trail outlined on **Map 41** on pages 184 and 185, creating the illusion of a huge sanctuary. The route is 9 miles long (14.5 kilometers).

Waterfall Glen is open daily from an hour after sunrise to an hour after sunset. Dogs must be leashed. The area is managed by the Forest Preserve District of DuPage County; telephone (630) 933-7200 or go to www.dupageforest.com.

For automobile directions, please turn to page 182. Walking directions also start on page 182.

FOR THE MOST PART, Waterfall Glen Forest Preserve is rolling terrain formed when the Wisconsin Glacier receded from the Chicago region about 12,500 years ago. Clay, sand, and rocks were picked up by the ice sheet as it advanced southward, and of course all of this material dropped out as the glacier melted, leaving a blanket of earth that covered the landscape. Randomly dotted with sloughs and marshes, this land surface is typical of the Chicago region, but in the southeastern part of Waterfall Glen, there is something different. Here streams have penetrated to bedrock as they descend toward the Des Plaines River, creating alternating ridges and ravines off the larger valley. This rugged zone was described as "broken" terrain by government surveyors in the 1840s.

The valley of the Des Plaines into which the ravines empty is a mile wide and more than a hundred feet lower than the upland, reflecting the erosive power of what once was a far bigger river than that seen today. As the Wisconsin ice sheet receded, the Des

Plaines was fed by a huge volume of meltwater. For a period even Lake Michigan drained to the southwest through the Des Plaines Valley.

The bedrock in the vicinity of Waterfall Glen is dolomite, a very durable variety of limestone. It was deposited as sediment between 500 and 400 million years ago when the low interior of the continent was flooded by a shallow sea extending from the Gulf of Mexico to Alaska. In the Des Plaines Valley near the towns of Lemont and Romeoville, quarrying became a major industry after the Illinois and Michigan Canal opened in 1848 and provided a means of transporting stone cheaply to the booming city of Chicago. Big pits were carved into the hillsides up and down the valley. At Waterfall Glen a Chicago builder named Edwin Walker operated three quarries for high-quality Lemont limestone—or Athens Marble, as it was called. Among Walker's many projects was the Chicago Water Tower, constructed in the mid-1860s from limestone quarried at Waterfall Glen.

Lumber operations were another locally important industry. From 1860 through the 1880s, the Ward Brothers' sawmill occupied a site on Sawmill Creek, although the stream was then called Hennebry's Creek.

DuPage County first began to purchase land at Waterfall Glen in 1925, when it bought 75 acres at Sawmill Creek. Here the Civilian Conservation Corps constructed a small waterfall during the Great Depression of the 1930s. The CCC provided work, income, and vocational training for unemployed single men. The organization was run on a semi-military basis by the War Department and assigned projects selected and supervised by the Departments of Agriculture and Interior. Living in barracks, the workers were organized into companies of about two hundred men. Base pay was $30 per month, and if a man's family at home was on relief, as was often the case, most of his wages were sent there. At its peak in 1935, the CCC had more than half a million men in over 2,600 camps working on forest and wildlife protection, flood control, soil conservation, and the development of federal, state, and local parks.

In 1973 the federal government gave DuPage County a huge doughnut-shaped area surrounding Argonne National Laboratory. The conveyance was made pursuant to the Legacy of Parks Program, by which surplus land at federal facilities is transferred

to local governments for park use. At 2,433 acres, Waterfall Glen is now one of the county's largest forest preserves.

≈   ≈   ≈   ≈

AUTOMOBILE DIRECTIONS: Waterfall Glen Forest Preserve is located southwest of Chicago. (See **Map 40** at right.) Directions from **Interstate 55** are given below.

To Waterfall Glen from Interstate 55: This highway is the extension of the **Stevenson Expressway** southwest toward Joliet. Leave the expressway at Exit 273A for Cass Avenue south toward Argonne National Laboratory. Go only a few tenths of a mile, then turn right onto Northgate Road. After just 100 yards, turn right into the parking lot for Waterfall Glen Forest Preserve.

≈   ≈   ≈   ≈

WALKING and BICYCLING: Map 41 on pages 184 and 185 shows a 9-mile loop at **Waterfall Glen Forest Preserve**, which completely surrounds Argonne National Laboratory.

To get started, locate the trailhead behind an information board and picnic area. Head straight into the woods and past another trail intersecting from the left (and by which you will return at the end). Cross a small bridge and continue on the wide hike-bike path, which climbs, dips, and winds through the woods, some-times passing side trails and at one point crossing old Kearny Road (now abandoned).
　　Eventually, the trail reaches Westgate Road. Bear right along the road until the trail reappears on the other side and continues through the woods. After bordering a railroad and passing a slough, the trail climbs gradually to Poverty Prairie. Turn right along a gravel road, then left at a parking lot.
　　After the trail descends into the valley of the Des Plaines River, continue along the bottom of the slope with a railroad on the right. At an intersection near a power substation, turn left onto a gravel road and go 80 yards, then bear right to continue on the hike-bike path, which eventually arrives at a set of valves on a gas pipeline right-of-way. Turn left along the right-of-way and go 90 yards, then turn right into the woods and continue to an information board above Rocky Glen.

[Directions continue on page 187.]

MAP 40 — Access to Waterfall Glen Forest Preserve

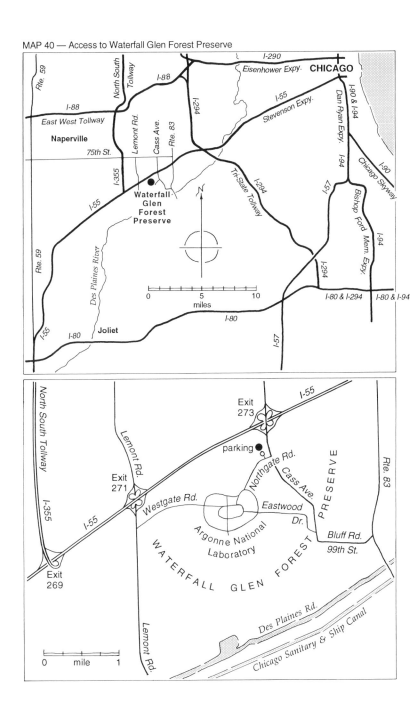

MAP 41 — Waterfall Glen Forest Preserve

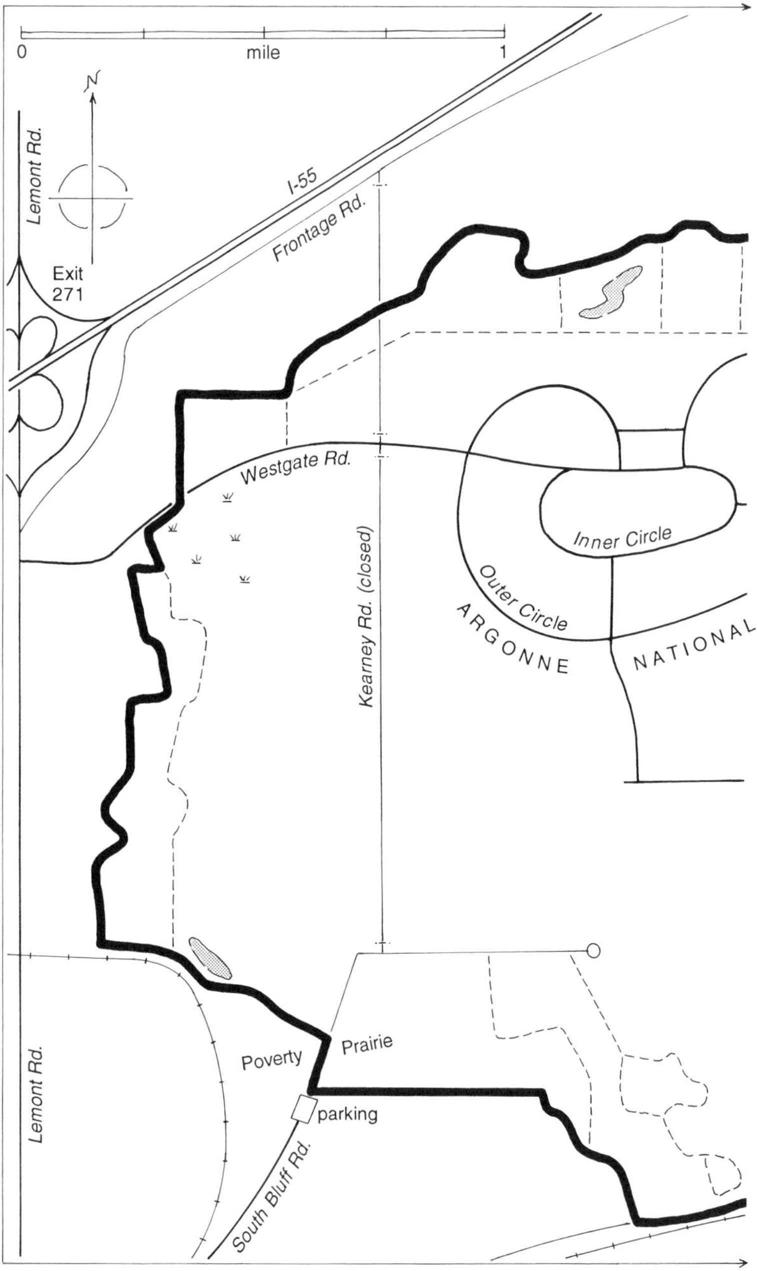

0   mile   1

N

Lemont Rd.

I-55

Frontage Rd.

Exit
271

Westgate Rd.

Kearney Rd. (closed)

Inner Circle

Outer Circle

A R G O N N E   N A T I O N A L

Lemont Rd.

Poverty   Prairie

parking

South Bluff Rd.

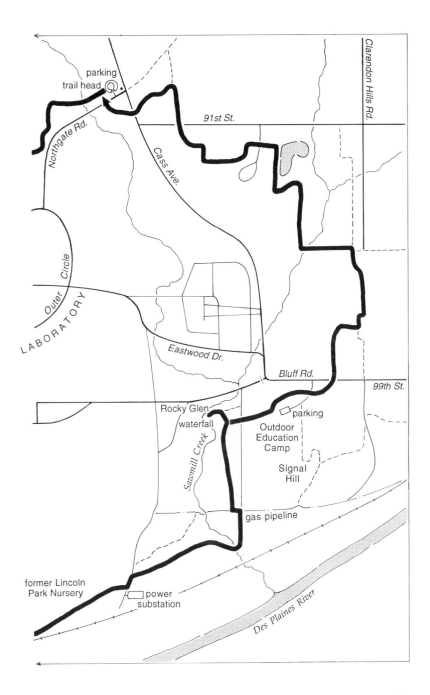

parking
trail head

Northgate Rd.

Cass Ave.

91st St.

Clarendon Hills Rd.

Outer Circle

LABORATORY

Eastwood Dr.

Bluff Rd.

99th St.

Rocky Glen

parking

waterfall

Outdoor
Education
Camp

Signal
Hill

Sawmill Creek

gas pipeline

former Lincoln
Park Nursery

power
substation

Des Plaines River

185

For a digression to a small waterfall at Rocky Glen, descend into the ravine. Afterwards, return to the information board and continue on the hike-bike path. After crossing a gravel road, the trail skirts to the left of a parking lot, crosses the entrance road to the parking lot, and then crosses Bluff Road (99th Street).

Follow the hike-bike path as it twists and turns through the woods, eventually passing a pond and crossing a small road. Use caution as the trail crosses 91st Street, Cass Avenue, and Northgate Road. Finally, at a T-intersection with the trail that you followed at the outset, turn right to the parking lot.

15

PALOS HILLS and SAG VALLEY

These huge forest preserves are located adjacent to one another southwest of Chicago at the confluence of the Des Plaines River and the Calumet Sag Channel.

Maps 43 and 44 on pages 197 and 198 outline two walks in the **Palos Hills** starting at the **Little Red Schoolhouse Nature Center**. Directions are on pages 194-196. The first walk is just 1.8 miles long (2.9 kilometers) in the vicinity of Long John Slough. The second walk is 5.3 miles long (8.5 kilometers) and explores forested hills dotted with marshes and ponds.

The parking lot at the Little Red Schoolhouse Nature Center opens daily at 8:00 a.m. From March through October, the lot closes at 5:00 on weekdays and 5:30 on weekends. During the rest of the year, it closes a half-hour earlier. Dogs are prohibited at the nature center. If you bring your dog, park at Country Lane Woods off 95th Street and take the circuit shown on Map 44.

Map 45 on page 201 outlines a route of 4 miles (6.4 kilometers) in the **Sag Valley** starting at the **Swallow Cliff Toboggan Slides**. Directions are on page 200. The trail explores the bluff and wooded highlands that overlook the Sag, through which Lake Michigan once drained to the southwest. The parking lot at Swallow Cliff opens daily at 8:00 a.m. and closes at sunset. Dogs must be leased.

The Palos Hills and Sag Valley are managed by the Forest Preserve District of Cook County. For information call the Palos Division at (708) 839-5617 or the Sag Valley Division at (708) 448-8532, or go to www.fpdcc.com.

WHEN I WAS A CHILD growing up near Chicago, I sometimes took a shovel—a real one, not a toy—to the beach, where I liked to play in a small stream that flowed across the sand and into Lake Michigan. First I would dam the stream. The dam, how-ever, had to be very long because the beach was flat and the impounded water quickly spread to form a large, shallow pool. Eventually, of course, the water overflowed at one point or another, and a trickle quickly became a torrent that washed a big hole in my dam. When all was done, what was left was a rivulet flowing across the sand as before, except that at one point the stream passed through a wide gap in the long, low, irregular ridge that had been my dam.

Something like this happened on a larger scale—a *much* larger scale—at the Palos Hills about 12,500 years ago, only then the dam was a long glacial moraine of which the Palos Hills are part, and the impounded water was glacial Lake Chicago, the predecessor of Lake Michigan. At the Palos Hills, the lake overflowed and broke through the moraine, carving a big gap through the hills in the area explored by this chapter.

Since the onset of the Ice Age—or Pleistocene Epoch—in North America about one million years ago, the Chicago region has been subjected to four major glaciations. In each case the continental ice sheet originated in the Hudson Bay region of northern Canada and from there spread in all directions. During each glacial incursion, the erosive action of immense lobes of ice widened and deepened the basins now occupied by the Great Lakes, which previously may have been broad valleys and lowlands created by an extensive river system. At their farthest advance, the glaciers extended beyond the margins of the present lakes, and at least one incursion (not the most recent) got as far as Kentucky and northern Missouri. Between episodes of glaciation, which lasted perhaps 50,000 to 70,000 years, there were longer periods of 200,000 or 300,000 years during which the climate became warmer and the glaciers melted.

The most recent ice sheet to invade Illinois is termed the Wisconsin Glacier. It advanced about 70,000 years ago and started receding about 12,500 years ago. An immense quantity of clay, sand, pebbles, and boulders that had been picked up and carried within the ice as it advanced was left behind as it gradually melted, covering the landscape with an uneven blanket of material. As it retreated, the glacier also left behind long, low, irregular *morainic ridges*. These formed where the glacier's forward movement was for a time matched by the rate at which the ice front melted. While the perimeter was thus stationary, debris from the melting glacier was deposited as a range of hills along the entire ice front, like piles of sand and gravel at the end of a conveyor belt—only in this case the "conveyor belt" was hundreds of miles wide. Later, as melting speeded up, the ice front receded farther north, then paused again and again to form more morainic ridges whenever melting and forward movement were in balance. The landscape of Illinois shows dozens of these ridges running more or less parallel with each other and with the shore of Lake Michigan. On a map the ridges appear to be arranged in festoons drooping southward.

The largest morainic ridge near Chicago is the Valpariso Moraine, frequently called a *morainic system* because it actually is composed of nine closely-spaced parallel ridges. The Valpariso Moraine is at its highest near Valpariso, Indiana and extends around the southern end of Lake Michigan in a large, U-shaped band of hills more then ten miles wide. The Palos Hills, which show the random hummocks, hollows, marshes, and ponds characteristic of moraines, are part of the Valpariso morainic system.

After formation of the Valpariso Moraine, the meltwater from the Wisconsin Glacier was trapped between the receding ice sheet to the north and the dam-like moraines to the east, south, and west. A lake—glacial Lake Chicago—was formed, rising to a height sixty feet above the present average level of Lake Michigan. A terrace and ridge of sand delineate the former beach. Termed the Glenwood beach, this ancient shoreline still is discernible today in many places. In the Chicago region, the Glenwood beach is located inland as much as ten miles from the present beach. The site of all of Chicago was under water, although Blue Island, lying immediately to the south of the city, was indeed an island. Settling to the bottom of the lake, silt formed the thick bed of lacustrine clay now found near the land surface throughout most of the city.

Full to overflowing with meltwater from the Wisconsin ice sheet, Lake Chicago found an outlet through the Valpariso Moraine at the Palos Hills. Spilling over the moraine, the torrent carved a gap—called by geologists the Chicago Outlet—through the heights. Actually, two channels developed in the vicinity of the Palos Hills, but they merged half way through the moraine to form a configuration resembling a Y tilted to the right. The northern arm of the tilted Y is now occupied by a section of the Des Plaines River; the southern arm is occupied by the Calumet

Sag Channel. The two valleys merge just west of the Palos Hills, and from there the Des Plaines River continues southwest through the Valpariso Moraine past Waterfall Glen (see Chapter 14). With the Des Plaines River to the north, the Sag Valley to the south, and glacial Lake Chicago to the east, the portion of the Palos Hills embraced by the arms of the Y was an island, now called Mt. Forest Island. On a larger scale, meltwater from what is now Lake Huron's Saginaw Bay flowed westward across central Michigan via the Grand River Valley and into Lake Chicago, swelling the volume of water that ultimately drained through the Chicago Outlet.

As the channel through the Valpariso Moraine got deeper, the level of Lake Chicago fell. For reasons that are the subject of ongoing debate among geologists, the drop in water level did not continue at a steady rate. Instead, after falling twenty feet, the level stabilized and another beach—the Calumet beach—was formed. For a period Lake Chicago stood at the Calumet level, but about 11,000 years ago, rapid erosion in the Chicago Outlet resulted in another twenty-foot drop in lake level. A new beach—the Toleston beach—was formed at the new level.

Lake Chicago remained at the Toleston level and continued to drain through the Palos Hills until a lower outlet to the north was uncovered by retreat of the ice front past the Straits of Mackinac about 9,500 years ago, at which time the lake fell seventy feet, far below its current level. This low level was possible because the land surface east of Lake Huron (in the vicinity of present-day Lake Nipissing and the Ottawa River) had been greatly depressed by the weight of the massive ice sheet, thus providing an outlet to the St. Lawrence Valley that bypassed Lake Erie, Niagara Falls, and Lake Ontario. However, relieved of its burden of ice, the land gradually rebounded. The outlet through the Ottawa River was closed, and Lake Michigan and Lake Huron returned to the Toleston level. In consequence, water again discharged through the Chicago Outlet between 4,000 and 3,000 years ago. At the same time, a new gap (termed the St. Clair Outlet) was eroded past the site of present-day Detroit at the southern end of Lake Huron. Because the St. Clair Outlet occurred in an area of unconsolidated clay, sand, and cobbles, erosion there progressed more rapidly than at the Chicago Outlet, which had long before reached the stratum of bedrock seen today at the bottom of the

Des Plaines Valley downstream from the Palos Hills. As erosion continued in the St. Clair outlet, the Chicago Outlet was abandoned, and Lake Michigan and Lake Huron gradually fell another twenty feet to their present level, which was reached about 2,000 years ago.

Although the northern arm of the ancient Chicago Outlet still carries the Des Plaines River, the stream is merely a trickle compared to the torrent that carved the valley through the hills. Running parallel with the river, the Chicago Sanitary and Ship Canal also occupies the northern arm of the outlet. And at the outlet's southern arm, the Sag Valley is now dry except for the man-made Calumet Sag Channel and a few soughs. But as you will see, the steep bluff at the Swallow Cliff toboggan chutes and the wide bottomland clearly indicate that a major river once coursed through the Sag Valley.

≈   ≈   ≈   ≈

AUTOMOBILE DIRECTIONS TO THE PALOS HILLS: This large forest preserve is located halfway between Chicago and Joliet just north of the Calumet Sag Channel. The trailhead is at the **Little Red Schoolhouse Nature Center**. (See •15-A on **Map 42** at right.)

Two approaches to the Palos Hills—from the **Stevenson Expressway** and the **Tri-State Tollway**—are described below. Walking directions start on page 196.

From the Stevenson Expressway (Interstate 55): Leave the expressway at Exit 279A for LaGrange Road southbound (Routes 12, 20, and 45). Go 3.2 miles, then turn right onto 95th Street and follow it west 1.2 miles to 104th Avenue. Turn left and go 0.6 mile to the entrance to the Little Red Schoolhouse Nature Center on the right.

From the Tri-State Tollway: Leave the tollway at the exit for 95th Street (Routes 12 and 20) and go west 3.5 miles on 95th Street, in the process ignoring the fact that Routes 12 and 20 turn right after two miles. Turn left from 95th Street onto 104th Avenue, then go 0.6 mile to the entrance to the Little Red Schoolhouse Nature Center on the right.

≈   ≈   ≈   ≈

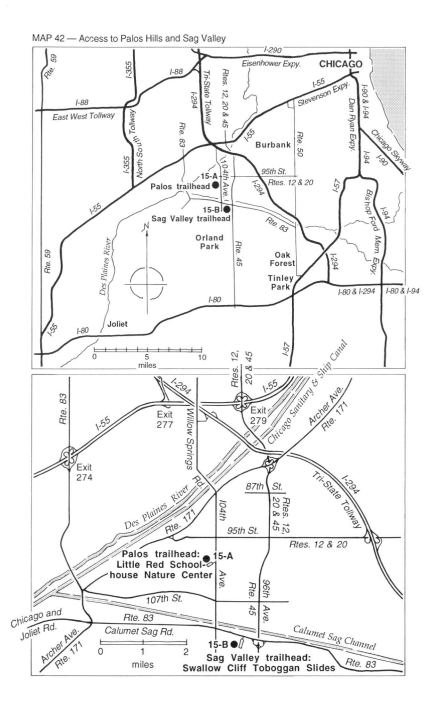

MAP 42 — Access to Palos Hills and Sag Valley

195

WALKING AT THE PALOS HILLS: Two routes are discussed below. Both start at the **Little Red Schoolhouse Nature Center**.

Map 43 at right shows the **Black Oak Trail**, which is only 1.8 miles long.

To get started, go to the rear of the schoolhouse and head downhill on the nature trail. At the water's edge, continue with Long John Slough on the right. At the next two trail junctions, fork right for the Black Oak Trail circuit, which eventually returns to the schoolhouse.

≈   ≈   ≈   ≈

Map 44 on page 198 shows a route of 5.3 miles through woods and past ponds and swamps east of 104th Avenue.

To get started, join a path almost directly opposite the front of the schoolhouse. Go 150 yards to a four-way trail junction. Turn left and follow the path across 104th Avenue. Continue as the trail curves left parallel with the road, then heads away from the road and into the woods to the left of the park headquarters compound.

Follow the gravel and cinder track as it curves through the woods. Ignore all narrow footpaths intersecting from left and right. Continue straight through an oblique four-way inter- section. (You will return later by the path intersecting from the left.)

Continue through the woods, at one point passing a trail intersecting from the right. Eventually, cross 95th Street. Continue through the woods and past Hogwash Slough on the left.

At a four-way trail junction, turn left. Pass to the right of Boomerang Slough (shown in the photograph on page 199). At a T-intersection with Old Country Lane, turn left. Follow Old Country Lane straight south back across 95th Street and across a road connecting two parking lots at Country Lane Woods. Eventually, at a four-way trail junction, turn sharply right to return to the Little Red Schoolhouse Nature Center by the path that you took earlier in the opposite direction.

≈   ≈   ≈   ≈

MAP 43 — Black Oak Trail at the Little Red Schoolhouse Nature Center

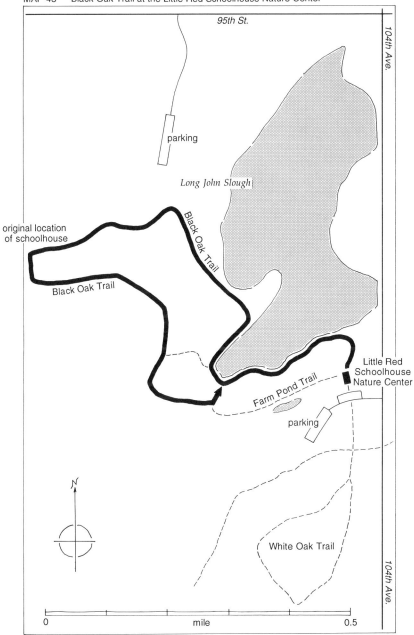

MAP 44 — Palos Hills Forest Preserve

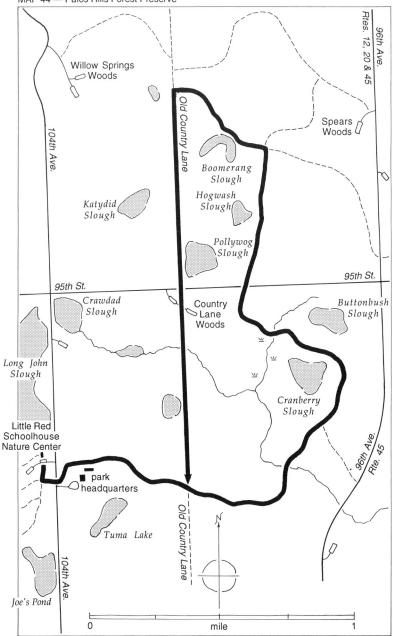

AUTOMOBILE DIRECTIONS TO THE SAG VALLEY: The trailhead is at the **Swallow Cliff Toboggan Slides**. (See •15-B on **Map 42** on page 195.)

Two approaches to the Sag Valley—from the **Stevenson Expressway** and the **Tri-State Tollway**—are described below.

From the Stevenson Expressway (Interstate 55): Leave the expressway at Exit 279A for LaGrange Road southbound (Routes 12, 20, and 45). Focusing on Route 45 and ignoring the fact that Routes 12 and 20 turn east at 95th Street, go south 5.7 miles. Immediately after crossing the Calumet Sag Channel, take the exit for Route 83. At the top of the ramp, turn left and follow Route 83 for 0.2 mile, then turn left into the Swallow Cliff Toboggan Slides and Winter Sports Area.

From the Tri-State Tollway: Leave the tollway at the exit for 95th Street (Routes 12 and 20). Go west 2.3 miles, then turn left to follow Route 45 south 2.5 miles. After crossing the Calumet Sag Channel, take the exit for Route 83. At the top of the ramp, turn left and follow Route 83 for 0.2 mile, then turn left into the Swallow Cliff Toboggan Slides and Winter Sports Area.

≈   ≈   ≈   ≈

WALKING AT THE SAG VALLEY: **Map 45** at right shows a route of 4 miles along the bluff and heights overlooking the Calumet Sag Channel. As shown on the map, there are also trails east of 96th Avenue, making possible a much longer walk.

To get started, go to the entrance to the parking lot for the **Swallow Cliff Toboggan Slides**. With Route 83 on the right, follow a path that curves left away from the road. At the foot of the bluff, turn sharply right and follow the wide path along the bottom of the slope. Continue straight past a parking area on the right and across 104th Avenue.

Follow the path as it climbs west of 104th Avenue, then snakes through the woods. At a junction with another path, turn left downhill. Continue as the tail winds, dips, and climbs through the woods. Eventually, cross back over 104th Avenue.

Pass a trail intersecting from the rear-right. Ignore minor side trails, but at a major fork in the path, bear left. At the next trail junction, turn left. Follow the trail to the top of the toboggan chutes and to stairs descending to the parking lot.

MAP 45 — Sag Valley at the Swallow Cliff Toboggan Slides

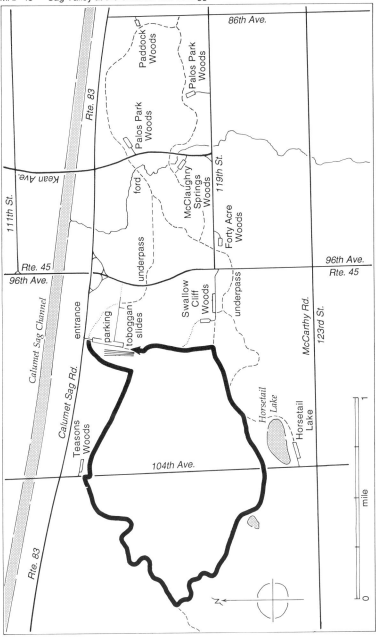

86th Ave.

Paddock Woods

Palos Park Woods

Rte. 83

Palos Park Woods

Kean Ave.

111th St.

ford

McClaughry Springs Woods

119th St.

Forty Acre Woods

underpass

Rte. 45

96th Ave.

96th Ave.
Rte. 45

Swallow Cliff Woods

underpass

Calumet Sag Channel

Calumet Sag Rd.

entrance

parking

toboggan slides

McCarthy Rd.

123rd St.

Horsetail Lake

Horsetail Lake

Teasons Woods

104th Ave.

Rte. 83

N

1

mile

0

201

16

ILLINOIS AND MICHIGAN CANAL

Completed in 1848, the Illinois and Michigan Canal stretched 96 miles from Chicago southwest to La Salle on the Illinois River. Although part of the canal has been obliterated since it stopped operating in 1933, there is still a remarkable hike-bike path called the I&M Canal State Trail between Joliet and La Salle, altogether totaling 61.5 miles (98.4 kilometers). Also discussed here is a separate 4-mile section southwest of Lockport.

Map 46 on page 218 gives an overview of the canal trail, and **Maps 48-51** on pages 220-223 provide more detail in four overlapping sections that are arranged from west to east.

The canal trail is open daily from dawn to dusk. Dogs must be leashed. Most of the trail is managed by the Illinois Department of Natural Resources. One good place to obtain information is Gebhard Woods State Park in Morris, through which the trail passes; telephone (815) 942-0796 or go to www.dnr.state.il.us and look for the link to state parks.

The I&M Canal Visitor Center in the historic Gaylord Building at Lockport has excellent exhibits on the waterway. For hours and information, telephone (815) 838-4830.

The M. J. Hogan Grain Elevator in Seneca is well worth touring. Built adjacent to the canal, it is shown in the photograph on page 211. For hours, telephone (815) 357-6197.

The Illinois Waterway Visitor Center east of Utica has exhibits on the canal, plus an observation platform overlooking a gargantuan lock on the present-day system of river navigation; telephone (815) 667-4054.

For automobile directions to a dozen access points along the canal, turn to page 215. Walking directions start on page 224.

THE ILLINOIS AND MICHIGAN CANAL follows the river channel carved at the end of the last glacial period, when Lake Michigan drained to the southwest until withdrawal of the ice sheet uncovered a lower outlet to the north. During the time that the lake emptied to the southwest, the torrent cut downward through the moraines near Chicago until the elevation of the gap is now only a dozen feet higher than Lake Michigan. The low terrain separating the Chicago River (which has its mouth at Lake Michigan) and the Des Plaines River (which flows southwest to the Illinois River) became the Chicago Portage used by Indians, European explorers, and fur trappers.

A canal at the Chicago Portage was first proposed by Louis Joliet and Father Jacques Marquette. In 1673 they reached the Mississippi River by way of the Wisconsin River. After going as far south as Arkansas, they returned northward to the Illinois River, then followed it upstream to the Des Plaines and across the portage to the Chicago River and Lake Michigan. This journey helped legitimate French claims not just to Canada, where they were well-established, but also to the Great Lakes and the Mississippi Valley, where the French foresaw an inland empire surrounding the nascent English colonies on the Atlantic seaboard. The official Jesuit report of the expedition states:

> According to the researches and explorations of Joliet, we can easily go to Florida in boats and by a very good navigation with slight improvements. There will be but one canal to make—and that by cutting only one half league of prairie from the lake of the Illinois [that is, Lake Michigan] into the St. Louis River [Illinois River], which empties into the Mississippi.

Nine years later, Robert La Salle also recommended construction of a canal linking Lake Michigan and the Illinois River after returning from his voyage all the way down the Mississippi to the Gulf of Mexico.

The French, however, never attempted to build a canal. Despite a policy that favored agricultural settlements, France's North American empire concentrated on trade with the Indians, mainly for beaver pelts, a light cargo. This commerce was conducted through numerous small trading posts on well-traveled rivers and portage routes. In the hands of the *voyageurs,* transportation was by bateaux—that is, simply large canoes. In consequence, a wagon road maintained by a few resident traders was all that was necessary to carry boats and cargo across the Chicago Portage.

French rule in North America lasted only a hundred years. By the Treaty of Paris, which in 1763 concluded the French and Indian War, Great Britain gained control of Canada, the Great Lakes, and the territory east of the Mississippi. In spite of the large part that England's colonial population had played in the victory, the movement of settlers into the interior of the continent was thereafter prohibited instead of encouraged. By a proclamation in 1763, King George III forbade the granting or taking of land west of the Appalachian Mountains, where, according to one cabinet minister, the populace would be "out of reach of government." Not until the colonies gained independence in 1782 and Congress passed the Northwest Ordinance in 1787 was a framework established for the orderly settlement, development, and government of the region bounded by the Ohio and Mississippi Rivers and the Great Lakes.

During the following three decades, several proposals to build a canal at the Chicago Portage were made by high federal officials, including Secretary of the Treasury Albert Gallatin in 1807, President Madison in 1814, and Secretary of War John C. Calhoun in 1819. In each instance, however, the plan was either ignored or rejected by Congress. The skepticism of congressmen from the Atlantic states is not surprising. In 1818, when Illinois was admitted to the Union, the population of the northern part of the state was still nearly all Indian. White settlements in Illinois were concentrated along the Ohio and Mississippi Rivers, and even the state capital was at Kaskaskia, south of St. Louis. When agents from Illinois and Indiana met at Chicago in 1821 to survey the boundary between their states, they found (aside from the federal garrison at Fort Dearborn) a village lacking "any kind of civil government" and consisting of only nine or ten houses, all occupied by traders—chiefly of French or French-Indian ancestry—and their families.

Proponents of a canal, however, had gained a huge concession when Illinois entered the Union. The state's northern boundary, which under the Northwest Ordinance was supposed to run west from the lower tip of Lake Michigan, was moved forty-one miles north so that an additional eight thousand square miles (an area about the size of Massachusetts) was included in Illinois rather than Wisconsin. This transfer was justified on the grounds that an outlet to the Great Lakes would bind Illinois to the upper

Midwest and the East Coast rather than to the southern states down the Mississippi, thus providing "additional security for the perpetuity of the Union," according to Representative Nathaniel Pope, a leading advocate for statehood and a canal. Pope also urged Congress to help Illinois build a publicly owned canal by donating to the state the land along the proposed route. Under the Northwest Ordinance, *all* land in frontier Illinois belonged initially to the federal government, which obtained title to it by a series of dubious treaties with the Indians. In particular, the land at the Chicago Portage had been ceded to the federal government in 1816 by a treaty with the United Tribes of the Ottawa, Chippewa, and Potawatomi.

In 1823 the Illinois legislature established a Board of Canal Commissioners, and four years later the state received a grant of federal land not only for the canal itself but also of every other square mile in a checkerboard swath ten miles wide along the entire length of the proposed waterway, provided the canal was begun in five years and completed in twenty. Construction costs were supposed to be financed by selling the state land. A survey of the canal route was begun, but in 1831 the state legislature instructed the commissioners to consider also an alternative proposal for a railroad. Construction of the first commercial railroad in America—the Baltimore and Ohio—had started in Baltimore in 1828 and after only two years the railroad's progress west toward the Ohio River clearly was outstripping the competing—and far more costly—Chesapeake and Ohio Canal, on which work had started the same day. When the survey engineer hired by the Illinois canal commissioners submitted his final report in 1833, he strongly recommended building a railroad, which by various estimates would cost a quarter or a third as much as a canal. A railroad could also run year-round, while a canal would be forced to close in winter. At the request of the Illinois legislature, Congress authorized the state to use the land donated by the federal government for either a canal or a railroad, and also extended by five years the time limit to start construction in recognition of the fact that the state still lacked the money to begin. Sale of the land had started in 1830, but the proceeds were disappointing and foreseeably would not be enough to pay for a canal. In this climate of skepticism and irresolution, the state abolished the Board of Canal Commissioners in 1833 and repealed all canal legislation.

For the next year Illinois debated what to do. The gubernatorial election of 1834 was run chiefly on the issue of a canal versus a railroad, and the canal candidate won. The canal proponents had raised the specter of a private railroad monopoly charging prohibitive freight rates; the canal, in contrast, would be owned by the state. Canal advocates also argued that a canal could move extremely heavy bulk cargo, such as grain, stone, and lumber, better than a railroad. Most importantly, the Erie Canal, completed in 1825, was proving to be an immense success. Already vessels arriving in Chicago from the Erie Canal's western terminus at Buffalo had jumped from 12 in 1832 to 180 in 1834, when Chicago's harbor was improved at federal expense. Platted in 1830 and incorporated as a village in 1833, Chicago was a booming frontier town.

In 1835 the Illinois legislature appointed a new Board of Canal Commissioners, which secured a loan of $500,000 to begin work. The commissioners hired William Gooding as chief engineer to design the canal and to supervise its construction. Previously, Gooding had worked on construction of canals in Ohio and the Welland Canal in Canada around Niagara Falls. The commissioners also decided that the Illinois and Michigan Canal should be built according to a "deep cut" plan by which the channel west from Chicago would be dug so deep that the water of Lake Michigan would flow by gravity through the South Branch of the Chicago River directly into the canal and from there through locks down the entire length of the canal to the Illinois River at La Salle, below which the river was deep enough for navigation by large boats to and from the Mississippi River. In 1836 advertisements were run in East Coast cities for laborers, drawing hundreds of Irish immigrants to a shantytown that sprang up at the head of the canal in Bridgeport (which is still the center of Irish influence in Chicago). In time recruiters even went to Ireland itself. After a raucous groundbreaking on July 4th, featuring beer, rum, howitzer salutes, ceremonial spadework, speeches, dancing, and even a brawl, contractors and gangs of shovelmen began work on the canal itself, and speculators started bidding up the price of land along the route.

Construction on the I&M Canal was plagued by financial problems. The work was much more difficult and expensive than anticipated. In many places, ledges of limestone and sandstone were encountered close to the surface. Rock and even the prairie soil, bound together by the roots of grasses, had to be blasted loose with black powder, then removed by hand with pick, shovel, scraper, and wheelbarrow. Even where the canal did not pass through marshes and swamps (and often it did), the soil became so soggy in spring that it was almost impossible to work with. Also, economic conditions turned bad. Financial panic and five years of depression engulfed the nation in 1837 just as the Illinois legislature passed an ambitious Internal Improvements Act that burdened the state with high taxes and strained its credit. Speculative land values collapsed. In 1839 the canal com-missioners ran out of money, and the canal was on the brink of abandonment. Work continued into 1840 solely because con-tractors accepted interest-bearing checks payable sometime. Contractors, in turn, paid their laborers with canal scrip that was accepted by merchants only at a discount. The state of Illinois, however, honored the scrip at full value in payment for state land, with the result that many laborers bought tracts and turned to farming. By 1841 work on the canal had altogether stopped while the government tried to borrow more money, but the next year, the state's credit deteriorated further when the Illinois State Bank failed and there was talk of repudiating the state's bonds. To revive the canal, the "deep cut" plan was dropped in favor of a far less expensive but more cumbersome "shallow cut" waterway. In 1845 work on the canal resumed after a group of investors from the East Coast and Great Britain agreed to supply funds to finish the project, provided payment of the loan was under-written by a special canal tax, and further provided that the canal was managed not by the state but by an independent board of three trustees, two of whom were selected by the investors.

Working and living conditions for canal laborers (who were mainly Irish but also came from French Canada, Germany, and Norway) were primitive. Often entire families occupied dirty, temporary huts. Crowded shanty towns, poor sanitation, polluted drinking water, and mosquito-infested marshes pro-duced epidemics of cholera, typhoid, malaria, and dysentery. An outbreak of cholera in 1845 was exceptionally ferocious, carrying off victims after little more than a day of illness.

Finally, on April 20, 1848, the waterway opened to navigation. As completed, the canal was 96 miles long, sixty feet wide at water level, thirty-six feet wide at the bottom, and six feet deep. It had fifteen locks (later reduced to fourteen) that compensated for a 140-foot drop between Chicago and La Salle. Under the shallow-cut system, the first two locks *raised* the boats from the level of Lake Michigan to the summit level of the canal (to which water had to be pumped up from the Chicago River), and the rest of the locks controlled the gradual descent along the valleys of the Des Plaines and Illinois Rivers to La Salle. Aqueducts carried the canal across several tributaries, including Aux Sable Creek and the Fox River. A different technique was used to cross the Des Plaines River at Joliet and the DuPage River at Channahon. In these places the rivers were dammed downstream from the spot where the canal crossed. The crest of each dam was built just high enough so that water in the reservoir was at the same level as water in the canal. Mule teams crossed the reservoir on a pontoon bridge that was simply a floating version of the tow path.

When the canal opened, it was mired in debt. It had cost about four times the original estimate for a shallow cut canal. Accrued interest on the backlog of unpaid checks, bonds, and loans swelled the total debt further. Moreover, the canal was on the verge of obsolescence as railroads demonstrated their superior versatility and ease of construction. In 1852 Chicago's first rail connection to the East opened. By 1854 a railroad ran parallel with the canal, and by the early 1860s more railroads met at Chicago than at any other spot on the globe. Nonetheless, under the management of the canal trustees, the waterway proved to be viable. Tolls not only covered annual operating expenses but also serviced the debt, which was entirely paid with interest by 1871. The trustees then turned the canal and more than $95,000 in surplus funds over to the state.

Together with the railroads, the Illinois and Michigan Canal contributed mightily to the growth of Chicago and other towns, such as Joliet, Morris, and Ottawa. Merchants built dozens of grain elevators and warehouses along the waterway. (Shown at right, one of the few remaining elevators is at Seneca. It is a fascinating place to visit. Also, stone warehouses still stand at Lockport and Utica.) At La Salle cargo was transferred to and from river steamers that plied the Illinois and Mississippi Rivers, and passengers too changed boats. Wheat, corn, barley, oats, salted

beef, bacon, hams, hides, lard, eggs and other farm products from points west and south were brought to Chicago by canal. One of the first boats to navigate the canal carried sugar from New Orleans bound for New York via the Great Lakes and Erie Canal. Building stone, coal, sand, gravel, lime, and cement were transported to the city from quarries, mines, and kilns near the waterway. Other cargo included locally produced ale, beer, whiskey, paper, glass, and iron. Lumber from Wisconsin, Michigan, and Canada and manufactured goods from the eastern part of the country—and even from Chicago itself (including, for example, locally manufactured McCormick reapers and other farm machinery)—were shipped down the I&M to the burgeoning towns located along the canal and the Illinois and Mississippi Rivers. Chicago was launched on its career as the great mid-continental shipping center where bulk cargo was off-loaded, processed, stored, commingled, sold, and re-shipped. When the canal opened, the city's population was about 20,000. By 1850 the population was 28,269, and in 1854 it was 74,500. By 1855 more than half the population of Illinois lived north of Springfield (which had been made capital in 1837), and the most densely populated area was along the I&M Canal.

Because the locks of the I&M were the narrowest part of the entire canal and river system, boats using the waterway were made to fit the locks closely. Each lock was 18 feet wide and 118 feet long, and the typical canal boat was not much smaller. Until supplanted by trains in 1853, passenger packets—which in the interest of speed had precedence at locks and narrow aqueducts—took about 23 hours to pass through the waterway. For boats loaded with 150 tons of cargo, the time was longer. On the Chicago River, the boats were ganged together and towed by small steamers, but on the canal each boat was pulled individually by a team of two to five mules hitched to long towlines. The teams worked in shifts, or "tricks," up to six hours long before being replaced by fresh mules from one of the many livery barns along the canal. A driver—frequently a boy as young as twelve or fourteen years—guided the team, either walking behind it or riding the rear animal. These boys were notorious for their precociously foul language and willingness to fight to make other boats give way in passing and at narrow places, although boats heading downstream were supposed to have the right-of-way.

Every boat also had a bowman who handled the lines and used a stout pole to fend off obstructions and to maneuver through the locks. There might also be a helmsman, or the captain might perform that job. The crew were employed by the captain and paid set wages; each captain, in turn, was either an independent contractor for the company that owned the boat or else he owned the boat himself. During the 1870s, mule-drawn barges were replaced by boats with screw propellers, but even these steam-powered craft traveled slowly to prevent their wakes from eroding the canal embankment.

Operating no boats other than a few dredges, the canal management focused on running the canal itself, for which it had several classes of employees. Most numerous were the locktenders, who lived in houses by the locks and were on call twenty-four hours a day to lock boats through whenever they arrived. The procedure for locking entailed closing and opening the gates and valves by hand in a set sequence. For example, after a boat heading down the canal had floated into the lock, the upstream gates were closed behind it and valves in the downstream gates were opened, draining the water into the canal below the lock and lowering the boat to that level. The valves were then closed, the downstream gates were opened, and the boat was towed out. For boats headed up the canal, the procedure was reversed: The water in the lock was raised by opening valves in the upstream gates after the boat was sealed in the lock. Alerted by the blast of a trumpet carried on each boat, the locktender would have the water at the right level and the appropriate gates open for the approaching boat. If a boat did not have to wait in line, the process of passing through a lock took somewhat less than half an hour, fifteen minutes of which were spent draining or filling the lock. During the 1860s one locktender reported locking through an average of thirty boats per day.

Other canal employees were canal walkers, who were assigned to a section of the canal and inspected it every day. They maintained the canal at its proper level by adjusting the waste gates that allowed excess water to drain into streams. The towpath walkers also examined the locks and aqueducts for damage or signs of weakening, and checked the banks for erosion and for burrowing animals, which it was their duty to shoot or trap. They noted items that needed attention, made temporary repairs as necessary, and in general tried to prevent small problems from becoming big ones.

Aside from the locktenders and the canal walkers, the I&M Canal had toll collectors stationed at Chicago, Lockport, Ottawa, and La Salle. According to a complex schedule of rates, the toll depended on the type of cargo and its final destination. The collectors also supervised the locktenders and towpath walkers in their section of the canal, and were in turn supervised by the general superintendent, whose office was at Lockport.

During the 1870s and '80s, traffic on the I&M Canal declined. In 1892 work began on the Chicago Sanitary and Ship Canal, which would be far larger than the I&M. By 1902 the Sanitary and Ship Canal extended from Chicago to Lockport, and traffic on the parallel section of the I&M ended. Between Lockport and La Salle, the old canal continued in use, but in 1919 work began to channelize the Des Plaines and Illinois Rivers downstream from Joliet. When the Illinois Waterway eventually opened in 1933, all of the Illinois and Michigan Canal was closed to navigation. Now from the towpath huge barges are often visible on the adjacent river system, which essentially is a larger canal with its own set of locks. In contrast to the 150-ton capacity of the old canal boats, today's barges can carry ten times as much, and one diesel-powered boat can push 15 barges or 22,500 tons. Cargo consists chiefly of stone aggregate, sand, cement, and fuel oil.

The recreational potential of the I&M Canal was recognized at the time of its closing. During the Great Depression of the 1930s, the Civilian Conservation Corps renovated the towpath and built picnic areas and shelters at parks along the former waterway. Even so, the canal deteriorated for forty years until 1974, when what was left was placed under the stewardship of the Illinois Department of Conservation (now the Department of Natural Resources). By then, however, parts of the canal were gone, most notably the eight miles nearest Chicago, which had been used as the right-of-way for the Stevenson Expressway. Other smaller sections had been transferred to local communities. Since 1974 these towns and the state have cleared and opened nearly all of the remaining towpath. As discussed in the directions below, the longest section is the 61-mile continuous run between La Salle and the outskirts of Joliet. Upstream from Joliet, there is another short section extending to Lockport. As this book goes to press, the section immediately above Lockport is not open, but there are a few more miles accessible to the public where the canal passes north of the Palos Hills.

≈   ≈   ≈   ≈

AUTOMOBILE DIRECTIONS: The directions below will guide you to a series of parking lots located at intervals along the **Illinois and Michigan Canal** between La Salle and the outskirts of Joliet. Also described is Lockport, where there are a museum and a short section of canal disjoined from the rest. The dozen access points are indicated by •16-A through •16-L on **Maps 46 and 47** on pages 218 and 219. For greater detail, refer to **Maps 48-51** on pages 220-223, showing the canal trail in four overlapping sections arranged in sequence from west to east, as indicated by the diagram on each map.

The automobile directions start on **Interstate 80**, which can be reached from Chicago via **Interstate 55** (the southwestward extension of the **Stevenson Expressway**). For the most part, I-80 runs north of the canal and parallel with it.

To the canal at La Salle (•16-A): Lock #14 in La Salle is at milepost 95 on the canal trail. **Panel 1** on page 219 may help with the following directions.

Leave I-80 at Exit 77 for Route 351 south toward La Salle. Follow Route 351 for 3.4 miles through La Salle, then turn right for the I&M Canal State Trail at Lock 14. Go 0.2 mile to the parking lot.

To the canal at Utica (•16-B): Utica is near milepost 91 on the canal trail. **Panel 2** on page 219 may help with the following directions.

Leave I-80 at Exit 81 for Route 178 and Utica. Follow Route 178 south through Utica for 2 miles—in the process you will turn left and right in town—then turn right onto West Canal Street and go one block to the I&M Canal parking lot.

To reach the **Illinois Waterway Visitor Center**, continue south on Route 178 beyond Canal Street for 0.6 mile, then turn left onto Dee Bennett Road and go 1.7 miles.

To the canal at Ottawa (•16-C): Ottawa is near milepost 81 on the canal trail. **Panel 3** on page 219 may help with the following directions.

Leave I-80 at Exit 90 for Route 23. Follow Route 23 south 1.7 miles to a bridge over the canal trail, then park nearby on one of the side streets.

To the canal at Marseilles (•16-D): Main Street in Marseilles is near milepost 74 on the canal trail. **Panel 4** on page 219 may help with the following directions.

Leave I-80 at Exit 97 for Marseilles. Go south on Main Street 3.4 miles to a bridge over the canal, then park on the street.

To the canal at Seneca (•16-E): Main Street in Seneca is near milepost 69 on the canal trail. **Panel 5** on page 219 may help with the following directions.

Leave I-80 at Exit 105 for Seneca. Go altogether 5.6 miles as you join Route 6 and follow it west toward Seneca. At the intersection of Route 6 and Route 170 (Main Street) in Seneca, turn left and follow Route 170 south 0.5 mile to the canal, then park on the street or in front of the nearby M. J. Hogan Grain Company elevator, now a park site and well worth visiting. (See the photograph on page 211.)

To the canal at Gebhard Woods State Park (•16-F): Gebhard Woods is at milepost 59 on the canal trail as it passes through the town of Morris. **Panel 6** on page 219 may help with the following directions.

Leave I-80 at Exit 112 for Morris and Route 47. Follow Route 47 south 1.1 miles, then turn right onto Route 6 westbound. After 0.5 mile, turn left onto Union Street (opposite Michael Street). Go 0.6 mile to a T-intersection, then turn right onto Hazel Court, left onto Vine Street, and then right onto Fremont Avenue at another T-intersection. After 0.4 mile, turn left onto Ottawa Street and follow it 0.2 mile to Gebhard Woods State Park on the left.

To the canal at Aux Sable Aqueduct (•16-G) Aux Sable is near milepost 53 on the canal trail. **Panel 7** on page 219 may help with the following directions.

Leave I-80 at Exit 122 for Minooka. Follow Ridge Road south through Minooka for 3 miles to Route 6. Turn right and go west on Route 6 for 1 mile to McClindon Road. Turn left onto McClindon Road and go 3.3 miles as it changes name to Cemetery Road after crossing the canal. The parking lot at Aux Sable is on the right 0.3 mile beyond an intersection with South

Tabler Road. (You may notice on the way to Aux Sable that there is another parking lot near the intersection with Hansel Road.)

To the canal at McKinley Woods (•16-H): McKinley Woods is near milepost 47 on the canal trail. **Panel 8** on page 219 may help with the following directions.

From the interchange where Interstate 80 and Interstate 55 cross, follow I-55 south toward St. Louis. Leave I-55 at Exit 248 for Morris and Route 6. Follow Route 6 west 3.5 miles, then turn left onto McKinley Road. Go 2.6 miles, descending steeply at the end to reach the lower parking lot, where a footbridge crosses the canal to the towpath trail.

To the canal at Channahon (•16-I): Lock #6 at Channahon is at milepost 44 on the canal trail. **Panel 8** on page 219 may help with the following directions.

From the interchange where Interstate 80 and Interstate 55 cross, follow I-55 south toward St. Louis. Leave I-55 at Exit 248 for Morris and Route 6. Follow Route 6 west 2.6 miles, then turn left onto Canal Street. After 0.3 mile, turn right onto Story Street and go just 0.1 mile to the I&M Canal parking lot.

If the lot here is full, go back to Canal Street and turn right. After 0.2 mile, turn right onto Bridge Street and continue 0.2 mile to a parking area on the left.

To the canal at Rock Run (•16-J): Rock Run is at milepost 38 on the canal trail.* **Panel 9** on page 219 may help with the following directions.

Leave I-80 at Exit 127 for Empress Road. Follow Empress Road south 0.5 mile, then turn right into Lower Rock Run Preserve, with access to the I&M Canal.

To the canal at Brandon Road (•16-K): Brandon Road is near milepost 35 on the canal trail. **Panel 9** on page 219 may help with the following directions.

Leave I-80 at Exit 130A for Larkin Avenue (Route 7) southbound and follow it 0.9 mile to a junction with Route 6. Turn left

---

* In the early 1900s, Rock Run was the site of an amusement park reached from Joliet by an excursion boat that ran four times daily. The park featured picnicking, croquet, bowling, dancing, and water slides.

[Directions continue on page 224.]   217

MAP 46 — Access to the Illinois and Michigan Canal

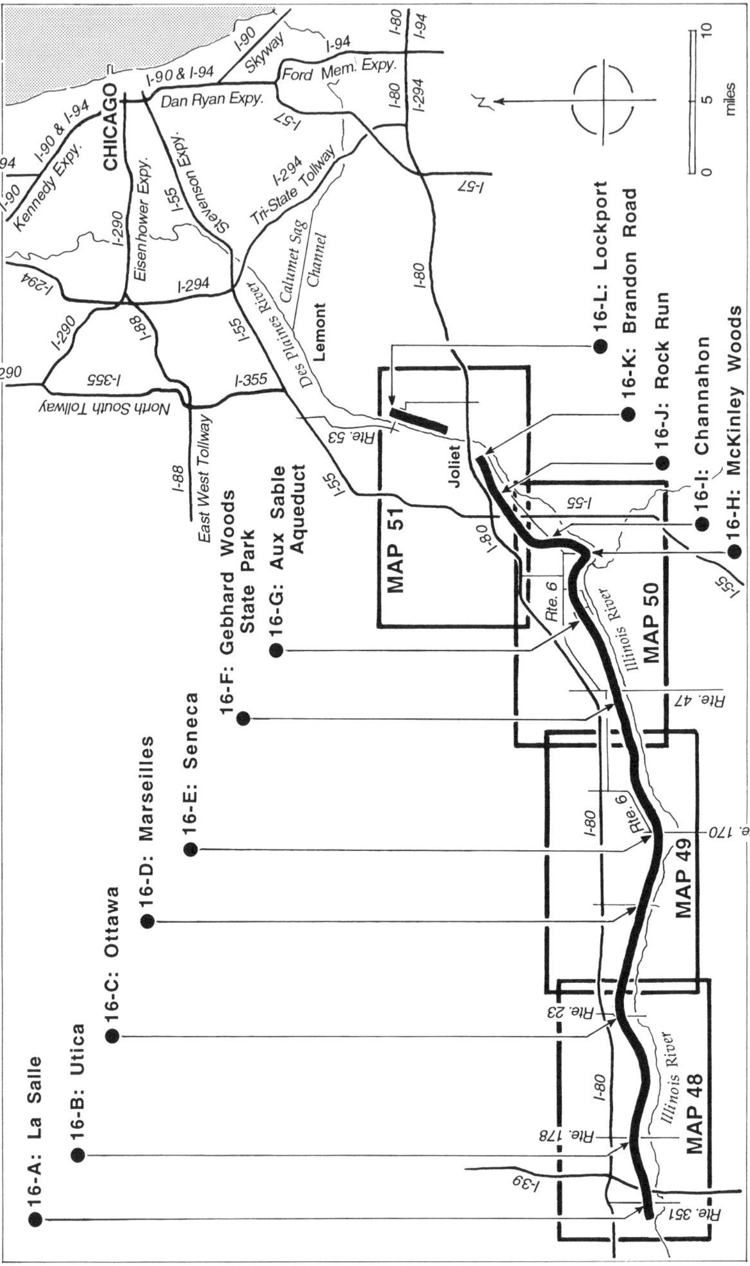

MAP 47 — Details showing access to the Illinois and Michigan Canal

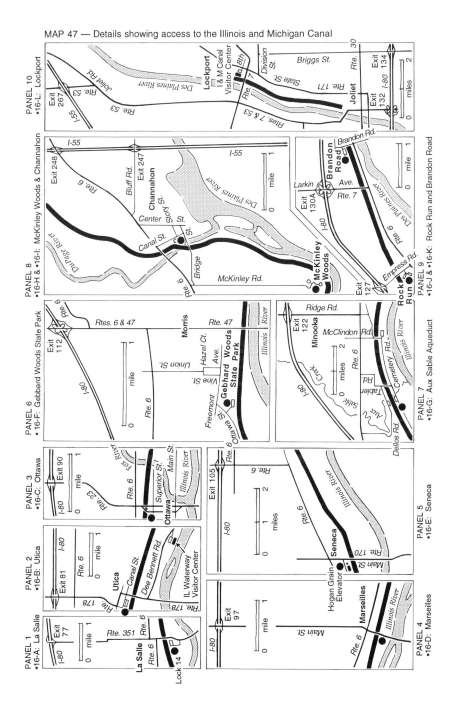

219

MAP 48 — Illinois and Michigan Canal

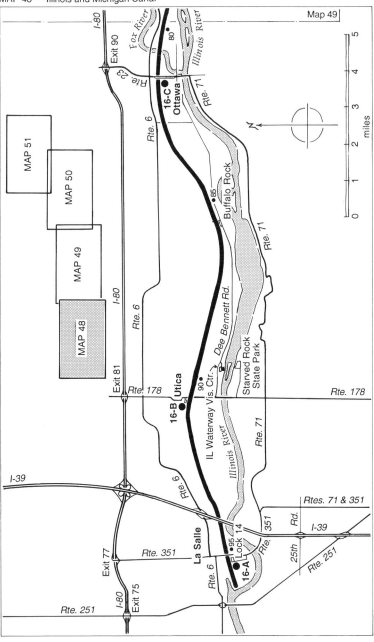

MAP 49 — Illinois and Michigan Canal

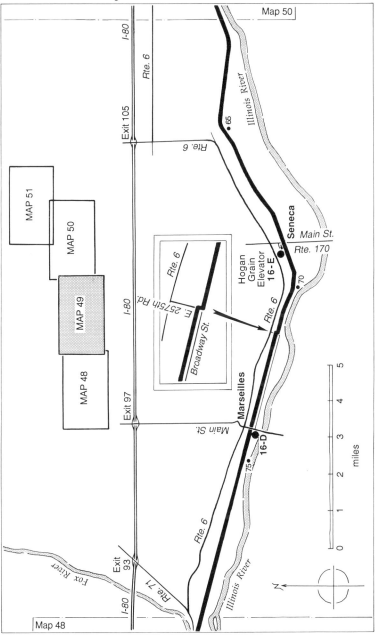

MAP 50 — Illinois and Michigan Canal

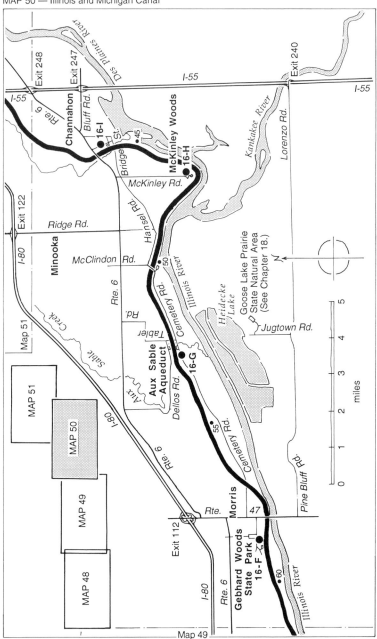

MAP 51 — Illinois and Michigan Canal

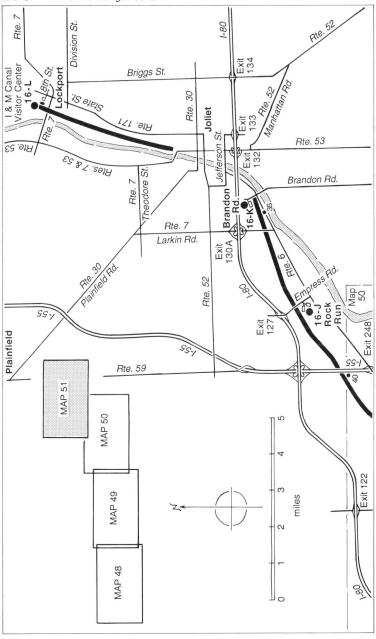

223

and follow Route 6 east for 1.1 miles, then turn left onto Brandon Road, then left again into the I&M Canal parking lot.

To the canal at Lockport (•16-L): Two approaches—from **Interstate 80** and **Interstate 55**—are described below. (See **Panel 10** on page 219.)

To Lockport from Interstate 80: Leave I-80 at Exit 134 for Briggs Street. Follow Briggs Street north toward Lockport 4.7 miles, then turn left at a T-intersection with Division Street. After 0.8 mile, turn right onto Route 171 (State Street). Go 0.6 mile, then turn left onto 8th Street and descend to the parking lot on the right in front of the railroad. The **Illinois and Michigan Canal Visitor Center** is in the Gaylord Building across the tracks, and beyond that is the canal trail, which leads left 3.5 miles to Joliet. There is no trail through Joliet. The canal there was obliterated and submerged by construction of Brandon Dam and the Illinois Waterway, which opened in 1933.

To Lockport from Interstate 55: Leave I-55 at Exit 267 for Route 53 south toward Romeoville. After 1.2 miles, bear right toward Lockport and continue on Route 53 for 5.4 miles, then turn left onto Route 7 toward Lockport. After 1 mile, turn left onto Route 171 (State Street), then left again onto 8th Street and descend to the parking lot on the right in front of the railroad. The **Illinois and Michigan Canal Visitor Center** is in the Gaylord Building across the tracks, and beyond that is the canal trail, which leads left 3.5 miles to Joliet. There is no trail through Joliet. The canal there was obliterated and submerged by construction of Brandon Dam and the Illinois Waterway, which opened in 1933.

≈   ≈   ≈   ≈

WALKING and BICYCLING: The Illinois and Michigan Canal State Trail is an outstanding artifact of Illinois history. Lift locks, locktenders' houses, aqueducts, warehouses, and towns that originated with the canal punctuate a walk or ride along the towpath, which sometimes overlooks the canal's present-day counterpart, the Illinois Waterway.

Map 46 on page 218 provides an overview of the 61.5-mile trail between La Salle and Brandon Road, just south of Joliet. It also shows the short segment below Lockport. In turn, **Maps**

48-51 on pages 220-223 give more detail in four overlapping sections arranged in sequence from west to east. The large dots on the maps (•16-A, •16-B, •16-C, and so forth) are the twelve access points discussed in the automobile directions.

No route is shown through Joliet, where the canal and towpath have either been obliterated or submerged by the far larger Illinois Waterway. Some bicycle clubs sponsor maps showing how to navigate through Joliet, but in my opinion riding or walking through town is not worthwhile.

Navigating the canal trail is problem-free: The route is unmistakable. The only possible exception is a small jog in the trail near milepost 72, illustrated by the inset on Map 49 on page 221.

Finally, **please note** that the trail occasionally crosses roads and parking lots, so use caution at all places where cars may be present.

17

STARVED ROCK STATE PARK
MATTHIESSEN STATE PARK

Located southwest of Chicago near Utica, Starved Rock State Park and Matthiessen State Park are like nothing else in the region.

Map 53 on page 233 outlines a walk of 4.8 miles (7.7 kilometers) at Starved Rock, where sandstone pinnacles, cliffs, and canyons border the Illinois River. From Starved Rock itself, follow the river upstream past Eagle Cliff to La Salle Canyon, then return along the rim of the bluff.

Map 54 on page 237 shows a walk of 7.5 miles (12 kilometers) at the eastern end of Starved Rock State Park. The route explores Ottawa, Kaskaskia, and Illinois Canyons, by far the largest in the region.

Map 55 on page 239 outlines a walk of 3.2 miles (5 kilometers) at Matthiessen State Park, where three footbridges cross the chasm and other trails follow the canyon floor.

Starved Rock and Matthiessen State Parks are open daily from 5:00 a.m. to 10:00 p.m. Pets must be leashed. **To avoid accidents**, stay back from the edges of cliffs and control your children closely. Both parks are managed by the Illinois Department of Natural Resources; telephone (815) 667-4726 at Starved Rock and (815) 667-4868 at Matthiessen, or go to www.dnr.state.il.us and look for the link to state parks.

For automobile directions, please turn to page 230. Walking directions for Starved Rock start on page 232 and for Matthiessen on page 238.

THE VIEW FROM STARVED ROCK looks over the Illinois River where it flows through a mile-wide valley that is nearly two hundred feet lower than the adjacent upland. Yet 100,000 years ago, there was neither a valley nor even a river here. Like so many other features in Illinois, the river, cliffs, and tributary canyons at Starved Rock and Matthiessen State Parks are the product, albeit indirectly, of continental glaciation.

Central Illinois occupies a region of sedimentary rocks formed at the bottom of a shallow sea that covered the center of the continent—although not all of it at the same time—in a series of inundations between 500 and 280 million years ago. During each inundation, sand and silt carried to the ocean by rivers settled to the bottom of the sea. Sand, which usually is deposited in river deltas or in water close to shore, was cemented by silica or other minerals to form sandstone, the main rock type in the vicinity of Starved Rock. Clay and silt, which remain in suspension longer than sand and thus settle to the bottom farther from shore, were compressed and consolidated by the weight of the deposits to form shale. Calcium carbonate, reaching the sea in solution and precipitated there either by organic agencies (such as in skeletons of minute marine animals) or by inorganic processes (such as warming of the water) settled farthest from shore and became limestone, as is seen at Waterfall Glen (Chapter 14) and in numerous large quarries in the Chicago region. Periodically, compressive forces within the earth's crust bowed the rock strata upward and elevated the mid-continent above the ocean. Plant material, later to become beds of coal, accumulated in freshwater swamps. The land was eroded, then re-submerged. Again and again the cycle of emergence, erosion, and submergence occurred, leading to the formation of distinct rock strata, some of which are now visible at the surface. Other rock material once overlay what now exists, but these higher strata were worn away during the period of prolonged erosion that preceded the glacial epoch.

Judging from old, buried river channels that have been discovered in the course of strip mining, road building, and other excavations, the pre-glacial drainage pattern in Illinois was very different than what presently exists. A river that drained the area now occupied by Lake Michigan may have flowed north to Hudson Bay. The lobes of ice that repeatedly advanced from Canada are thought to have followed the shallow valley of this river upstream, gradually scooping out the lake basin. At one time a major river flowing from north to south—a predecessor of the Mississippi River—was located about thirty miles to the west of Starved Rock, and a large tributary flowed from east to west about ninety miles to the south. During the successive invasion of continental glaciers, however, these river valleys were filled with clay, sand, and boulders carried and deposited by the ice sheets. Diverted from their channels, the rivers found new courses across the landscape after the glaciers melted. This re-arrangement happened repeatedly with each incursion and recession of the ice. Only after the retreat of the last ice sheet (the Wisconsin Glacier) got underway about 12,500 years ago did the Illinois River assume its present course from the vicinity of Joliet to Depue, located about fifteen miles west of Starved Rock. At Depue the river joined an older channel and abruptly turned south, as seen today.

As the last ice sheet receded during a period that went on for thousands of years, a series of meltwater torrents, far more volu-minous and powerful than the region's present-day rivers, churned through the Illinois Valley. The flow, however, fluc-tuated in response to various factors. In one often repeated scenario, *proglacial lakes* formed when meltwater was trapped between the ice mass to the north and long ridges (termed *moraines)* of clay, sand, and cobbles to the south. This earth ma-terial had been scraped up and carried forward by the glacier, then dumped along the perimeter of the melting ice. Often these moraines were miles thick and hundreds of miles long, in effect forming huge dikes that held in the meltwater. Of course, the accumulation of water in large lakes behind the moraines produced periods of reduced outflow through the Illinois Valley, followed by episodes of rampant erosion when the lakes breached the moraines. Also, the flow varied as the recession of the ice uncovered other channels that drained part of the meltwater elsewhere. One period of great flow was the Kankakee Torrent, when ice lobes occupying the present-day basins of Lake Michi-gan, Lake Huron, and Lake Erie cumulatively discharged melt-water from parts of Illinois, Wisconsin, Indiana, and Michigan down the Illinois River. The erosive power of the Kankakee Torrent increased the width of the Illinois Valley by half a mile and lowered the valley floor to the level of what is now the top of Starved Rock and Eagle Cliff. The Kankakee Torrent was followed by a series of floods from glacial Lake Chicago (the precursor of Lake Michigan) after the water broke through the moraine at the Palos Hills, as described in Chapter 15. By the time the Lake Chicago outlet was last abandoned, perhaps as recently as two thousand years ago, the river bed at Starved Rock had been lowered to very nearly its present level.

The downward erosion of the main valley in turn led to development of tributary canyons by increasing the gradient—and hence the erosive energy—of small streams where they joined the larger river. Following vertical cracks in the bedrock, the tributary streams entrenched themselves in a pattern that reflects the rectilinear jointing characteristic of sandstone formations. (For example, notice how La Salle Canyon and the stream that carved it make several right-angle turns as they approach the Illinois River.) Erosion was slow while the tributary streams cut into the layer of firmly-cemented, resistant sandstone that now forms the rims of the canyons, but once the streams penetrated to the less firmly cemented material below, erosion was rapid and deep canyons with vertical walls quickly developed. Waterfalls with plunge pools at the bottom have been formed where streams plummet over the upper layer of resistant rock and cut into the relatively soft lower layers. The canyon walls and riverside cliffs also show differential erosion. Weakly cemented layers have receded while the more strongly cemented layers have endured and now stand out, producing a corrugated appearance seen in the photograph on page 226.

≈   ≈   ≈   ≈

AUTOMOBILE DIRECTIONS: Starved Rock State Park and **Matthiessen State Park** are located close to one another 80 miles southwest of Chicago. (See **Map 52** at right, where •17-A, •17-B, •17-C indicate three separate walks starting at different trailheads.) Directions via **Interstate 55** and **Interstate 80** are given below.

To Starved Rock and Matthiessen from Interstate 55: This highway is the extension of **Stevenson Expressway** southwest out of Chicago and past Joliet. Leave I-55 at exit 250B for Interstate 80 west toward Des Moines, then follow the directions in the next several paragraphs.

To Starved Rock and Matthiessen from Interstate 80: This highway runs east-west between Gary, Indiana and Des

MAP 52 — Access to Starved Rock and Matthiessen State Parks

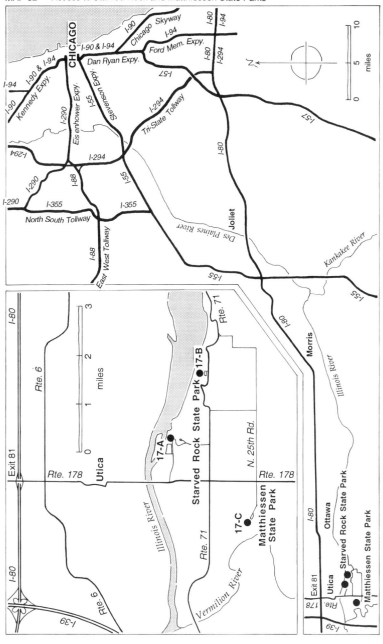

Moines, Iowa. Follow I-80 west past exits for Morris, Seneca, Marseilles, and Ottawa. Leave the expressway at Exit 81 for Route 178. Follow Route 178 south 3.4 miles, in the process turning left and right through Utica.

•**17-A:** This walk is outlined on **Map 53** at right. To reach the trailhead, turn left into **Starved Rock State Park** after crossing the high bridge over the Illinois River. Follow the entrance road 0.8 mile to the huge parking lot on the left for the visitor center and hiking trails. Walking directions start at the bottom of this page.

•**17-B:** Leading to **Ottawa, Kaskaskia, and Illinois Canyons**, this walk is shown on **Map 54** on page 237. To reach the trailhead, continue on Route 178 past the entrance to Starved Rock State Park. Go 0.8 mile to a four-way intersection with Route 71. Turn left and follow Route 71 for 2.5 miles to a parking lot on the left. Walking directions start on page 236.

•**17-C:** This walk at **Matthiessen State Park** is outlined on **Map 55** on page 239. To reach the trailhead, stay on Route 178 past the entrance for Starved Rock. Go another 1.8 miles (in the process you will go straight through a crossroads with Route 71), then turn right into the Dells Area of Matthiessen State Park. Follow the entrance road 0.8 mile to the parking lot. Walking directions start on page 238.

≈   ≈   ≈   ≈

WALKING AT STARVED ROCK STATE PARK: The cliffs and canyons at this park are more like something out of the Southwest than the flatlands of Illinois. To avoid injury to yourself and your family, and to minimize damage to the soft sandstone formations, please stay on the trails.

Map 53 at right shows a route of 4.8 miles starting at **Starved Rock itself**. Much of the route is via wooden stairs and paved paths that provide safety and prevent excessive wear on the environment. As you explore the more remote canyons, the trails become more rugged and natural.

To get underway, go to the trailhead behind the souvenir shop, which in turn is behind the huge visitor center. Follow a wide

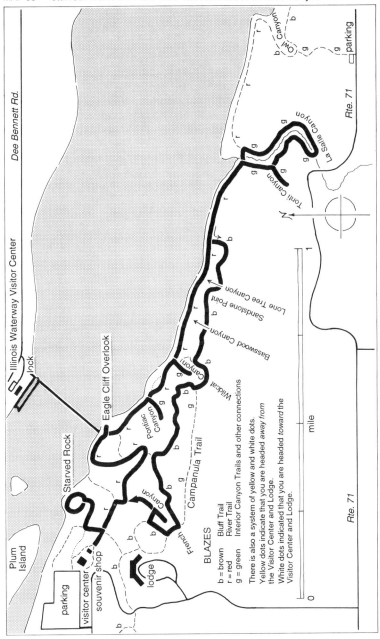

BLAZES

b = brown   Bluff Trail
r = red   River Trail
g = green   Interior Canyon Trails and other connections

There is also a system of yellow and white dots.
Yellow dots indicate that you are headed away from
the Visitor Center and Lodge.
White dots indicated that you are headed toward the
Visitor Center and Lodge.

233

path of crushed stone a few dozen yards, then turn left up a flight of wooden steps. Follow the signs to the top of Starved Rock.

From the top of Starved Rock, return by the way you came. At the foot of the last flight of stairs, turn left for the hiking trails. For the next 1.5 miles, follow the red-blazed **River Trail**, with occasional digressions into canyons on green-blazed spur trails. (As for yellow blazes, they merely indicate that you are going away from the visitor center and lodge. Wnite blazes indicate that you are headed back.)

The River Trail leads past the Fishing Cove Trail on the left, then forks left for **Lover's Leap** and **Eagle Cliff**. From the observation deck at Eagle Cliff, return by the way you came for 100 yards, then turn left down some stairs. At a trail junction, fork left and continue to descend. With the Illinois River on the left, follow the red-blazed path to the mouth of **Pontiac Canyon**, where a spur trail leads right to the headwall.

Continue on the River Trail, at one point bearing right where the trail splits and then rejoins. At **Wildcat Canyon** there is another worthwhile spur trail leading to the headwall.

Pass an intersection with the brown-blazed Bluff Trail, to which you will later return if you follow the route described here.

Continue on the River Trail at least as far as a large foot-bridge over a cove. Without crossing, turn right and follow a green-blazed trail up **La Salle Canyon**. After crossing a small bridge, turn right to explore **Tonti Canyon**, then return and continue up La Salle Canyon. Eventually, make a U-turn to the left below large cliffs at the head of La Salle Canyon (shown in the photograph on page 226), then return along the opposite side of the canyon.

At the mouth of La Salle Canyon, turn left across the big bridge. With the Illinois River on the right, follow the River Trail back to the junction with the **Bluff Trail**, where a long flight of stairs leads to the rim of the valley. Bear right at the top and follow the Bluff Trail around the top of **Lone Tree Canyon**, past **Sandstone Point**, and around the head of **Basswood Canyon**.

At a junction where stairs ascend from the right, turn left to follow the Bluff Trail boardwalk around the head of **Wildcat Canyon** (but first take a look from the platform perched on the brink). Continue past the Campanula Trail intersecting from the left. Pass the head of **Pontiac Canyon**. At a trail intersection with a boardwalk, turn left and continue along the rim of the bluff toward the lodge.

Eventually, cross a small bridge at the head of **French Canyon**, then turn right. Continue on the brown-blazed Bluff Trail past a path intersecting from the left. At the next junction, where the Bluff Trail veers left toward the lodge, fork right onto a trail that descends steeply on stairs. At the bottom of the stairs, turn right to explore French Canyon, then return past the stairs and curve left to the visitor center.

≈   ≈   ≈   ≈

Map 54 at right shows a route of 7.5 miles leading to some of the larger and more remote canyons at Starved Rock State Park.

To get started, follow the wide path as it winds through the woods and descends via stairs to a trail junction above the head of **Owl Canyon.** Turn right and continue with Owl Canyon below on the left, then follow the high bluff bordering the Illinois River. After skirting around **Hennepin Canyon**, there is a short spur leading left to **Hennepin Canyon Overlook.**

Continue with the river on the left, at one point forking left to stay on the bluff trail, now blazed green. Eventually, follow stairs down to Route 71. After crossing the road, continue as the trail descends steeply. At the bottom there is a trail junction. Turn right and pass below the huge **Council Overhang**. At a fork in the trail, bear right to explore **Ottawa Canyon** or left into **Kaskaskia Canyon**. Both are worth seeing.

Return past the Council Overhang to the trail junction at the mouth of the canyons below Route 71. Bear right and continue across a bridge and along the foot of the bluff that rises to the right. Pass through a parking lot, then continue along the foot of the bluff and through a second parking lot. At this lot, join the trail that leads through the woods and up **Illinois Canyon**, which ends in a pool and a narrow gorge.

I suggest that you stop here and return by the way you came, as indicated by the bold line on the map. However, for a longer and more strenuous outing, you may want to return via the route shown by the dotted line, which follows the rim of the canyons. **A warning**, however, is in order. This is not a trail for children, nor for anybody when conditions are wet, snowy, or icy. In places the trail runs within a few feet of the precipice, and unlike elsewhere in the park, there are no guardrails. In particular, the switchback that climbs steeply out of Illinois

MAP 54 — Starved Rock State Park: from Owl Canyon to Illinois Canyon

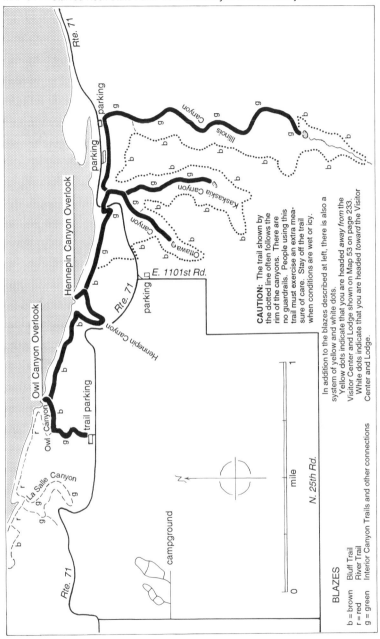

CAUTION: The trail shown by the dotted line often follows the rim of the canyons. There are no guardrails. People using this trail must exercise an extra measure of care. Stay off the trail when conditions are wet or icy.

In addition to the blazes described at left, there is also a system of yellow and white dots.
Yellow dots indicate that you are headed *away from* the Visitor Center and Lodge shown on Map 53 on page 233.
White dots indicate that you are headed *toward* the Visitor Center and Lodge.

BLAZES

b = brown   Bluff Trail
r = red   River Trail
g = green   Interior Canyon Trails and other connections

237

Canyon requires caution. Also, part of the trail follows Route 71 before crossing the road and returning to the trail junction near the Hennepin Canyon Overlook.

≈   ≈   ≈   ≈

WALKING AT MATTHIESSEN STATE PARK: Map 55 at right shows a route of 3.2 miles in an area that is less visited than Starved Rock yet provides a similar opportunity for canyon exploration. Please bear in mind, however, that the dells are sometimes flooded after heavy rain.

To get started, descend the long flight of stairs from the parking lot. After crossing a bridge over the canyon, turn right at a T-intersection, then immediately fork right down some stairs. Follow the streambed up the canyon, then climb stairs to the left. Fork right at the first opportunity in order continue upstream along the bottom of the canyon and past the small waterfall shown on page 8.

Eventually, climb stairs out of the canyon. At the top, pass a trail—the rim path—intersecting from the left-rear. Bear right across a bridge at the dam for Matthiessen Lake, then continue on a path that at first is concrete, then gravel.

At the next intersection, turn right to follow the contour of the slope around the head of a canyon. Pass through a four-way junction with the stairs that you descended at the outset. At the next stairs, descend to the right toward yet another bridge.

Before crossing the bridge, descend more stairs to the bottom of the canyon, where a path of sorts leads upstream a few hundred yards, then ends at a wall. This is perhaps the most scenic and impressive section of the canyon.

Return up the stairs, then cross the bridge. Again climb, bearing right at the top. Eventually, turn right across the bridge that you used at the outset. Climb straight up the long flight of stairs to the parking lot.

MAP 55 — Matthiessen State Park: Dells Area

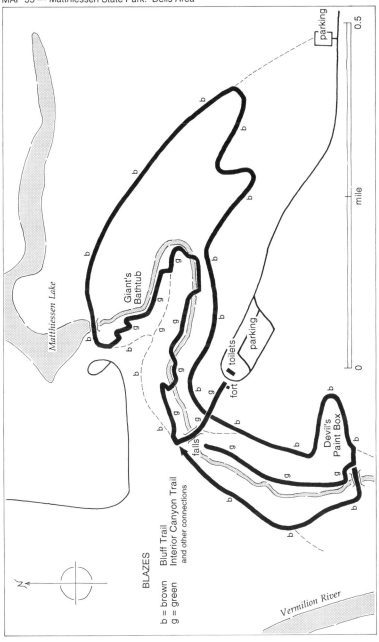

239

18

GOOSE LAKE PRAIRIE

Located southwest of Chicago near Morris, the huge expanse of grassland at Goose Lake Prairie evokes what the first settlers saw in much of northern Illinois when they started to pour into the region 170 years ago. Here you can fare far out into the prairie. **Map 57** on page 248 outlines two routes, one about 5.3 miles long (8.5 kilometers) and the other 3.5 miles (5.6 kilometers). The wide, mowed paths pass through a variety of prairie plant communities that chiefly reflect varying moisture but also a tendency to form stands of different species. In addition to the grasses there are numerous broad-leaved flowing plants that bloom one after another spring through early September. And in the fall, the grasses turn yellow and bronze. If you can, come on a breezy day to enjoy the sound and movement of the prairie —and also to beat the heat, which at midday in summer can be fierce in this treeless environment.

Goose Lake Prairie State Natural Area is open daily from sunrise to sunset. The visitor center is open from 10:00 to 4:00. Pets must be leashed. The area is managed by the Illinois Department of Natural Resources; telephone (815) 942-2899 or go to www.dnr.state.il.us and look for the link to state parks.

For automobile directions, please turn to page 246. Walking directions start on page 249.

THERE IS VERY LITTLE PRAIRIE LEFT in the Prairie State. The grassland that once typified about 60 percent of Illinois—and an even higher percentage west and south of Chicago—is now seen chiefly in parks and forest preserves where big bluestem grass, blazing star, prairie dock, and other native plants have been reestablished to show what the region looked like before the prairie was plowed and planted into oblivion. And at a very few places—Goose Lake is one of them—patches of the original prairie have survived because they were too wet for the cultivation of crops. Even after being drained, Goose Lake was used merely for pasture and later for mining clay and coal. The 2,500-acre site is now the largest prairie remnant in Illinois.

The tall-grass prairie formerly covered an immense triangular area at the middle of the continent. One corner was in northwestern Indiana, another corner in southern Manitoba, and the third corner in Oklahoma. To the west the tall grasses gave way to the sparser, shorter grasses of the Great Plains. Within the prairie area, most forests were limited to major stream valleys, although scattered groves of oak and hickory sometimes occurred on knolls and ridges, where the soil had a lower peat content and was not as soggy as the poorly-drained flatlands and hollows.* Also, thickets of hawthorn, crabapple, quaking aspen, and wild plum sometimes encroached on the grassland, as occurs at Goose Lake Prairie now.

How the grassland originated and remained largely treeless for thousands of years has been the subject of much research and debate. Although ample rain falls on the eastern prairie (an average of about thirty-three inches annually in Illinois), a warm, dry period that followed the retreat of the last continental glacier about 12,500 years ago may initially have fostered the spread of grasses because they tolerate drought better than trees do. And even today the prairie region periodically experiences extreme, protracted droughts that belie the average-rainfall figures.

In any case, once the prairie was established, a variety of factors enabled the grassland to hold its own against woody invasion. The chief factor was fire, often started by Indians and probably also sometimes by lightning. In order to attract grazing animals to the fresh grass that sprouts in the spring after each blaze, Native Americans set prairie fires as a regular practice. They also used fire to drive bison and pronghorn to places where they could be killed by hunters, stampeded over bluffs, or herded to a

---

* Published in 1868, the *Geological Survey of Illinois* states: "The proportion of prairie to wooded land [in Cook County] is a little greater than two to one. The timber is distributed in belts, of varying width, along the water-courses and on the shore of the lake, with frequent groves or timber islands in the open prairie." In DeKalb, Kane, and DuPage counties to the west, the proportion of prairie to forest was estimated at three or four to one.

small area where they would trample each other in panic. Many accounts written by early European explorers and settlers speak of the annual fires lit by Indians. La Salle, for example, mentioned in 1682 the autumnal prairie fires set by the Illinois natives. And even as late as 1823, William Faux, an English farmer touring the area to evaluate prospects for British emigrants, described widespread fires, "darkening the air, heavens, and earth, filling the whole horizon with yellow, palpable, tangible smoke, ashes and vapour." Fires swept over any given expanse of prairie every few years, feeding on the accumulation of dry, dead leaves. These fires killed the seedlings of most woody plants but not the grasses themselves. Growing from underground stems (or rhizomes) and drawing nourishment from roots that penetrate six feet or more below the surface, the grasses quickly sprouted back after each blaze. In fact, studies show that as much as ninety percent of each plant's mass may be underground, where it is simply unaffected by fire. Fire even appears to stimulate the growth of prairie vegetation. Now, recognizing the importance of fire in prairie ecology, the staff at Goose Lake sets carefully controlled fires early each spring in different sections of the park, before birds begin to nest and the grasses begins to grow.

In addition to fire, other factors helped to keep the prairie free of trees. Bison and pronghorn hindered the growth of woody plants by trampling and grazing on the seedlings and rubbing themselves against young trees. The dense root systems of the prairie plants made it difficult for seeds of trees to sprout and grow. The grasses exhausted the available water near the surface so that there was little left for seedlings. Also, before ditches were dug to drain large areas for agriculture, much of the prairie was unsuited for trees because it was soggy or even covered with water for two or three months every spring.

The dominant plant of the tall-grass prairie is big bluestem, also called turkey foot grass because its three-pronged seed head resembles a bird's foot. It is an excellent forage crop and often was used by the settlers to feed livestock. Found in rich, moderately drained soils, big bluestem produces a seed stalk as much as six or eight feet tall. Despite its annual seed head, this grass propagates itself mainly by rhizomes that spread underground to establish new plants. In this way, large areas are occupied and tenaciously held against competing plants.

Indian grass is another widespread native prairie plant, similar in appearance to big bluestem except in mid-August, when reddish-brown tassels form at the ends of the seed stalks—a spectacular sight in areas with large stands. Yet another common plant is switch grass, which has a slight bend in the stem at the joints or nodes. Indian grass and switch grass both thrive in disturbed areas, but Indian grass favors somewhat dry soil and switch grass prefers moist soil.

In the mid-range of moisture, northern prairie dropseed grows to a height of two feet in areas that are not overshadowed by taller grasses. In the fall, the leaves of dropseed curl to form little corkscrews. Its seeds have an odor resembling buttered popcorn.

In low, undrained areas, other grasses take over: predominantly cordgrass and blue-joint grass, both of which can tolerate prolonged flooding during spring and early summer and long dry spells during the late summer and fall. Cordgrass is the tallest prairie grass; its seed stalks commonly reach eight to twelve feet. Its finely serrated leaf edges are very sharp and can cut like a knife. In July flowers that resemble combs appear along the top foot of the stalks. Blue-joint grass, which has coarse, bluish-green leaves, forms white seed heads when it blooms early in July.

In areas of very dry, sandy soil, shorter grasses predominate. Here, little bluestem and side-oats grama are most abundant, growing to knee height when mature. Common in the western prairie, little bluestem has roots that penetrate to a depth of twenty feet and enable it to survive severe drought. On the driest sites, muhley grass and blue and hairy grama are likely to be found, growing not more than a few inches high. All of these dry grasses are bunch grasses: they grow in tight bunches which increase in diameter only slightly each year. The plants occupy just a small portion of the ground surface, leaving bare soil between, but the roots and leaves reach out into the intervening spaces, hindering other plants from growing there.

Aside from various grasses, the prairie vegetation includes numerous forbs—a catchall term meaning broad-leaved, flowering plants. Many are members of the daisy and pea families. Their flowers dominate the prairie scene before the tall grasses bloom. Like the grasses, the forbs are perennials, growing afresh each year from roots that may live for decades and that enable them to

survive episodic fires and droughts. Again, different forbs thrive in different areas, depending mainly on the degree of moisture in the soil. For example, in dry areas sunflowers, goldenrod, flowering spurge, partridge pea, and different varieties of aster often occur among bunches of little bluestem. At the other end of the moisture spectrum, water hemlock, hedge nettle, and blue vervain commonly grow among prairie cordgrass.

Finally, at Goose Lake Prairie, there are areas of weeds, meaning European and Asian plants such as ragweed, milkweed, wild carrot, and broom grass. These non-native plants are opportunists, growing quickly in areas disturbed by over-grazing, farming, and construction, and they maintain their advantage by going to seed early.

≈   ≈   ≈   ≈

AUTOMOBILE DIRECTIONS: Goose Lake Prairie is located near the town of Morris southwest of Chicago. (See **Map 56** at right.) Two approaches—from **Interstate 55** and **Interstate 80**—are described below.

To Goose Lake Prairie from Interstate 55: I-55 is the extension of **Stevenson Expressway** southwest past Joliet toward St. Louis.

Leave I-55 at Exit 240 for Lorenzo Road. Follow Lorenzo Road west 6.9 miles—along the way it becomes Pine Bluff Road—then turn right onto Jugtown Road at the entrance to Goose Lake Prairie and Heidecke Lake. After 1 mile, turn right toward the visitor center and the Goose Lake Prairie Natural Area. Go 0.5 mile to the large visitor center parking lot.

To Goose Lake Prairie from Interstate 80: I-80 runs east-west between Gary, Indiana and Des Moines, Iowa. There is an interchange with Interstate 55 near Joliet.

Leave I-80 at Exit 112 for Morris and Route 47. Follow Route 47 south 3.2 miles, then turn left onto Pine Bluff Road. After 5.2 miles, turn left onto Jugtown Road at the entrance to Goose Lake Prairie and Heidecke Lake. After 1 mile, turn right toward the visitor center and the Goose Lake Prairie Natural Area. Go 0.5 mile to the large visitor center parking lot.

≈   ≈   ≈   ≈

MAP 56 — Access to Goose Lake Prairie State Natural Area

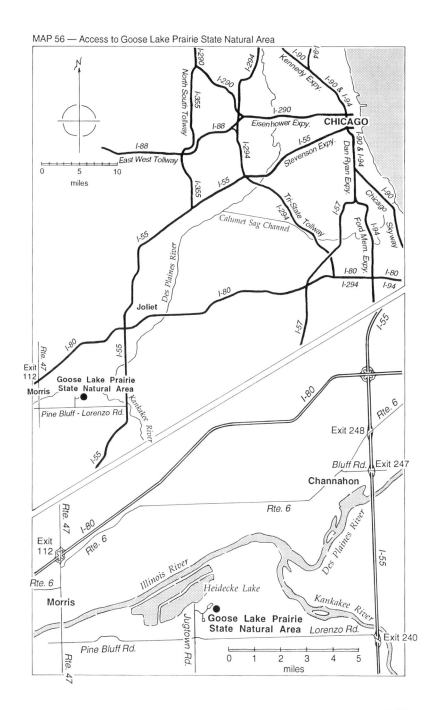

MAP 57 — Goose Lake Prairie State Natural Area

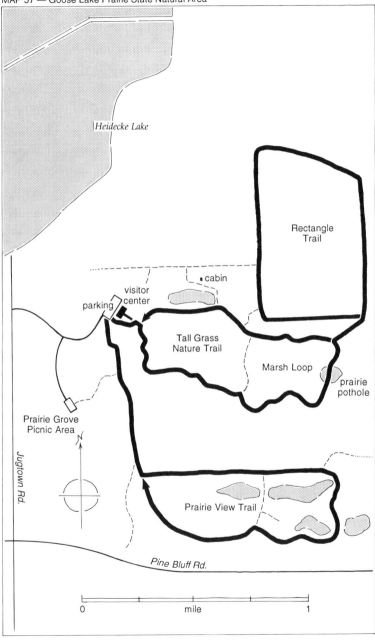

Heidecke Lake

Rectangle Trail

cabin

visitor center

parking

Tall Grass Nature Trail

Marsh Loop

prairie pothole

Prairie Grove Picnic Area

N

Jugtown Rd.

Prairie View Trail

Pine Bluff Rd.

0   mile   1

WALKING: Map 57 at left shows two walks at **Goose Lake Prairie**.

The longer walk—5.3 miles—starts behind the visitor center. You can get there by passing through the building or by skirting around it to the right, where a sign at the corner of the parking lot says, "To trails."

From the information board at the end of a long ramp, follow the **Tall Grass Nature Trail** to the right. At an intersection with the **Marsh Loop**, bear right to cross a prairie pothole on a boardwalk (if it is open). Bear right repeatedly to go all the way around the **Rectangle Trail**, then return to the visitor center visible in the distance.

The shorter walk—3.5 miles—is the **Prairie View Trail**. It starts at the right-hand side of the parking lot as you face the visitor center, not far from corner. Follow the grassy track south toward distant Pine Bluff Road and some low hills. Eventually, fork left and continue clockwise around the circuit. At times the trail may pass through narrow gaps in the reeds. Continue across some mounds. These and the ponds that they overlook are the remnants of a strip mine.

After completing the circuit, return to the visitor center visible in the distance.

19

INDIANA DUNES STATE PARK

Located at the southern end of Lake Michigan approximately midway between Gary and Michigan City, this park offers some of the best walking in the greater Chicago region. **Map 59** on pages 260 and 261 outlines a circuit that for a time follows the crest of high dunes overlooking the lake. Eventually the trail descends to the beach, then heads inland in order to return through the woods sheltered among the back dunes. Altogether the loop is 5.5 miles long (8.8 kilometers). It includes a few short stretches that are strenuous where the trail climbs the sand slopes.

Indiana Dunes State Park is open daily from 7:00 a.m. to 11:00 p.m. Dogs must be leashed. An admission fee is charged. The park is managed by the Indiana Department of Natural Resources; call (219) 926-1952 or go to www.in.state.us/dnr. and look for the link to state parks.

For automobile directions, please turn to page 258. Walking directions also start on page 258.

"THE PROVINCE OF ECOLOGY is to consider the mutual relations between plants and their environments," wrote Henry Chandler Cowles in an article summarizing his research into the plant communities of the Indiana Dunes and other dunes regions bordering Lake Michigan in the late 1890s. Today ecologists include both plants and animals within their purview, but as a graduate student at the University of Chicago and later as a professor of botany there, Cowles focused on ways that plants show special adaptations to the physical and climatic properties of their sites. An outgrowth of Darwinism, this subject was at the forefront of botanical research and was already under investigation by some European botanists on whose work Cowles built.

When a modified version of Cowles' doctoral thesis was serialized in 1899 in the *Botanical Gazette*, it attracted worldwide attention among botanists. Cowles went on to write other leading articles in the developing field of plant ecology, and in 1912 he presented in London a well-received paper on his fifteen years of study at the Indiana Dunes. The following year, when Cowles organized the International Phytogeographic [plant geography] Excursion to America, all of the visiting European botanists put the Indiana Dunes—along with the Grand Canyon, Yosemite, and Yellowstone—on their lists of places that they most wanted to see.

Cowles regarded the Indiana Dunes as a living laboratory ideally suited to ecological studies. "Plant formations should be found which are rapidly passing into other types by reason of a changing environment," he wrote, and pointed out that no land-form is more changeable than a sand dune. Accordingly, he examined not only the features that enable some plants to survive and thrive where others fail, but also the dynamic rise and fall of distinct plant communities as their physical surroundings change—for example, as sand dunes grow or deteriorate or advance inland. Stressing the mutuality of the relationship between plants and their environment, he studied how plants themselves contribute to change in local topography, soil, and other conditions, and how these modified conditions favor the rise to dominance of yet entirely different plant communities than were formerly present. This displacement of one biotic community by another is called *ecological succession*, and as Cowles pointed out, it can continue through several stages until change becomes so slow—depending, perhaps, on shifts in the climate itself—that a virtual equilibrium is achieved between the physical environment and the climax community of plants and animals.

One of Cowles' favorite pedagogical exercises was to conduct visitors and students through a succession of plant communities, starting at the bare beach and ending in the mature deciduous forest of the backdunes. This sequence in space is a metaphor for sequence in time. By walking inland the visitor can pass through stages of ecological succession that in all likelihood occurred in the backdunes at various times in the past. After all, the forested backdunes once were vacant beach and then grassy foredunes before they became far removed from Lake Michigan. This movement of the shore is due mainly to two factors: a dramatic drop in water level between 3,000 and 2,000 years ago (as de-scribed in Chapter 15) and the arrival of more and more sand at the southern end of Lake Michigan, to which it is washed by the longshore current produced by northerly winter winds. In any case, as you walk from the beach through the dunes and down into the woods, notice the shifts in vegetation that correspond to the changing environmental factors of light intensity, temperature, wind, soil, water, and topography.

Cowles divided the beach into three zones: the lower beach that is washed by summer waves and lacks established plants; the middle beach that is washed by winter storms and inhabited by plants that live for only one season; and the upper beach where dune formation starts because of the presence of hardy perennial plants. Beginning, then, with the annual plants of the middle beach, one common species is sea rocket, a succulent (that is, water-filled) member of the mustard family. Although only a few yards from the water's edge, the middle beach is a very dry environment because of the glaring sun, the nearly constant wind warmed by heated sand, and the porosity of the sand itself, through which rainwater quickly percolates. Accordingly, sea rocket shows several adaptations to its dry environment: fleshy stems and leaves that store water, a glossy leaf surface that helps to retain moisture, and disproportionately long, bushy roots to reach the water table.

Other pioneer plants of the middle beach are bugseed, winged pigweed, and seaside spurge. Bugseed is stiff with many branches and plump, narrow leaves that expose minimal surface to the sun. Similarly, winged pigweed has narrow, pointed leaves that resemble miniature holly. Seaside spurge has tiny leaves and hides from the wind by growing flat along the sand in a spreading mat. A large supply of latex in its leaves helps to preserve moisture.

Dune formation starts at the upper beach where, safe from winter storms, perennial plants establish a firm hold. The perennials catch windblown sand to form small mounds that swell into foredunes as the vegetation spreads. Chief among the dune-building plants is marram grass, growing in dense clumps and tufts. Although marram grass produces a seed head each fall, the plants spreads mainly by *rhizome propagation*. Pushing outward from each established plant, underground stems sprout new roots and shoots. The rhizomes from a single plant sometimes spread as far as twenty feet. Together the underground stems and dense roots of many plants form a tight matrix that binds the sand so that it resists erosion even by waves. As the dunes grow vertically, the marram grass simply grows with it, keeping pace with the surface by pushing up fresh leaves from the buried central stem—a process called *internodal elongation* because the stem lengthens itself as necessary between leaf nodes. Marram grass is thus ideally suited to thrive in the unstable dune environment. In fact, when the sand surface becomes stabilized, the plant shows a decline in vigor because the underground stems, which continue to grow upward, get too near the surface and dry out.

In the shelter behind the front rank of marram-grass dunes, other grasses appear, including little bluestem bunchgrass and sand reed. Little bluestem bunchgrass, so-named because of its bright blue joints, shows some ability to adjust to a shifting surface by internodal elongation, but it lacks underground runners and so can sprout only from seeds. Sand reed, on the other hand, spreads by underground runners but lacks the ability to elongate its stem. Also, the rhizomes of sand reed tend to dive deep for moisture rather than to grow parallel with the surface. This adaptation serves it well when the dune is eroding, but when sand is accumulating, sand reed sometimes suffocates. As the buried grass decomposes, it provides nutrients for other plants and even trees, including the pioneering cottonwoods, sometimes called common cottonwood or Eastern cottonwood, a member of the poplar family that includes aspens.

Frequently seen along the foredunes and sandy slopes fronting the lake, cottonwoods have wide, almost triangular, coarsely-toothed leaves. Like marram grass, these trees are major dune-builders because they can adjust to the changing sand surface. Cottonwood seeds require a sheltered, damp depression in which to sprout, but once the young trees are established, their foliage creates a windbreak that results in the deposition of drifting sand. Engulfment by sand would kill most trees, but cottonwoods can tolerate being buried. As the sand piles up and the water table rises within the growing dune, cottonwoods avoid suffocation by sprouting adventitious roots from successively higher levels of their trunks and branches. In this way, cottonwoods keep pace with a growing dune of their own making. What looks like stubby brush atop a dune may actually be the tip of a century-old, fifty-foot tree, as is sometimes plainly seen when the sand is blown away again, exposing a cottonwood that has a trunk and branches shaggy with roots. These exposed roots can, in turn, form stems and sprout leaves. Cottonwood dunes tend to have steeper sides than marram-grass dunes because cottonwoods cannot spread sideways by underground runners, nor will their seeds sprout in the dry dune sand.

Other successful dune plants are two shrubs: sand-dune willow, with thick, small leaves adapted to the dry environment, and sand cherry, with reddish bark, narrow leathery leaves that turn bright red in the fall, and fruit that grows one to each stem. Both shrubs frequently are found behind the front rank of marram-grass dunes. Like cottonwood, sand-dune willow can sprout adventitious roots and can tolerate being buried and unburied. Like marram grass, sand cherry spreads by underground runners. Studies of sand cherry indicate that the roots of its seedlings tend to follow organic matter left by the burial of dune grasses.

The farther you walk into the foredunes, the greater becomes the variety of plants, including wormwood, wild rye, sand thistle, sand cress, goldenrod, milkweed, red osier dogwood, fragrant sumac, poison ivy, grapes, and many other plants, shrubs, and scrubby trees that are not unique to the dune region. One surprising plant, however, is the prickly-pear cactus, with round fat pads. Abundant in the desert regions of the Southwest, the cactus finds a similarly appropriate niche in the dry, sandy wastes of the dunes.

Along much of the lakeshore at the Indiana Dunes, the transition from the grassy, scrubby foredunes to the forested backdunes is fairly abrupt, since the mature woods often start immediately atop or behind the ridge of high dunes fronting the lake. But at the various blowouts along the shore, the transition is more confused and complex. Blowouts are places where the wind has breached the barrier of foredunes. Channeled through a narrow gap, the wind then scours out a huge, amphitheater-like bowl. The high dunes are pushed back in a horseshoe-shaped bulge, and established forests are buried by the advancing dunes. Eventually the blowout becomes so big that the concentrated effect of the wind is dissipated, and the blowout is stabilized by vegetation.

As plants colonize the blowout, most of its low, uneven center is covered by the same species seen at the foredunes, including grasses, cottonwoods, willow, and sand cherry. In the hollows at the center of the blowout, organic debris from decaying plants accumulates more quickly than elsewhere, and a few oaks may grow here from acorns dropped by chipmunks and squirrels. From the ridges adjacent to the blowout, evergreens such as juniper, jack pine, and perhaps even white pine spread downward into the blowout bowl. More striking than the living trees, however, are the dead ones in so-called tree graveyards (see page 262). These gray, dried relics show where forests were buried by the advancing dunes and then uncovered as the dunes moved inland. Sometimes a dark line across the sandy slopes indicates a stratum of humus from which the former forest grew.

As just noted, at the top of the high dunes is a zone that often is occupied by a community of evergreens: juniper (both the slender, vertical redcedar and the low, spreading common juniper), jack pine (with stiff, short needles, two to each fascicle), white pine (five long, soft needles to each fascicle), and bearberry (with papery, reddish stems and small, paddle-shaped leaves). These are among the first trees and shrubs after cottonwood to become established on the windward slopes and crests of the high dunes near the lake, and they often are seen strung out in a long, narrow band that forms a buffer sheltering the deciduous forest of the backdunes. The evergreens sometimes occur on the backdunes as well, but the dense shade cast by the deciduous trees makes it very difficult for juniper and pine seedlings to compete successfully. The trees of the deciduous forest, however, have difficulty tolerating exposure to the wind, cold, and dryness of the high front dunes, and so there the evergreens find a niche for themselves.

The jack pines at the Indiana Dunes are an isolated colony located more than sixty miles south of any other stand of jack pine in the Great Lakes region. They are present here as a relic of the last glacial period, when the climate of the entire Midwest, particularly near the ice sheet, was colder than at present. Most northern plants retreated with the glacier, but at the Indiana Dunes the jack pines remain because environmental conditions— the meager soil, exposure to driving wind, and lack of water—in many ways resemble conditions farther north, where water is abundant but frequently unavailable because it is frozen as ice.

Jack pine is so well adapted to the cold and physiological drought experienced by plants in the windy, ice-bound taiga that its range extends farther north into Canada than any other pine. Transpiration is minimized and resistance to cold is maximized by its short needles that have a cuticle so thick that it forms half the bulk of the leaf. Jack pines have singularly low nutritional requirements, and so can grow in dune sand, with its negligible humus.

Associated with jack pine is bearberry, another plant common in Arctic regions. Bearberry is a low, woody creeper of the heath family, and once established, it provides cover that protects the young pines—which, of course, must grow from seeds—until they are big enough to survive on their own. Like marram grass, bearberry spreads by sending up new shoots from underground runners. Its growth, however, is slow; while it can adjust to some instability of the dune surface, it cannot survive a rapid accumulation of sand.

Sheltered from the wind by the high front dunes, the region to the rear is a suitable environment for a deciduous forest of oak, hickory, ash, maple, and other trees and shrubs that are not required to show any special tolerance to the shifting topography, drought, cold, or sterile soil that characterize the dunes nearer the lake. Here the terrain has been stabilized by vegetation that over the centuries has produced sufficient leaf litter and humus to support a rich and diversified forest. The various plant communities of the deciduous forest show only the usual differences between damp hollows, dry hilltops, north and south slopes, and other such conditions, as described in Chapter 9. And among the deciduous forests are occasional ponds, marshes, and bogs, each with its characteristic communities of plants. (For a discussion of bog vegetation, see Chapter 3.)

Of course, all is not static, even in the backdunes. Where the high front dunes are moving inland because of blowouts, the deciduous forest will simply be buried until the forward slope of the advancing dunes are captured by grass, cottonwood, willow, cherry, and other dune-stabilizing plants. But absent an incursion by a migrating dune or the occurrence of an extraneous catastrophe such as fire, blight, or insect infestation, the deciduous forest is the dominant plant complex among the back dunes, as it is throughout the Chicago region.

≈   ≈   ≈   ≈

AUTOMOBILE DIRECTIONS: Indiana Dunes State Park is located at the southern end of Lake Michigan. (See **Map 58** at right.) Two approaches—via the **Chicago Skyway** and the **Tri-State Tollway**—are described below. Remember, of course, that the state park is distinct from the Indiana Dunes *National Lakeshore*, which is the subject of Chapter 20.

To Indiana Dunes State Park via the Chicago Skyway (Interstate 90): From downtown Chicago, follow the Dan Ryan Expressway south, then exit onto the Skyway for Interstate 90 east to the Indiana Toll Road. Eventually, after about 37 miles on the Skyway and toll road, leave I-90 at Exit 31 for Route 49 toward Chesterton. After paying the toll, turn left onto Route 49 and follow it north 5.9 miles straight into Indiana Dunes State Park. From the gate house, continue 0.1 mile, then turn right toward the campground and Wilson Shelter. Go 0.8 mile, then turn left into the parking lot for the Wilson Shelter.

To Indiana Dunes State Park via the Tri-State Tollway (Interstate 294): Follow the tollway toward Indiana. Eventually, the Tri-State Tollway becomes Interstate 80 and Interstate 94 eastbound into Indiana. **Stay on I-94** past Exit 16—i.e., so as to avoid the Indiana Toll Road (I-80 and I-90). Finally, leave I-94 at Exit 26B for Route 49 north toward the Indiana Dunes. Go north on Route 49 for 2.6 miles straight into Indiana Dunes State Park. From the gate house, continue 0.1 mile, then turn right toward the campground and Wilson Shelter. Go 0.8 mile, then turn left into the parking lot for the Wilson Shelter.

≈   ≈   ≈   ≈

WALKING: Map 59 on pages 260 and 261 shows a moderately strenuous circuit of 5.5 miles at the **Indiana Dunes State Park**. In addition, of course, there is the opportunity for an easy walk along the beach at the foot of the high dunes.

To get started, locate the trailhead to the left of an eight-foot-high boulder where Trails 8, 9, and 10 enter the woods. For nearly a mile the route shown on Map 59 follows **Trail 9**, first forking right where Trail 8 diverges to the left, then forking left away from Trail 10 (by which you will return at the end).

                                        [Directions continue on page 263.]

MAP 58 — Access to Indiana Dunes State Park

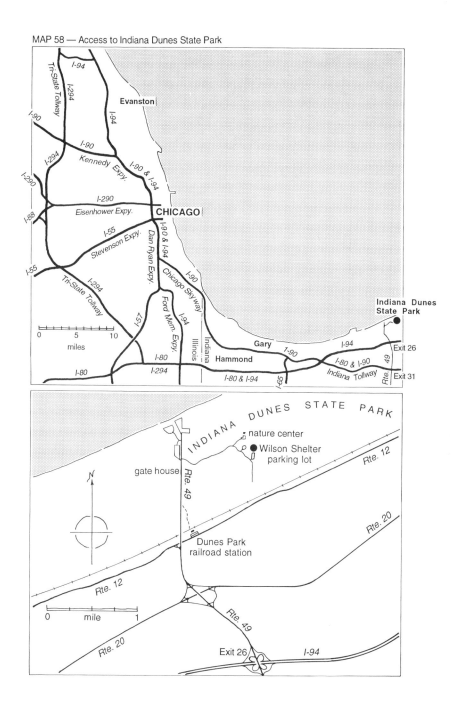

MAP 59 — Indiana Dunes State Park

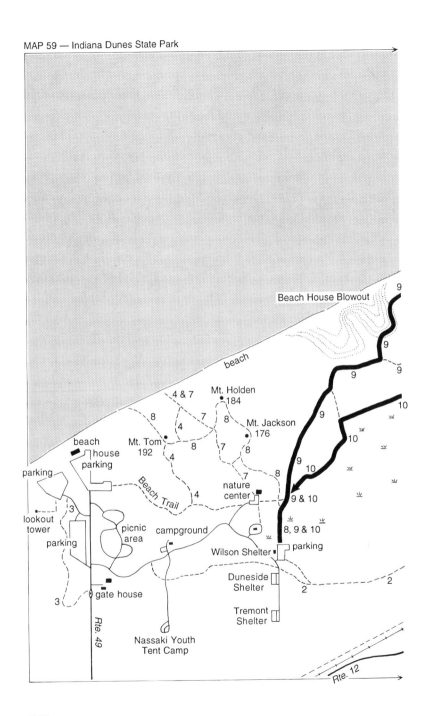

Beach House Blowout

9

9

9

9

beach

10

Mt. Holden
●184

4 & 7

8   7   8   Mt. Jackson
4   ● 176

9

beach
house
parking   Mt. Tom   8   7

192
10

parking   4   7   8   10

9 & 10

nature
center

Beach Trail   4

lookout
tower   3

picnic   campground
parking   area

8, 9 & 10

9 & 10

parking

Wilson Shelter

3   gate house

Duneside
Shelter   2   2

Rte. 49

Tremont
Shelter

Nassaki Youth
Tent Camp

Rte. 12

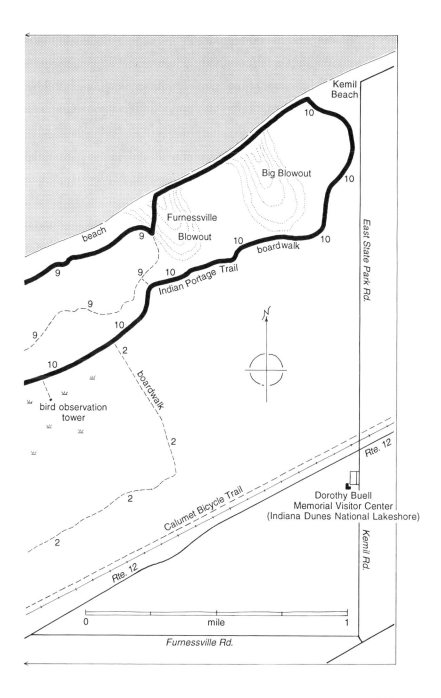

Kemil Beach

10

10

Big Blowout

10

Furnessville Blowout

beach

9

10

boardwalk

10

9

9

Indian Portage Trail

10

9

9

10

2

boardwalk

10

bird observation tower

N

East State Park Rd.

2

2

Calumet Bicycle Trail

Rte. 12

Dorothy Buell
Memorial Visitor Center
(Indiana Dunes National Lakeshore)

2

Rte. 12

Kemil Rd.

0   mile   1

Furnessville Rd.

261

Follow Trail 9 through the woods, at one point passing a path intersecting from the right. Pass high dunes encroaching on the woods from the left.

When Trail 9 splits—i.e., both prongs are identified as Trail 9—turn left and climb the dune. At the top, bear right to follow the rim of Beach House Blowout. With Lake Michigan on the left, continue along the crest of the high dunes on Trail 9.

Eventually, Trail 9 arrives at the Furnessville Blowout. As the path curves inland, **leave Trail 9** by turning sharply left to follow an unmarked trail to the beach.

With the lake on the left, follow the shore east. Go nearly three-quarters of a mile. At the Big Blowout, the high dunes disappear behind the much lower foredunes. Continue along the beach past the Big Blowout to a place where **Trail 10** meets the beach. This juncture is marked by a post and perhaps also by a fan of foot tracks issuing from the dunes.

Follow Trail 10 steeply uphill over the high, forested dunes. As you continue on Trail 10, you will cross a boardwalk where sand is spilling into the woods at the back of the Big Blowout. Eventually, bear left at a trail intersection, then bear right past the junction with Trail 2. At a T-intersection, turn left to stay on Trail 10. Immediately after Trail 9 intersects from the right-rear, fork left. Pass Trail 8 merging from the right-rear and continue to the parking lot.

20

INDIANA DUNES NATIONAL LAKESHORE

The national lakeshore stretches in pieces from Gary to Michigan City. Listed below are three walks that show the best of the dunes. There are of course many other trails that you can learn about at the **Dorothy Buell Memorial Visitor Center**, which is located at the intersection of Route 12 (the Dune Highway) and Kemil Road, as shown on **Map 60** on page 275.

Map 61 on page 277 outlines a walk that starts at **Mt. Baldy**, a huge migrating dune shown in the photograph at left and also on page 271. From the summit you can descend to Lake Michigan and walk along the beach for a round-trip of 3.5 miles (5.6 kilometers).

Map 62 on page 279 shows the outstanding **Cowles Bog Trail**. It passes along the edge of wetlands, over forested dunes, then along the beach and back through the woods for a circuit of 4 miles (6.4 kilometers).

Map 63 on page 281 outlines the **Inland Marsh Trail**, which wanders 3 miles (4.8 kilometers) through a landscape of irregular, wooded ridges overlooking wetlands among the dunes.

The trails at the Indiana Dunes National Lakeshore are open daily from 8:00 a.m. to sunset. Dogs must be leashed. The national lakeshore is administered by the National Park Service, a unit of the U.S. Department of the Interior; telephone (219) 926-7561 or go to www.nps.gov/indu.

For automobile directions to the Dorothy Buell Memorial Visitor Center, please turn to page 274. From there, refer to pages 276 and 278 for directions to the various sites.

INDIANA DUNES NATIONAL LAKESHORE was authorized by Congress in 1966, half a century after the idea was first reviewed at a public hearing held by the Department of the Interior. In 1916 the land under consideration was still virtually empty and untouched, stretching twenty-five miles from Gary to Michigan

City. By the time the federal park actually was created, the area was a patchwork of steel mills, power plants, harbors, and residential developments strung out at intervals along the shore.

At first the impetus to preserve the Indiana Dunes came mainly from Chicago, where rampant growth had produced, during the late nineteenth and early twentieth centuries, a countervailing movement for municipal parks and county forest preserves. Under the leadership of landscape architect Jens Jensen and other Chicago-based conservationists, the dune country at the southern tip of Lake Michigan was identified as one of the nearby areas most worth keeping in its natural condition. In 1911 the conservationists organized the Prairie Club, which sponsored frequent excursions from Chicago to the Indiana Dunes via electric trolley and railroad. In 1914 the Prairie Club allied itself with other local organizations to form the Conservation Council of Chicago, and preservation of the Dunes became the council's first project. The council asked wealthy individuals and institutions to endow a Dunes arboretum and similar projects, but had no success. Nonetheless, the Conservation Council 's persistent publicity campaign, which included illustrated lectures, guided hikes, and even theatrical productions in the Dunes, developed strong support for preservation of the Indiana Dunes among Chicagoans and some Indianans. Most local residents, however, were adamantly opposed to the idea.

Opposition to a Dunes park was centered in Indiana's Porter County, where the main stretch of undeveloped Dunes land was located. This area was still a rural backwater, and local leaders and businessmen longed for industrial development. Nonetheless, U.S. Senator Tom Taggart, who had implemented Indianapolis's first park plan while major in the late 1890s, sponsored a Senate resolution in 1916 authorizing a study by the National Park Service of "the advisability of the securing by purchase or otherwise, all that portion of the counties of Lake, LaPorte, and Porter in the State of Indiana bordering on Lake Michigan and commonly known as the 'sand dunes' together with the cost of acquisition and maintenance."

Although seemingly straightforward, Taggart's proposal was out of the ordinary in several respects. At that time, Congress had never spent any money whatsoever to buy land for the national parks. Rather, the great national parks, starting with

Yellowstone in 1872, had all been created from land already in federal ownership or donated by state governments. Also, the National Park Service, established by Congress in 1916 and under the direction of Chicagoan and Prairie Club member Stephen Mather, had formulated standards for the national parks to which the Indiana Dunes did not conform. National parks were supposed to be monumental examples of natural grandeur. Park policy called for immense, pristine areas far removed from population centers—a policy that prevailed at the National Park Service until, nearly fifty years later, President John F. Kennedy and Secretary of the Interior Stewart Udall initiated a new national park policy that stressed the development of smaller, recreation-oriented parks near large cities.

Although the Indiana Dunes region was merely a sandbox compared to the existing national parks (all of which were in the West), Mather worked hard for a few months to support the Dunes park proposed by Senator Taggart. At a hearing held in Chicago, there was a lengthy litany of support for a park, although one witness cautioned that Congress "is singularly uninterested in national parks and there is no precedent for buying land for such a purpose." Disregarding precedent, Mather filed a report a month later endorsing federal purchase of twelve thousand acres of Dunes land at a cost of $2.6 million. The federal government, however, was preoccupied with America's entry into World War I, and Mather's report never received congressional consideration. Moreover, Senator Taggart was defeated in his bid for re-election in the fall of 1916, and no Indiana politician took his place in support of a federal Dunes park.

Although Congress was indifferent to a Dunes national park, within a few years a much smaller park was created at the state level. In 1916 Indiana was one hundred years old, and the celebrations included the formation of a State Park Memorial Committee to identify areas worth preserving in commemoration of the state's centennial. The chairman and chief mover on the committee was Richard Lieber, a wealthy retired businessman turned conservationist. Lieber convinced the Indiana Federation of Women's Clubs and other local organizations to appoint their own state park committees to solicit contributions to buy three state parks in the centennial year. Indiana's governor even declared a Park Contribution Week, and Lieber personally raised large sums from his wealthy friends. Altogether, however, only enough money was received to buy two state parks, both in central Indiana.

Indiana's first state parks proved to be immensely popular and established the precedent for still more state parks. Appointed state forester, Lieber persuaded the Indiana legislature in 1918 to create a Department of Conservation, of which he was made director. In 1919 a state representative from Gary introduced a bill to establish the Indiana Dunes State Park. The bill produced no immediate result, but in 1920 construction of the Dunes Highway (present-day Route 12) added a sense of urgency that something must be done to protect the Dunes from the development that the road would surely bring. That same year the National Dunes Park Association—chief proponent of a federal preserve—gave its support to a state park as the next best thing.

In 1921 a bill to create a state park reached the floor of the Indiana legislature but failed to pass, in part because opponents in Porter County were unwilling to accept any park that included more than three miles of frontage on Lake Michigan instead of the nine miles suggested by the preservationists. Park advocates, led by Lieber and Bess Sheehan, chairman of the Dunes Park Committee of the State Federated Women's Clubs, spent 1922 gathering public support for a Dunes park. Meanwhile, residential development at the Indiana Dunes continued as the communities of Dune Acres and Ogden Dunes were established. In 1923 legislation to create a Dunes state park was again introduced, and after intense lobbying by its supporters, a three-mile park was approved on the last day of the legislative session. To implement the legislation, Lieber struggled to augment the $105,000 annual appropriation with private contributions, and he succeeded in raising several hundred thousand dollars from wealthy philanthropists, including Julius Rosenwald, president of Sears, Roebuck & Company, and Judge Elbert Gary, chairman of the board of U.S. Steel. By 1927 the state completed purchasing the two thousand acres that comprise Indiana Dunes State Park.

Creation of the state park ended, for more than twenty years, all effort to establish a larger federal park in the Indiana Dunes. The issue lay dormant because for decades there was no industrial expansion into the Dunes. First the Great Depression intervened, then World War II. During this period 3,600 acres of spectacular duneland fronting the beach between the communities of Ogden Dunes in the west and Dune Acres in the east—a section called the Central Dunes—remained unchanged and apparently unthreatened. But after the war the Midwest boomed and became a tremendous market for steel, principally for use in automobiles and large appliances like refrigerators, washers, and dryers. In 1956 the Bethlehem Steel Company began quietly to buy large holdings in the Central Dunes from land speculation companies that had held the property since the early 1900s, and in 1962 Bethlehem announced plans to build a billion-dollar, fully integrated steel works on its newly acquired land.

Bethlehem's plans were contingent on the development of a publicly financed harbor at Burns Ditch, a small waterway that had been carved through the Dunes when the Little Calumet River had been relocated in 1926. Ever since the excavation of Burns Ditch, big business in northern Indiana had dreamed of a major public port to stimulate industrialization and the export of farm products. The harbor project gained plausibility after work began in 1955 on the St. Lawrence Seaway, which promised direct shipping access to the world. In 1957 Bethlehem gave the State of Indiana's Board of Public Harbors and Terminals a purchase option for 260 acres of waterfront duneland. Enthralled at the prospect of a major port, Indiana officials foresaw "7,00 three-year jobs for the building trades; 15,000 direct jobs in the steel mills; 25,000 jobs in service, allied industries, transportation and miscellaneous occupations; $2 billion in home and industry construction; and federal condemnation costs of $50 million"—if, that is, the Army Corps of Engineers would approve the harbor and the federal government pay for it. According to the cost-benefit studies conducted by the Corps of Engineers, the feasibility of a port depended on its heavy use by a major Bethlehem mill, but Bethlehem would not promise to build such a plant until a publicly financed port was a certainty. Indiana, the federal government, and Bethlehem Steel each wanted the others to demonstrate their commitment by building first.

Meanwhile, Bethlehem's land acquisitions had sparked a renewed effort to save the Central Dunes for a national park. The same factors that made the site attractive to Bethlehem—its large size, lake frontage, and lack of development—also made the area the most suitable section of duneland for preservation. Moreover, by the early 1960s there was precedent for the National Park Service to buy waterfront areas. In 1961, at the urging of the new Kennedy administration, Congress had authorized creation of the Cape Cod National Seashore, the first national park to be acquired with congressionally appropriated funds.

Indiana politicians at the local, state, and national levels were overwhelmingly behind the proposal for a harbor and steel mill, so park advocates had to look out of state for a spokesman to lead their crusade in Congress. In 1957 the Save the Dunes Council, which had been trying for five years to raise private funds to buy duneland, enlisted the aid of Illinois Senator Paul Douglas, who had a weekend house in the Dunes. Douglas tried to persuade Indiana's senators to sponsor park legislation, but they declined, and so in 1958 Douglas introduced the first of a long series of bills designed to protect and preserve the still unspoiled Central Dunes in Porter County.

Douglas's first proposal called for a federal reservation of nearly four thousand acres with 3.5 miles of shoreline, including the land targeted by Indiana for a port and the land purchased by Bethlehem Steel. The Indiana press, politicians, and industrial spokesmen responded with outrage, accusing Douglas of carpet-bagging, of trying to be the "third senator from Indiana," of representing Chicago's commercial interests that sought to prevent Indiana's industrial development, and of wanting a park outside Illinois to be patronized by blacks from Chicago's South Side. Douglas's first bill never even received a hearing from the Senate committee responsible for national parks. Nonetheless, Douglas and the Save the Dunes Council, under the leadership of club-woman Dorothy Buell (who followed in the footsteps of Bess Sheehan and for whom the present-day visitor center is named) continued to amass popular support for a national lakeshore park.

Soon, however, a series of major projects got underway in the Dunes, and together these works spelled the end of a national park in the Central Dunes. In 1959 Bethlehem Steel swapped some of its land with the Northern Indiana Public Service Company in order to enable NIPSCO to build a $30 million coal-fired power station that would supply electricity to the proposed Burns Harbor Steel Mill. At the same time that construction

began on the NIPSCO plant, the Midwest Steel Company, which owned land to the west of Bethlehem, started work on a $100 million finishing plant. Although a port was not essential to the Midwest plant, Midwest nonetheless wanted a port and could be counted as among potential users whose business would help to justify port construction. In 1960 Midwest and Bethlehem agreed to contribute $4.5 million to Indiana to help pay for part of the port's installations. Then, in a decision termed by one observer as a "crucial and Machiavellian" maneuver, Bethlehem Steel commenced to destroy the Central Dunes for park use while still not committing itself to build a steel mill. In 1961 Bethlehem announced that it had contracted to sell 2.5 million cubic yards of sand to Northwestern University to be used as fill for the expansion of Northwestern's campus into Lake Michigan. The sand would be taken from the proposed harbor site, which was soon sold to the State of Indiana. Actual sand mining began in April 1962, and when it was completed, the state undertook to start construction of the Port of Indiana, which at long last had been approved by the Corps of Engineers after repeated hearings called to address the objections of the harbor's opponents.

Finally, in December 1962, after Senator-elect Birch Bayh promised that he would support proposals for a federally funded port, Bethlehem Steel announced plans to begin construction of its steel mill as soon as possible. By July 1963, giant earthmovers were leveling the Central Dunes to create an immense plateau fourteen feet above lake level. By 1965 Bethlehem had a finishing mill running, and in 1969 Bethlehem's integrated plant became a reality when the first coke oven began operation.

Construction of the Bethlehem plant and Burns Harbor broke the stalemate by which the steel company and park advocates both vied to determine the fate of the Central Dunes. Defeated, the park proponents turned their attention elsewhere. As early as 1961, Indiana's Senator Vance Hartke had introduced a bill which proposed a park of six thousand acres, entirely excluding the Central Dunes, but park partisans had attacked Hartke's proposal as a sellout to industry. By mid-1963, however, the Central Dunes had been flattened, and the Kennedy administration, which had been subjected to fierce lobbying from advocates for both a park and a port, announced a quintessential political compromise. At the President's request, the Bureau of the Budget recommended federal funding for construction of Burns Harbor and also for an 11,700 acre Dunes park.

Two years later, on October 27, 1965, Congress passed a public works bill that included the Burns Harbor project, but a proviso stipulated that no funds would be appropriated for the harbor until both houses of Congress had voted on the proposed Indiana Dunes National Lakeshore. A year later, on October 14, 1966, Congress authorized a 6,539 acre federal park containing no land in common with the original Douglas proposal, having 5,161 acres less than recommended by the Kennedy compromise three years earlier, and split into two main sections separated by a huge industrial complex.

Since congressional approval in 1966, plans for the Indiana Dunes National Lakeshore have been slowly implemented and expanded. Six years passed before the National Park Service judged that it had purchased enough land to establish the park formally. Secretary of the Interior Walter Hickel under President Nixon continued the Kennedy/Udall policy of developing small, recreation-oriented national parks near large cities, but after Hickel resigned in protest against the Vietnam War, the Nixon administration and subsequent presidents pulled back from the urban and near-urban park concept, ostensibly to reduce budgets. Nonetheless, at the urging of Porter County's first Democratic representative in forty-two years, Congress voted to enlarge the national lakeshore by 3,300 acres in 1976 and by 500 acres in 1980. On both occasions the expansion was voted over the opposition of the National Park Service, which thought that the land in question was too expensive. Indeed, during the tenure of James Watt as Secretary of the Interior during Ronald Reagan's first term, a serious effort was made within the Interior Department to disestablish and eliminate the lakeshore park. Watt called the new urban national parks "merely minor playgrounds" that never should have been authorized in the first place. Although de-authorization was thwarted, land acquisition at the Indiana Dunes slowed still further as Watt held back funds and curtailed condemnation proceedings. However, Watt's campaign against the national lakeshore proved to be entirely out of step with popular sentiment supporting the park. After Watt resigned under the pressure of nationwide reaction against his anti-park, anti-conservation policies, funds were made available to complete authorized acquisitions at the Indiana Dunes National Lakeshore, and since then Congress has authorized the purchase of still more land.

And now for a straight editorial pitch. In the course of writing my various Country Walks books, I have seen a great many parks serving some of the nation's largest cities (which, of course, are going to get larger—very much larger—during the coming centuries). With its lake frontage, mountainous sand dunes, swamps, bogs, and wooded hollows, the Dunes region is unsurpassed for scenic and recreational value. In the future, the survival of the Dunes as public parkland will seem a miracle: a godsend to millions of people. So after your visit, if you think that the national lakeshore is worth expanding and improving, write or e-mail your congressperson. Tell your representative what a good time you had and that funds should be made available to create more coherent boundaries and gradually to eliminate small residential and commercial inholdings.

≈   ≈   ≈   ≈

AUTOMOBILE DIRECTIONS: Indiana Dunes National Lakeshore is located east of Gary at the southern end of Lake Michigan. (See **Map 60** at right, where •20-A, •20-B, and •20-C indicate three separate walks.)

Two approaches to the national lakeshore—via the **Chicago Skyway** and the **Tri-State Tollway**—are described below. The directions will take you to the **Dorothy Buell Memorial Visitor Center**, which provides a good introduction to the area. From the visitor center, there are separate directions to the various sites, as described on pages 276 and 278.

To Indiana Dunes National Lakeshore via the Chicago Skyway (Interstate 90): From downtown Chicago, follow the Dan Ryan Expressway south, then exit onto the Skyway for Interstate 90 east to the Indiana Toll Road. Eventually, after about 37 miles on the Skyway and toll road, leave I-90 at Exit 31 for Route 49 toward Chesterton. After paying the toll, turn left onto Route 49 and follow it north 5 miles to the turnoff—it is on the left—for Route 12 and the National Lakeshore. At the bottom of the ramp, turn right and follow Route 12 east 3.1 miles, then turn right onto Kemil Road and right again into the visitor center parking lot.

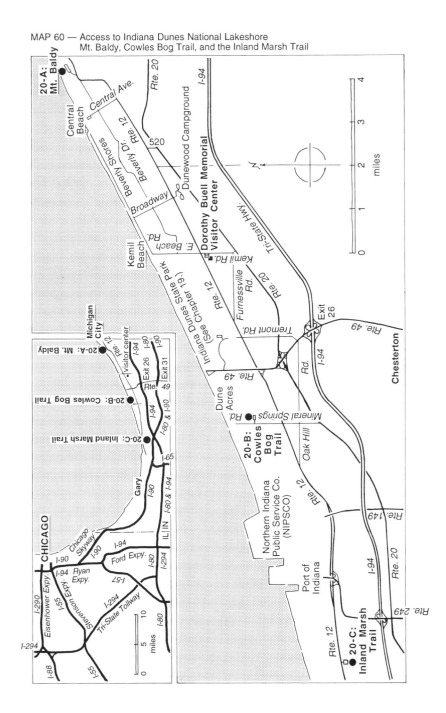

275

To Indiana Dunes National Lakeshore via the Tri-State Tollway (Interstate 294): Follow the tollway toward Indiana. Eventually, the Tri-State Tollway becomes Interstate 80 and Interstate 94 eastbound into Indiana. **Stay on I-94** past Exit 16—i.e., so as to avoid the Indiana Toll Road (I-80 and I-90). Finally, leave I-94 at Exit 26B for Route 49 north toward the Indiana Dunes. Follow Route 49 north 1.6 miles to the turnoff—it is on the left—for Route 12 and the National Lakeshore. At the bottom of the ramp, turn right and follow Route 12 east 3.1 miles, then turn right onto Kemil Road and right again into the visitor center parking lot.

≈   ≈   ≈   ≈

MT. BALDY is located at •20-A on **Map 60** on page 275. To drive there from the visitor center, turn left out the parking lot and then right onto Route 12. Follow Route 12 east 5.4 miles to the Mt. Baldy entrance on the left.

Walking at Mt. Baldy: Map 61 at right shows a route over Mt. Baldy and along the beach. The round-trip distance is 3.5 miles.

To get started, locate the trail at the back of the "buses only" area to the left of the lavatories. Follow the path and signs to the summit and from there descend to the beach.

With the lake on the right, walk as far as the stone rip-rap at Lake Front Drive, then return by the way you came.

≈   ≈   ≈   ≈

THE COWLES BOG TRAIL is located at •20-B on **Map 60** on page 275. To drive there from the visitor center, turn left out the parking lot and left again onto Route 12. Follow Route 12 west 4.4 miles, then turn right onto Mineral Springs Road at a sign for Dune Acres. After 0.6 mile, turn right for the Cowles Bog parking lot just before the Dune Acres gate house. Go 0.1 mile to the parking lot itself.

Walking at Cowles Bog: This is one of the best dune environments at the national lakeshore. **Map 62** on page 279 shows a 4-mile route past the wetlands, across forested dunes, along the beach, and back through the woods. However, on summer weekends, the beach here is often crowded with boats.

MAP 61 — Mt. Baldy

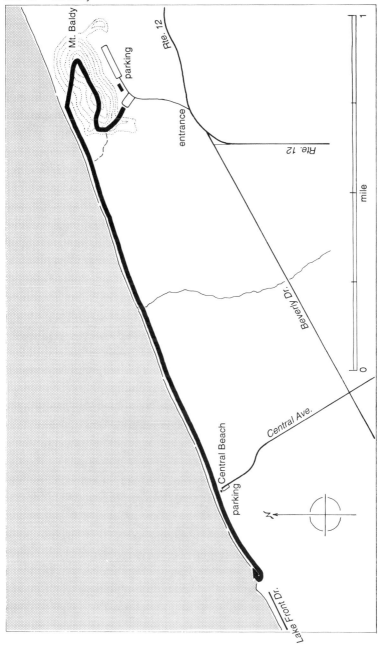

Mt. Baldy

parking

Rte. 12

entrance

Rte. 12

Beverly Dr.

Central Ave.

Central Beach
parking

Lake Front Dr.

1

mile

0

N

277

To get started on the **Cowles Bog Trail** shown at right, follow the entrance lane from the parking lot back to Mineral Springs Road. The trailhead is on the opposite side of the road.

Follow the trail through the woods, across a boardwalk, and along the back side of a dune ridge. At a trail junction, turn right uphill over the ridge. Continue past a large bog on the left and across other ridges.

At a T-intersection, bear right and continue as the dunes get bigger near the lake. Eventually, descend to the beach. With Lake Michigan on the right, follow the beach for a quarter-mile toward the NIPSCO power plant.

The trail that returns into the dunes is marked by a small sign and perhaps also by foot tracks. Climb steeply up the huge dunes and gradually downhill as the trail winds through the woods. At a trail junction, bear left to return towards Cowles Bog. At the next intersection, turn right and go back to the parking lot by the way you came.

≈   ≈   ≈   ≈

THE INLAND MARSH TRAIL is located at •20-C on **Map 60** on page 275. To drive there from the visitor center, turn left out the parking lot and left again onto Route 12. Follow Route 12 west 10.3 miles to the Inland Marsh parking lot on the left.

Walking at the Inland Marsh: The little-used trail outlined on **Map 63** on page 281 provides a quiet walk of 3 miles past wetlands and along sinuous dune ridges now covered with woods.

To get started, head out the back of the parking lot and straight through some flats where the sand dunes were removed before the national lakeshore was established. After nearly half a mile, the trail turns right and climbs into the dunes, levels off, and soon splits. Fork right to continue along the marsh edge, through scrubby growth, and across a boardwalk.

At the top of a hill, bear left and continue a few yards to a trail junction. Bear right and continue around the large loop. Eventually, pass near Stagecoach Road as the trail begins to circle back along the crest of the wooded dunes.

At a T-intersection atop a ridge, turn right. At the next trail junction, bear right to return to the parking lot.

MAP 62 — Cowles Bog Trail

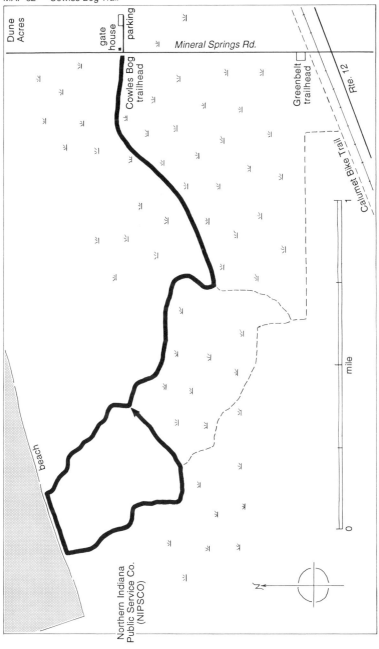

MAP 63 — Inland Marsh Trail

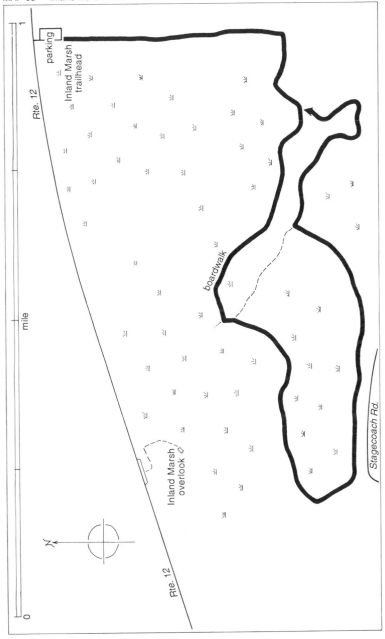

INDEX OF SITES AND TRAILS

IF YOU LIKE THIS BOOK, you or your friends might also enjoy some of the other guidebooks listed below. All follow the same format. These guides are widely available at bookstores and outfitters, and also from online booksellers.

COUNTRY WALKS NEAR BOSTON
"An invaluable paperback, profusely illustrated with photographs and maps. . . Possibly the best few dollars you could ever spend"—*Boston Globe* • "My favorite trail guide"—*Boston Phoenix*

COUNTRY WALKS NEAR WASHINGTON
Dozens of outings explore national, state, and local parks and hike-bike trails located within an hour's drive of the U.S. capital. Each chapter includes an overview, detailed directions, one or more maps (there are sixty in all), and extensive commentary.
"Cream of the local outdoors-guide crop"—*Washington Post* • "The happy union between a utilitarian and historically informative guide"—*Washington Times*

DAY TRIPS IN DELMARVA
The Delmarva Peninsula, which consists of southern Delaware and the Eastern Shore of Maryland and Virginia (hence Del-Mar-Va, in local parlance), is one of the most fascinating vacation areas in the nation. *Day Trips in Delmarva* emphasizes the region's historic towns, scenic back roads, wildlife refuges, undeveloped beaches, and routes for car touring, hiking, and bicycling.
"The best organized, best written, most comprehensive and practical guide to the Delmarva Peninsula"—*Easton Star Democrat* • "An infinitely enjoyable book"—*Baltimore Magazine*

COUNTRY WALKS & BIKEWAYS
IN THE PHILADELPHIA REGION
This guidebook explores the Delaware Valley's parks, wildlife refuges, and trail networks, including eighty-five miles of canal trails along the Delaware River.

COUNTRY WALKS NEAR BALTIMORE
"A model of pith and practicality. . . . The maps excel."—*Baltimore Sun* • "A favorite and handy reference"—*Maryland Magazine*